Attachment Theory and the Teacher–Student Relationship

D1477468

How teachers form and maintain classroom and staffroom relationships is crucial to the success of their work. A teacher who is able to accurately interpret the underlying relationship processes can learn to proactively, rather than reactively, influence the dynamics of any class. These are skills that can be taught. This invaluable text explains how adult attachment theory offers new ways to examine professional teaching relationships, classroom management and collegial harmony: equally important information for school leaders, teacher mentors and protégés.

Attachment Theory and the Teacher–Student Relationship addresses three significant gaps in the current literature on classroom management:

- the effects of teachers' attachment style on the formation and maintenance of classroom and staffroom relationships;
- the importance of attachment processes in scaffolding teachers' and students' emotional responses to daily educational tasks; and
- the degree of influence these factors have on teachers' classroom behaviour, particularly management of student behaviour.

Based on recent developments in adult attachment theory, this book highlights the key aspects of teacher–student relationships that teachers and teacher educators should know. As such, it will be of great interest to educational researchers, teacher educators, students and training teachers.

Philip Riley is a Senior Lecturer in school leadership and mentoring in the Faculty of Education, Monash University, Australia. He is also a registered psychologist and an experienced teacher at both primary and secondary level.

Attachment Theory and the Teacher–Student Relationship

A practical guide for teachers, teacher educators and school leaders

Philip Riley

Routledge
Taylor & Francis Group

LONDON AND NEW YORK

First edition published 2011
by Routledge
2 Park Square, Milton Park, Abingdon, Oxon, OX14 4RN

Simultaneously published in the USA and Canada
by Routledge
270 Madison Avenue, New York, NY 10016

Routledge is an imprint of the Taylor & Francis Group, an informa business

© 2011 Philip Riley

Typeset in Bembo by Exeter Premedia Services

British Library Cataloguing in Publication Data
A catalogue record for this book is available from the British Library

Library of Congress Cataloging-in-Publication Data
Riley, Philip, 1957-
Attachment theory and the teacher-student relationship : a practical guide
for teachers, teacher educators and school leaders / Philip Riley.
    p. cm.
Includes bibliographical references and index.
1. Teacher-student relationships.   2. Attachment behavior in children.
3. Educational psychology.   I. Title.

    LB1033.R54 2011
    371.102'3—dc22

                            2010006471

ISBN10: 0-415-56261-9 (hbk)
ISBN10: 0-415-56262-7 (pbk)
ISBN10: 0-203-84578-1 (ebk)

ISBN13: 978-0-415-56261-4 (hbk)
ISBN13: 978-0-415-56262-1 (pbk)
ISBN13: 978-0-203-84578-3 (ebk)

To my secure bases, Andrea and Dad, without whom this book would have been just another passing thought.

Contents

List of illustrations

Figures

Tables

Acknowledgements

I have been extraordinarily lucky to meet and work with so many wonderful people. This book is in one sense the culmination of all of those personal and professional experiences. However, it would not have seen the light of day without a great deal of help from a brilliant group of people I have come to know and learn from over the years. First and foremost, I owe a great debt of gratitude to my partner Andrea Gallant. She is my secure base. Having first inspired me to undertake the study that led to the book she also read countless drafts, questioned, probed and challenged my ideas so that the final draft of the text actually says what I wanted it to say. There were many other important people along the way, including most of my teachers. Even the ones I disliked taught me a great deal about the teaching and learning process.

As a beginning teacher I was lucky to have Margaret Lyttle as my first Principal. She had an immense effect on me first as a teacher, later as a school leader and now as a researcher. She was the first person to introduce me to attachment theory. Margaret encouraged all the teachers she came into contact with to view students through their developmental history as well as the curriculum, and never to lose a sense of wonder about them. She had many wise words and sayings that have stayed with me over the years and I recount three here that frame this book in a profound way. During staff meetings she often reminded teachers "You are teaching for the children of the children you teach." This was and remains a very powerful statement and one that I always try to keep in mind. Margaret also advised, "All you need to really teach well is a shady tree to sit under and a stick to make marks in the earth." Having understood the powerful effects of intergenerational transfer of behaviour, Margaret saw teaching as the building of strong bonds between adults and children;[1] a way of breaking the cycle of negative transfer. Like Margaret, I also believe that the best teaching is also preventative psychology, a deeply human experience for both teachers and students, and that done with integrity allows people to fulfil their human potential.

The third of Margaret's sayings that stayed with me was, "You have to decide whether you want to make a better world for the people or better people for the world...because you can't do both." I have always struggled with this statement, sometimes believing it to be true and at other times believing that we should all be doing both. Like all great ideas that are never truly captured and tied down, revisiting them over the years has proved energising and growth promoting. And like all great leaders Margaret set the conditions for growth but left the growing up to you.

There are so many others without whose help this book would be far less than it is: Professors Bernie Neville and Ramon (Rom) Lewis, who read the first iteration of the text, offering many valuable suggestions and challenging me to improve it; Dr Coral Brown for her depth of knowledge about psychological processes, insights into people, deep understanding of attachment, careful reading and many suggested improvements to some of the cases, and as being a wonderful supervisor; Bruce Hunter for providing the necessary conditions in which I was able to have the ah-ha moment that led to the book; my colleagues Associate Professors Len Cairns, Helen Watt and Paul Richardson for many hours of conversation and support while we probed the issues. I am indebited to the team at Routledge, in particular Dr. Kate Reeves, for her close reading of the text. I am also indebited to Helen Neville for the production of the index. Finally I would like to thank all the teachers who worked with me both formally and informally, engaging with the ideas and providing me with many insights that have greatly improved the text. Their wish to become better teachers was inspiring and their faith in me as a potential catalyst for this was humbling.

Foreword

A note about gender

Throughout the book the feminine gender is used to represent all people while keeping the grammar manageable. This is not to imply that teaching is or should be increasingly done by women as current trends indicate. In fact I believe there is very good evidence to suggest that more men should be teaching. Studies reported by Hrdy (2009) show that males involved in childcare of all types have increased levels of prolactin and decreased levels of testoterone, and that the most violent societies are the ones that have extreme sex segregation. She believes men are a largely untapped source of nurture in many societies. If more men were teaching, societies would increase male nurturing.

A note about educational leadership

There are two distinguishing features of educational leadership that differ from the leadership of many other professions. First, educational leaders generally move up from the shop floor, beginning their careers as classroom teachers and moving through the ranks to leadership positions. The second distinguishing feature lies in the nature of teachers' work. Teaching is also a form of leadership. Teachers are the leaders of their classes. This means that formally appointed educational leaders lead leaders, not followers. Yet for their leadership to be effective teachers must be followers also, at least to a certain extent. This structure creates a number of challenges for educational leaders and for the teachers as leader-followers.

Teachers practice leadership from their first day in the classroom. When they are appointed to formal school leadership positions they bring all of this experience of leadership, albeit with children, to the role. This is not to underplay the significant new challenges that leading adults demands of educational leadership. However, as will be outlined in the text, leadership in the context of schools and teaching are almost interchangeable in terms of attachment theory. The rapidly growing literature on leadership conceived as an attachment relationship attests to this, but until now this has not been applied to educational leadership. Therefore, as the teacher–student relationship has many similarities to the leader–follower relationship, when one is mentioned in the text, it generally applies to both. However, mentioning both repeatedly would make the text cumbersome and awkward, so usually only one form is listed for ease of reading, not reasons of substance. When specific differences between the two occur they are specifically mentioned.

A note about the case stories

To protect participants, the case stories in Chapter 5 necessarily omit important developmental, classroom and organisational information that could identify individuals. Unfortunately, this is often the information that most clearly demonstrates the connection between attachment needs and teachers' experiences. However, these connections can still be recognised in the cases, albeit not quite as clearly as I would have liked to convey.

Introduction

Why teachers need to know about attachment theory

The 3Rs: relationship, relationship, relationship

This book essentially rests on two premises: the first is that the traditionally conceived foundations of education, the 3Rs (Reading, wRiting and aRithmatic), are not the foundations at all. In fact they can only be built on an even more fundamental set of 3Rs: relationships (*Relationship* from the student's perspective, *Relationship* from the teacher's perspective, and the priority given to *Relationship* formation and maintenance from school leadership). For a school to function effectively and for students to learn effectively both sets of 3Rs must be in place. The second premise that underlies this book is that too little attention has been paid to the fundamental 3Rs by educators. The aim of this book is therefore to address this by applying what we have learned about how relationships are formed and maintained to the very specific context of the classroom. So, to begin at the beginning …

A baby learns to speak (the foundations of reading and writing) to communicate with people; to maintain important relationships and to begin to form new ones. As the child grows, reading and writing facilitate and enhance communication *with others*. They are a means to an end, not an end in themselves. Without someone to speak to, an infant's speech is delayed. Similarly, it will be argued that without a sound working relationship between teachers and students, very little effective learning will take place.

This is by no means the first, and will not be the last book to stress the importance of classroom relationships. Carl Rogers (1983, 1990), the founder of the person-centred approach to teaching, provided much empirical support for the proposition that teacher–student relationships are fundamental to understanding classroom behaviour by teachers as well as students, and directly affects student outcomes. His work has been confirmed in many studies (R. Lewis, 2001, 2006, 2008; Wanzer & McCroskey, 1998; West, 1994) including a recent meta-analysis of 119 studies with 355,325 students ranging from 1948 to 2004 (Cornelius-White, 2007).

So when the back to basics movement calls for a return to the 3Rs, it is to the teacher–student relationship that we should look first. I encourage those of you who disagree with this premise to read on. I think you will find that the proposition is justified. Understanding attachment theory, and in particular adult attachment theory, changes your understanding of all school based relationships. These new understandings are then put to practical use, by outlining new ways to form, maintain and if necessary re-examine existing professional relationships in the school context.

This book had dual antecedents. The first emerged from many conversations I had with pre-service primary (elementary) teachers, when I began teaching adults following my move from the school setting to teacher education. It seemed that many pre-service teachers had an insatiable desire to discuss issues surrounding class-room discipline and curriculum matters. As our conversations progressed and I got to know them better, what emerged was an underlying level of anxiety about their ability to function in the classroom that appeared to go well beyond the challenges of management and curriculum. They talked about their future students, children they were yet to meet, with a kind of awe. It was as though they were entrusting to these unknown students power over their futures as teachers. I was surprised by how many of the pre-service teachers worried that they might not be "liked" by their future students and the extent to which this affected their approach to formal study. This fear appeared to be distinctly different from classroom management and curriculum implementation concerns.

As I puzzled on this I realised that this fear, albeit subterranean, was especially interesting in light of the fact that most of the pre-service teachers told me they were motivated to teach because they "loved kids" and therefore wanted to work with them. It dawned on me that for many of the students, this statement held a powerful unstated corollary: it appeared that at a fundamental level, they not only loved kids but also wanted or perhaps needed to be loved by them. The fear that they may not be loved by their students seemed to be a powerful force that dictated a great deal of their approach to learning how to teach, but was rarely if ever artic-ulated, and therefore remained unexamined. Having spent the previous 16 years as a teacher and in school leadership roles this level of anxiety by pre-service teachers was intriguing. It resonated strongly with my experience of colleagues in schools but had never been clearly articulated in that setting either.

I had spent the first nine years of my teaching career as a primary (elementary) teacher, and the next seven exclusively in secondary schools. I had noted that primary and secondary school teachers appeared to be "cut from a different cloth", in that secondary school teachers in my experience were not as interested in whether the students loved them as many primary teachers are, but they too held deep fears about their students. They appeared more interested in whether they had the ability to inspire students to love the subjects that they taught, and worried about their own level of content knowledge: "What if the students know more than me? I will lose their respect. Then what will happen?" For secondary teachers, gaining and maintaining respect from students was a powerful motivator, as was the fear of losing respect, and seemed as strong as the need to be loved and fear of losing love in primary teachers.

The second antecedent of this book came from the discovery of the litera-ture documenting self-reports of teacher aggression.[1] As I read about the level of aggression that some teachers show and the subsequent long-term harm for students I wondered about the levels of fear that were shown by pre-service teachers and whether there might be a connection. At the time I was completing my studies for full registration as a psychologist. This entailed weekly discussions with my supervisor about the cases I was dealing with and their relation to the theories of human behaviour introduced in the formal classes. During one of these sessions we were discussing potential reasons for the high level of complaint some of the probationary psychologists were making about the course we were all undertaking. My supervisor said, "We [the organisation] have forgotten about attachment theory; you [students] have had too many teachers and don't feel properly connected to any of them". As we discussed how this paradigm fitted the facts we concluded that the complaints appeared to be sophisticated *separation protest*[2] behaviours. This was an "ah-ha" moment. If probationary psychologists, adults who were highly trained to work with people in difficult situations and circumstances, could display separation protest behaviours so easily, and perhaps entirely unconsciously, perhaps teachers could too; particularly teachers who needed their students to "love them" or "respect them". In extreme cases the absence of student love or respect might provoke teachers to unconsciously punish students in an attempt to gain or regain it. It was then that I realised that attachment theory explained classroom processes more thoroughly and effectively than current educational theories in use.

So I found myself at the beginning of a new teaching career in the tertiary sector wondering about the impact that fear, love and anger may have on the way teachers approached their work. These concepts are rarely dealt with in the educational literature, although recently this is beginning to change. Experienced teachers know the power of these emotions in the classroom but they are usually overlooked in teacher education courses, which place more emphasis on learning theory and cognitive processes. This is a mistake, because without an understanding of the raw emotions involved in teaching, and adequate training in how to look after one's self and the students during moments of intensity, teachers are placed into intensely emotional environments ill equipped to deal with the strong emotions when they inevitably arise.

Having trained and worked as both a teacher and a counselling psychologist I have been struck with the similarity of the issues facing teachers and counsellors who work with young people. Yet only counsellors receive specific training in how to manage themselves and their students/clients in difficult situations. Teachers are left to work it out for themselves, or vote with their feet and leave, perhaps harbouring feelings of failure to boot. This seems nonsensical when we have the courses that would adequately prepare them already in operation.

These skills are taught to all the other relational professions, and should be taught to teachers too. This became the starting point for the book: helping teachers to deal with the emotional aspects of their work by understanding their underlying processes. The most important emotion to deal with first is anger. This is the emotion that holds the most immediate potential danger in the classroom and is fundamentally entwined with attachment processes on which this book is based. Where does anger come from and how should teachers manage it?

Is anger a "thing-to-be-managed"?

When anger appears in the classroom, whether instigated by students or teachers, its presence reveals significant information about the relationships between the students and the teacher. When teachers experience anger while interacting with students, this can be extremely useful information for further exploration and deeper understanding of classroom processes. This is personal, subjective and intersubjective information, often operating just below the level of conscious awareness. Roffman (2004) proposed that anger is a relational emotion that need not, but all too often does, lead to aggression. He suggests anger is a dynamic interaction between people and therefore lies between them, rather than inside individuals. Its emergence is therefore a signal of a difficulty arising between people. So when teachers explore anger without acting on it, it is a useful way of examining classroom relationships. Traditionally teachers have been taught to avoid the anger: to "manage" it, usually a euphemism for repressing it (Sutton & Wheatley, 2003). This conceptualises anger as a "thing"; something which exists independently and is therefore manageable without reference to relationships. Anger management for individuals results from this conception, rather than relationship interventions. This is an attempt to keep everyone safe if it is successfully carried out, but does not lead to understanding how and why anger emerged and re-emerges between people.

This approach to anger decreases the likelihood of the teacher seeing it coming next time and doing something about diffusing it early. If teachers were able to engage with the angry feelings, without acting on them, the context in which they emerge becomes a pathway for understanding previously difficult aspects of the relationship. Roffman (2004) makes the point that while anger is conceived of as a "thing-to-be-managed" (p. 161) it remains distant and dangerous: a "thing" to be avoided and not something that resides within and between people. He argues that to deny anger is to deny the self, and ultimately the chance of a flexible and responsive working relationship between teacher and student. He suggests that if anger is reconceptualised as an "in-relation-to phenomenon" (p. 164) it becomes a potential pathway to understanding a relationship difficulty. Thus, a starting point for an exploration of teachers' experiences of difficulties with classroom management might well be what, or who, makes them angry in the classroom, and what makes them angry outside of it. In this way anger becomes a useful ally, an energising emotion. As long as it remains separated from behaviour, anger can inform teachers about the dynamics of their classrooms in ways previously unavailable, or unacknowledged. Anger without reflection leads inevitably to poor outcomes: aggressive behaviour and fear in both teachers and students. Worse still, without reflection anger primes[3] both teachers and students for more anger: the slippery slope.

Teacher anger has only rarely been researched (Sutton & Wheatley, 2003). Teacher aggression is also under-researched, particularly in the West (Sava, 2002). This book attempts to address this aspect of teachers' work in some detail. Reflecting on Roffman's (2004) point that anger lies between people brings us back to relationships as the key to understanding. All roads lead to Rome. So we must look further than single emotions and look to the dynamics of relational interaction as the fundamentals of teaching and learning.

Brief outline of the book

Teaching is a high stress occupation (Friedman, 1994, 2006; Johnson et al., 2005; Kyriacou, 2001; Kyriacou & Sutcliffe, 1978; Piekarska, 2000; Wilhelm et al., 2000). It is often highly charged emotionally. This book includes a careful examination of the particular stresses that teachers face and patterns of teacher behaviour and their underlying motivations. The outcome is a series of suggestions for more efficacious ways to support teachers so they can do their best work: help their students achieve their potential.

Attachment theory is outlined in detail in Section I. The aim is to explain how it informs teachers about teaching. Attachment is the most comprehensive theory describing human relationships (Hrdy, 2009). And recent developments in the study of adult attachment have expanded the understanding of attachment processes beyond childhood: reciprocal or dyadic attachment. Beyond childhood attachment, which is largely established by three years of age, individuals who make up an attachment dyad may sometimes take the role of care seeker and sometimes care giver, depending on the context at any given moment. This was an important development of the original conception of attachment as a one-way bond between a permanent care seeker such as a small child on one hand, and the permanent care giver such as a parent on the other (Hazan & Shaver, 1987). A fundamental premise, outlined in detail in Section I, is that the teacher–student relationship is dyadic, not unidirectional, in attachment terms. Chapters 1 and 2 develop the argument for increasing teachers' knowledge of the psychodynamic processes underlying classroom behaviour, using dyadic attachment as the theoretical base.

Self-reports of teacher aggression and stress are discussed in Chapter 3, as is the link between stress and the attachment behavioural system. While it has been known for some time that increasing levels of stress can also lead to increases in aggression, attachment theory offers credible explanations for aggressive behaviour by teachers, due to the particular types of stress associated with the teaching process; namely a complex suite of behaviours collectively known as *separation protest* (Bowlby, 1975). Helping teachers to view feelings of aggression, whether acted on or not, as a variant of Roffman's (2004) in-relation-to phenomenon, allows them to deepen their understanding of the dynamics in their classroom and therefore draw on alternative management strategies.

Section II (Chapters 4–6) reports on research findings in relation to teachers and attachment theory. First, teacher responses to self-report attachment questionnaires are analysed in Chapter 4 and qualitative approaches to the issues of attachment, teacher motivation, self-reports of aggression in the classroom and corrective emotional experiences are outlined in Chapters 5 and 6. In Chapter 5, a new methodology for studying the issues, Contextual Insight-Navigated Discussion (CIND pronounced *k*IND), is outlined and five vignettes from teachers who undertook the process are presented as case studies. In Chapter 6, CIND is adapted to provide mentoring training for new school leaders by their experienced colleagues in a train-the-trainer model. Again vignettes are presented, not this time as case studies, but aggregated responses from many participants.

In the final part of the book, Section III covers the issues that have arisen as a result of the conceptual understandings and the research findings presented in sections I and II. The implications of the work are discussed in sections: pre-service education; changes to professional development for classroom management and mentoring; school leadership; and the implications and future directions for researching the area.

Chapter 8, "Further into attachment theory", contains technical information which adds more detail and expands some of the more complex concepts covered in the first seven chapters. It is included for the reader who would like to know more about the theory and the development of the CIND model for working with teachers psychodynamically.

Expanding the 3Rs

Two further assumptions underpin this book. Both have been drawn from psychodynamic literature. The first is that interpersonal interactions are based on conscious and unconscious processing. Therefore they have both subjective and intersubjective content. This has also been largely overlooked in terms of classroom relationships but is just as true in a classroom setting as in any other. The subjective experience of all parties in a relationship is as crucial to understanding the dynamics of that relationship as any other information. The second assumption is that by taking a psychodynamic view of the issues, concentrating on the underlying drives related to experiences and the meaning derived from the experiences, new tools for understanding and managing professional relationships in schools can be developed.

A brief word about methodology

The disciplines of psychology and education focus this book, as both have research evidence pertaining to relationships. However, my aim is to bring the two disciplines into a closer alignment. Partly this was because each discipline has a great deal to offer the other, and partly also because I am persuaded by Knox's (2003) argument that cross disciplinary approaches create exciting opportunities for perceiving issues in new ways. The delineation between the two disciplines is far from distinct, filled as it is with constructs and methodologies that overlap. Each discipline makes use of quantitative and qualitative methodology and the use of "mixed methods" is becoming more common as an enhancement to understanding. Therefore I have attempted work "between and within competing and overlapping perspectives and paradigms" (Denzin & Lincoln, 2005, p. 6). Quantitative methods offer perspectives on trends among teachers, but cannot provide definitive answers to some of the more pressing questions. Through qualitative research triangulation[4] a deeper, more complete view of the whole context for individual teachers was sought, while acknowledging that it could never be fully achieved. In this I was guided by the words of Nelson and colleagues who noted that "the choice of research practices depends on the questions that are asked, and that depends on the context" (Nelson et al., 1992, p. 2).

Neither psychology nor education as research disciplines have an agreed "gold standard" methodology for studying the complex suite of behaviours, interactions, intra- and inter-personal motivations that take place in classrooms across the world daily. Nor do I purport to lay claim to one. I simply attempted to bring all the skills at my disposal, as a former school teacher, current university lecturer and practicing psychologist, to bear on the issues apprehended through personal experience, reflexive practice, professional engagement with teachers and the literature.

Part I

Attachment theory

Chapter 1

Attachment theory and the classroom

Overlapping space

Attachment was once a very controversial theory of human development. Applying it to education may ignite a new controversy, as it represents a very different lens through which to view professional relationships in schools and challenges the way teachers have viewed their roles as educators. In this chapter and the next, I present a broad outline of the whole theory before concentrating on the specific components relevant to teachers' and school leaders' professional relationships. To date these concepts have remained largely within the domain of psychology. Yet the concepts are equally relevant to educators of all descriptions. By delineating this overlapping space between psychodynamic psychology and education, my aim is to explain the teaching process in new and useful ways to teachers, pre-service teachers, their mentors and leaders.

The reasons for undertaking this approach are threefold. First, by becoming aware of the mechanisms of attachment, teachers will be better informed about the processes of relationship building. This is a crucial aspect of professional practice, not usually included in pre-service teacher education. Second, the importance of the teacher's role as the *secure base* for students in the classroom, and the leader's role as secure base for the teachers in the staffroom becomes clear. These are important because they explain the *how* and *why* of teachers' work. The lack of a secure base predicts aggression in children (Sroufe, 2005) and may also explain why some teachers report becoming aggressive with their students. Third, if the overlapping theoretical space of psychology and teaching is a potential source of new tools for predicting and explaining positive and negative teacher and student behaviour, it deserves to be carefully examined.

The attachment behavioural system

> [The attachment behavioural system] comprises a reciprocal set of behaviours shown by care-seeker and caregiver in which they are aware of and seek each other out whenever the care-seeker is in danger due to physical separation, illness or tiredness.
>
> (Holmes, 1993b, p. 218)

Attachment theory is a homeostatic one, designed to regulate emotional distance and felt security in which the caregiver and care seeker endeavour to stay close enough to each other to remain comfortable. Just as the bodily functions of temperature regulation or blood pressure are maintained between appropriate limits for good health, attachment is a system of the regulation of "distance or accessibility ... to clearly identified persons ... maintained by behavioural instead of physiological means" (Bowlby, 1988a, p. 29). The attachment behavioural system appears to be hierarchical with the list of preferred carers starting with the parents at the top, closely followed by grandparents, siblings, aunts and so on. For each bonded unit, principally the family, the child forms its own unique hierarchy. In evolutionary terms attachment equals survival for the infant who is too helpless to meet his or her own survival needs. This makes attachment such a powerful system of connection between people.

Attachment behaviour

Attachment and attachment behaviour are not the same. An attachment is the bond felt by the care seeker for a particular individual who is thought by the care seeker to be "better able to cope with the world" (Bowlby, 1988a, p. 27). The desire to remain close to the care seeker, particularly in times of stress, persists across time. The various behaviours that the care seeker uses to remain in close proximity to the caregiver are known as attachment behaviour. Attachment behaviour in the care seeker is triggered by actual or imagined separation from the caregiver. It is most obvious when a person is frightened, sick or simply fatigued (Holmes, 1993b, p. 68). At other times the behaviour is less obvious. "Nevertheless for a person to know that an attachment figure is available and responsive gives him a strong and pervasive feeling of security, and so encourages him to value and continue the relationship" (Bowlby, 1988a, p. 27).

The attachment bond

> There is no such thing as a single human being, pure and simple, unmixed with other human beings. Each personality is a world in himself, a company of many. That self ... is a composite structure ... formed out of countless never-ending influences and exchanges between ourselves and other. These other persons are in fact therefore part of ourselves ... we are members of one another.
>
> (Riviere, 1955)

For normal development, a baby, lacking the ability to meet its own survival requirements, seeks proximity to a caregiver or is in great danger of injury, starvation or worse. Attachment is mediated by looking, hearing, holding and its goal is felt security, which produces a relaxed state in the infant so that it can get on with the developmental task of exploring the world around it. However, a missing, unresponsive, abusive or neglectful caregiver inhibits curiosity in the infant and can provoke feelings of aggression, vigilance and despair (Ainsworth, 1982; Bowlby, 1975). The baby's survival is at stake, and it must make a strong enough connection with at least one caregiver to achieve this. Therefore, babies respond powerfully to faces and face-like objects from birth and come to recognise the importance of the primary caregivers through repeated exposure to these very important faces (Knox, 2003). Equally, adults respond to babies' need for proximity by responding to crying, gurgling, smiling and similar behaviours.

While the care-seeking behaviour appears to be innate, the relationship bond formed between a particular baby and its caregivers is learnt through repeated exposure to each other. It is a sensible survival mechanism for the species as a whole. This *affectional bond*, according to Bowlby, is the basis upon which the baby forms all other relationships, including the teacher–student relationship. More recent research has questioned this deterministic aspect of the theory, by suggesting that inner working models are not static but subject to change throughout the lifespan as a result of experience (Bartholomew, 1994; Fonagy et al., 1996; Fraley & Shaver, 2000; Gillath et al., in press; Kobak & Hazan, 1991; Masiello, 2000). However, these researchers agree that the primary attachment remains a powerfully robust influence on subsequent relationships. For teachers the fact that attachment is not static is good news, as it offers the opportunity to provide security and hope of a better future to insecurely attached students. This is equally good news for leaders who are able to provide security for followers.

Childhood attachment: the development of the attachment bond

The development of the attachment system starts at birth, with the baby's intense interest in and responsiveness to the human face, and continues throughout life. It moves through a period of 'set goal attachment' (six months–three years) which is described by Bowlby as analogous to the setting of a thermostat: the infant must keep close enough to the caregiver, who is seen as the *secure base* to return to if exploration goes awry. During this period the infant will express *separation protest*, described by Bowlby (1975) as a danger signal alerting the caregiver that the distance between them has become too great. It operates somewhat like a heat seeking missile.

By the age of three years, as the child acquires language and the sophistication that comes with it, she begins to form reciprocal relationships in which negotiation, pleading, bribing and charm are added to the repertoire of behaviours used to maintain proximity to the caregiver. It is at this stage that the child's *internal working models* are formed. The models or prototypes are used by the child to engage with the world. The model contains three broad dimensions: the first aspect is a self-representation, the second, a physical world representation and the third is an other representation (Knox, 2003). By the age of three years the child is recognisably *securely* or *insecurely* attached to her caregiver (Ainsworth & Bowlby, 1991; Bowlby, 1982). Although there is some augmentation of the internal working model as the child develops, once constructed at approximately three years of age, it becomes the basis for all other relationships formed by the child, including relationships with teachers when she reaches school age. It has also been shown to be relatively stable into adulthood (Bartholomew, 1994; Hazan & Shaver, 1987) and perhaps is the basis of the relationships teachers form with students. Each of these ideas will be developed in more detail below, and the mechanism by which teachers may be vulnerable to separation anxiety from their students will be examined. However, it is first important to understand secure attachment.

Secure attachment

A *secure* attachment is based on the caregiver responding consistently and predictably to the child's needs, producing an internal working model of confidence in self and others, allowing her to gradually develop her own independence. The caregiver is able to predict what the child needs and through empathy keeps the child in mind when interacting with her. Thus the caregiver makes the world a safe and secure place to explore, but not perfectly so. While the caregiver does many things for the young child, the task of intuiting when and how to let the child struggle to achieve a desired goal for herself is also very important. By doing this, the caregiver allows the child to learn about her developing self-efficacy in dealing with the physical and social environment. As these experiences are learnt, the child's explorations away from the caregiver become rewarding also, because they were suited to her abilities and desires. Winnicott (2002) described this process as the caregiver empathically failing the child. In contrast, the child who has to fend for herself too much through lack of forethought or empathy by the caregiver, whose explorations from the carer are unfulfilling, dangerous or worse, soon learns not to venture out and loses curiosity about the environment in which she finds herself. This has serious implications for the child and her teachers when she reaches school age.

Insecure attachments: avoidant, ambivalent

If the child has been in a relationship with a caregiver who has been unpredictable or rejecting the child will develop an insecure attachment style. Insecure attachments lead the child to attempt to minimise her unmet needs for attachment in order not to experience the pain of separation when it occurs. Insecure attachments were originally conceived in two ways: *avoidant* or *ambivalent*. A third style, the much rarer *disorganised*, was added later for children who displayed aspects of both ambivalent and avoidant attachment (Ainsworth, 1989). In the extreme form avoidant and/or ambivalent people are wary and distrustful of others and of their own feelings and intuitions about relationships. They are more likely to become defensive to protect themselves from the pain of not having their genuine attachment needs met. Often this is accomplished by convincing themselves, through cognitive and affective restructuring (Brown, 2002) that they do not have attachment needs (avoidant) or they may become clinging and controlling in intimate relationships (ambivalent). This can lead to some or all of the following in the young child: distant contact with the caregiver even when able to be close; excessively clingy or submissive behaviour; role reversal where the child tries to comfort the caregiver; hyper vigilance; anger and despair (Bowlby, 1975).

Unfortunately, the links between severe forms of insecure attachment patterned in childhood by abusive or neglectful attachment figures predict violence in later life quite routinely (Appleyard et al., 2005; Shulman et al., 1999; Sroufe, 1986, 2005; Yates et al., 2003). This pathological form of separation protest is a perversion of normative aggressive responding by children when faced with separation from their primary attachment figures.

Separations: a structural part of every school day

In an attachment dyad such as the teacher–student dyad many separations occur as a normal function of the schooling system. These separations are beyond the control of both the teacher and the students: timetables, weekends, holidays – just to name a few. Each separation raises the possibility of separation anxiety, and each reunion provides the opportunity for a corrective or confirmatory emotional experience. Children from a secure home base who enter the school system to find a dependable and consistent teacher learn that home/school separations are not permanent, can be tolerated and that the reunion with a consistent attachment object can be a pleasure: something to look forward to. Further, the child learns that a consistent and dependable teacher can be a secure base at school, a home away from home. This strengthens her security and builds both self-efficacy and curiosity away from the home environment. This is the best-case scenario for transition to school.

Insecurely attached children, on the other hand, are much more likely to spend a great deal of time at school, in the initial stages at least, either anxiously awaiting and fearing the reunion with their attachment object, or trying desperately to connect with the teacher as a substitute attachment object for an inconsistent parent and therefore needing constant reassurance from her that all is well. The insecure child is also unconsciously searching for a corrective emotional experience from school through peers and teachers. Some will find that school does satisfy this need. If the child has an avoidant attachment style by the time she reaches school, she is likely to appear independent, perhaps overly so, and may seem to settle quickly into routines. However, over time she may show herself to be overly rigid in adhering to the routines, overly stoic when in need of emotional support, and avoiding of the offers of friendship from peers and support from teachers. Each of these children has less emotional energy that can be directed toward the making of secure affectional bonds with both the teacher and her peers, and a reduced curiosity about the interesting developmental challenges that school affords.

Attachment impacts on motivation to become a teacher

The insecurely attached child tends to seek out a substitute caregiver who can provide a corrective emotional experience through a secure, long-term attachment

(Brown, 2002). Such a person may very often be a teacher. If a relationship formed with a teacher afforded the child a corrective emotional experience, then it may also consciously influence a later decision to join the profession: a wish to help others achieve the same successful outcome. However, it is also possible that the corrective emotional experience found at school was incomplete. In this case the child may unconsciously seek to repeat this experience of felt security by remaining in the classroom for as long as possible. The wish to remain in the classroom to assuage attachment needs may also lead to an unconscious motivation to become a teacher, but in a quite different way. This teacher is looking to receive rather than give security. A teacher motivated primarily by this need would be vulnerable to separation protest behaviours if she did not receive the 'felt security' from students and/or colleagues. This argument is developed further in Chapter 2.

Attachment theory also offers an alternative theoretical unconscious motivation to remain in the classroom: safety. Ainsworth and colleagues (1978) described the inverse relationship between insecure attachment and curiosity, with insecurely attached children displaying less exploratory play. These children do interact with the world as they develop, but are likely do so reluctantly in many instances. For some, once they find a sense of security at school through mastery of the environment by understanding the structures and routines of the typical school day they may come to think of school as a safe haven and wish to remain within its walls: as teachers. This also goes some way to explaining the resistance to school wide change by teachers that is often evident in schools (Herr, 1999; Kelchtermans, 2005; Marshak, 1996; Gitlan & Margonis, 1995).

The underlying concepts of attachment theory

Loss

The fundamental concepts of attachment theory are loss and the fear of losing the attachment figure or object.[1] As distance from the attachment figure increases so does the fear that one is not safe. For young children it is physical distance, and becomes emotional distance with development. The threat of the loss of the attachment figure, through increased distance, whether physical or emotional, creates a particular type of anxiety in the child: *separation anxiety*. Separation anxiety is "anxiety about losing, or becoming separated from someone loved" (Bowlby, 1988a, p. 29). From an ethological perspective separation anxiety is a signal of increased risk to the organism, and therefore falls within a class of self-protective responses to environmental triggers.

Attachment behaviours result from separation anxiety. Bowlby was the first theorist to identify anxiety as a normal rather than pathological developmental response to environmental circumstances. The ultimate fear is abandonment, one of the greatest fears we know (Fraley & Shaver, 1997; Holmes, 1993b; Holtzworth-Munroe et al., 1997; Hoshmand & Polkinghorne, 1992; Macnab, 1991a, 1991b; Mann, 1981, 1991; Teyber, 2006). The separation only need be threatened to provoke anxiety in the child. Once activated the anxiety leads to a variety of behaviours designed to return the caregiver to a comfortable proximity. These behaviours are covered by the umbrella term *separation protest*. Taken together the anxiety and the resulting behaviours are a major component of the attachment behavioural system.

Separation anxiety, separation protest and aggressive behaviour

In attachment terms separation from the caregiver is a threat of physical, and later psychological, annihilation. The young are relatively helpless and therefore in need of protection. In all herding species the older, more competent members of the group protect the young and vulnerable. Bowlby was the first to suggest a built-in safety mechanism that the young could employ to alert their caregivers to potential dangers. Nature gave each of us from birth the ability to communicate angry protests at separations, born of anxiety. By crying, calling out, screaming, and with development cajoling and manipulating, the young become adept at bringing the caregivers back. Bowlby (1975) also noted that separation anxiety and aggressive responding fit together like a hand in a glove.

The striking thing about this angry response born of separation anxiety is that it is directed at the attachment figure. The child's aim as care seeker is to reduce the likelihood of the caregiver moving beyond the "comfortable" distance in future. In effect the caregiver receives an aggressive punishment for raising the level of anxiety in the care seeker by distancing herself. This has important correlates in classrooms and staffrooms. It explains why teachers and students may become aggressive with each other in some situations. Separation protest is a normal part of relational behaviour, but its behavioural correlates can vary widely. They can range from quite appropriate admonishment and admitting to fear that the relationship may be in jeopardy, to inappropriate wielding of power and threat designed to keep the attachment figure close through fear. Separations are a natural part of relationships. Caregivers cannot possibly meet all of the attachment needs of the care seeker. Sometimes separations last longer than either member of the dyad wishes. But how long is too long? What happens to the child when a separation from a caregiver continues for too long?

Despair, mourning and defences

When the anxiety of separation is not restored by a reunion, separation protest behaviours eventually subside. Separation protest behaviours give way to mourning and despair. Bowlby was first to write about healthy mourning (Bowlby et al., 1952). By carefully studying the behaviour of young children and babies separated from their caregivers over long periods, such as enforced stays in hospital during a period when parental visits were restricted to once per week, mainly because the children became so upset at the parting, Bowlby constructed the theory of the next stages of the attachment behavioural system. He developed a model based on stages of mourning, beginning with *separation protest*, which unresolved leads to *despair* and *detachment* phases. Once he had identified the attributes of healthy mourning it was possible to closely identify unhealthy or pathological mourning.

Healthy mourning allows for the gradual coming to terms with the loss at a pace that suits the individual, dealing with the anger, the yearning for reunion, the sorrow and eventually the acceptance that while the person may never return she can remain alive in the memory. Unhealthy mourning can trap the person in a cycle of anger and neglect which Bowlby called *defensive exclusion* (Bowlby, 1988a). This concept has a meaning very similar to Harry Stack Sullivan's concept of *selective inattention* and what Freud described as repression (Spiegel, 1981). Using information-processing theory Bowlby reclassified the Freudian internal view of psychoanalytic defensive structure into an interactionist, epigenetic model of defensive processes, defensive beliefs and defensive activities (Bowlby, 1980). His recasting of these structures may prove pivotal to understanding aggressive relational behaviour in classrooms and in leadership–followership exchanges.

Detachment

Detachment has two functions in attachment theory. The first is the psychological letting go of an attachment object that is a healthy part of the mourning process. This happens after the actual loss of an attachment object. With the death of a loved one for instance, a period of grief is healthy and eventually leads to the detachment from the lost attachment object, and an internalisation of the person in the memory of the bereaved. In healthy mourning, the detachment process allows the person who has lost an attachment object to internalise that person psychologically, and therefore keep them close, but in a realistic way. The actual person is lost but the warm memories and feelings are retained, and reframed. Brown (2002) describes this process as a form of cognitive and affective restructuring.

The second function of detachment is a pathological protection mechanism. Some individuals who have not received adequate nurture and care attempt to deny to themselves that their attachment needs exist. "I'm OK. I don't need anyone's help." This form of detachment happens in two ways, usually but not always unconsciously. The first is that the person denies or ignores her attachment needs as a defensive, protective measure in an attempt to lessen the internal perception of separation anxiety. This is akin to the *denial stage*, the first of Parkes' (1986) attributes of grieving. The second form of detachment is a change in the orientation toward others. This can take many forms given the environmental conditions. However, the underlying pattern of behaviour is one of distancing from other people. When this behaviour is extreme, the individual tends to deny herself the chance to have a close enough bond with another person who might provide a secure base for a corrective emotional experience that would eventually lead to increased feelings of attachment security. This is almost always an unconscious act, which Bowlby named *perceptual defence* and wrote about extensively in the third volume of his trilogy on attachment (Bowlby, 1988c).[2] Briefly, Bowlby discussed the idea of unconscious processes shaping behaviour and influencing a person's state of mind when he suggested the term perceptual defence: "painful feelings [such as unmet attachment needs] are kept out of awareness but may nevertheless influence a person's state of mind and behaviour" (Holmes, 1993b, p. 223). The idea that a student or teacher can prevent information coming in via the senses from reaching consciousness is very important for teachers to come to grips with. This is particularly so in conjunction with the concept of corrective emotional experiences discussed later, and the concept of the secure base, which follows.

The secure base phenomenon

First described by Ainsworth (1967), Bowlby came to regard the *secure base* as the central feature of good parenting. Others are now using this concept far more widely. For instance Popper and colleagues are developing theories of leadership based on the principles of good parenting (Popper, 2004; Popper & Mayseless, 2003; Popper, Mayseless, & Castelnovo, 2000). As teachers are also leaders this concept is crucial to the understanding of the teacher–student relationship. When a parent is responsive to the needs of the child, the child is able to confront the developmental task of discovering and interacting with the world in the knowledge that if she should overstep the mark in some way, become frightened or injured, or simply tire and need rest, the parent, as secure base figure, will be there to rescue and/or comfort her. As the name suggests, the secure base, or safe haven as it is sometimes referred to, is a solid, predictable home base, most often the primary attachment object, from which the child leaves to explore the world and to which she returns for comfort, nurture and safety when needed. It is the child's ability to predict with accuracy where the parent will be, through the consistent responsiveness to the child's emotional as well as physical needs, that promotes the feeling of the secure base in the child (Ainsworth, 1982; Crowell et al., 2002; Roisman et al., 2004).

Attachment, as a complex sociobiological system, is used by the child and the caregiver essentially as a control mechanism, similar to other homeostatic systems located within the central nervous system (Bowlby, 1988b). The child who "knows" that she can venture into the world with a support team on hand if needed is more likely to explore the world around her. This is not the case for the child who fears loss of the attachment figure if she moves away from it to explore.

These two modes of expectation about the world are no less true of the adult, except that the adult can feel secure in the knowledge of emotional proximity or felt security, whereas the very young child needs physical proximity. One only needs to reflect on who one feels most comfortable with and with whom one feels a sense of unease to determine one's secure base. This is because we feel most comfortable with people who understand us; who are attuned to our attachment behaviours, respect and act on them to make us feel safe, by being predictable. As Bowlby pointed out, "No parent is going to provide a secure base for his growing child unless he has an intuitive understanding of and respect for his child's attachment behaviour" (Bowlby, 1988a, p. 12).

Substitute the word teacher for parent as secure base in the classroom and leader for parent in the staffroom and attachment theory offers a new perspective on what is needed to enable the students to feel secure in the classroom. However, teachers deal with many more students at the same time than parents do. This is a significant difference and needs to be considered by teachers as they think about how to manage students with varying attachment styles. Teachers have to deal with students presenting with very different developmental histories than they have personally experienced. This is not the case with parents, who tend to pass on the same or similar attachment styles to their offspring.[3]

The inner working model

The internal working model forms a set of implicit rules, beliefs and expectations about the environment, self and others. This is used to predict the attitude and behaviour of others, for a predictable world is one in which the self can be safe (Knox, 2003). Bowlby drew on the disparate research findings of information theory, information flow and cybernetics, which was later to become known as cognitive psychology (Beck et al., 1979; Buxton, 1985; Craik, 1943; Knapp, 1986) to suggest that the higher species needed to have a set of understandings or cognitive map of the world for survival within it. He saw this model as being divided into two parts. The first he called the *environmental* model. This incorporated information such as the laws of physics and enabled the prediction and manipulation of the external world. The second he termed *organismal*. This is a personal model telling the individual about her place in the environment. Jeremy Holmes summed up well: "We carry a map of self, and others, and the relationship between the two … The map is built up from experiences and is influenced by the need to defend against painful feelings" (Holmes, 1993b, p. 221).

"Once built, evidence suggests, these models of a parent and self in interaction tend to persist and are so taken for granted that they come to operate at an unconscious level" (Bowlby, 1988a, p. 130). The securely attached person is able to amend and update her working model over time as relationships with others change. However, the insecurely attached person is less able to change her internal working model because of defensive exclusion, like perceptual defence, outlined earlier. This defence mechanism operates to obstruct incoming information discrepant with the internal working model and therefore denies experiences that may promote secure attachment. It operates in the same way that unconscious perceptions (priming) change behaviour (Dixon & Henley, 1991; Mikulincer et al., 2002; Mikulincer et al., 2005).

The child uses the inner working model as a prototype for subsequent relationships she forms. Therefore the child expects subsequent relationships with significant others to have a similar quality to the primary attachment relationship. It is Bowlby's contention that the attachment system, through the internal working models, comes into play throughout life, whenever we feel under threat, stress or fatigue. This is a useful model for teachers when thinking about the relationships they form with their students and why some of these relationships seem more difficult than others.

For example, if the inner working model decrees "I am not worthy of praise" then praise offered by a friend or colleague creates emotional dissonance within the person who must reduce it by either changing her inner working model to include positive judgements of self by others, or by rejecting the praise of others as incorrect. The person who rejects praise for a job she clearly did well may be coping with the emotional dissonance the praise caused by denial of her efforts as worthy. To experience the praise would be to make the world a less predictable and therefore less safe place. This is important information for teachers to consider when contemplating when and how to encourage students to strive to be the best they can be.

Emotional response sets: scaffolding and attachments: the internal context of teaching

Scaffolding has become a common metaphor in education. Teachers, environments and programmes scaffold learning. It is equally true that the emotional responses of children are scaffolded by attachment figures. When it comes to attachments scaffolding emotions, scaffolding should not to be viewed in a strictly Vygotskian sense, although it has a number of similarities (Vygotsky et al., 1997, 1998). It is not a structure erected at the zone of proximal development to be later dismantled as the person moves out of that zone, but rather is the relational environment in which people find themselves.

The scaffolds are the outwardly functioning expression of inner working models, and contribute to the sharing of emotional information and therefore the adjustment of any individual's model. In a sense the scaffold is the potentiality of each individual to act and react to the emotional world guided by those who have been entrusted with their care, because they cannot do it on their own. It is a useful term in this context because it is a solid and yet transitory structure, semi-permanent, rather than fixed, changeable with will but unlike a foundation, able to be modified without destroying the structure itself. It is a good representation of that part of the inner working model that mediates emotional responses to the environment. In that sense it is also relatively predictable.

An example of emotional scaffolding may provide a clearer explanation of how it operates. If one spends time watching young children at play, interacting with each other and their parents, inevitably a child will slip or fall and hurt herself. As long as the injury is not too severe the situation is ambiguous for the child and she will look to the parent's reaction to gauge the severity of the fall. Bowlby (1982) suggested that what the child is seeking is a response set from her parent: guidelines about how to behave in this new situation where the child feels the ambiguity as discomfort. The child asks, in a glance to the parent, "Something has happened to me and I am confused about how to react: Is this a fall big enough for me to cry and feel hurt? Is it time for me to receive comfort from you because I have gone beyond my level of self-soothing, or should I pick myself up, dust myself off and go back to playing?"

Attachment theory proposes that the parent's reaction to this new and ambiguous situation, the fall, is the emotional scaffold. Importantly, it is the scaffold, not the fall that determines the child's response. As the child sees the parent's reaction to the fall, she incorporates that into her response set by creating a new network of associations: the event the fall represents becomes associated with the environmental and physical sensations and perceptions (bumps, grazes, cuts etc.), and with the child's perception of the parental response to them. In effect the child is waiting for response cues from the parent that she will be able to replay in similar events (if my parent seems agitated or frightened by the event, I should stop what I am doing, cry and associate my new physical feelings (scratches, cuts or bruises) with that level of response; if my parent seems untroubled by the event I should return to play). As the child negotiates daily life with multiple caregivers to provide the framework for emotional reactions to the myriad events of life, so the internal working model is constructed and modified over time through the scaffolding of emotions evoked in response to ambiguous or neutral environmental stimuli.

Having outlined the broad constructs of childhood attachment, in the next chapter the theory is expanded with the development of adult attachment. This more complex model is outlined and the relevance of the theory for explaining the dynamics of school classrooms and staffrooms should become clear.

Chapter 2

Adult attachment theory and the teacher–student relationship

The focus of this chapter shifts to the processes of attachment that are more difficult to observe: adult attachment. Evidence will be presented to demonstrate that these processes form the structure of the student–teacher relationship rather than the more simple unidirectional attachment processes of early childhood. Once adult attachment processes are understood by teachers, school leaders and teacher educators they become: better observers of the dynamics of classroom and staffroom processes; more aware of what is going on when plans go astray; and importantly, better able to deal effectively with the novel situations that inevitably arise. It must be remembered, however, that these processes are situated in the person doing the observation just as much as the observed, and behove one to "firstly know thyself".

Attachment and inner working models do not stop developing at the age of three years. Not withstanding the workings of perceptual defence, which can inhibit positive movement in attachment style, the inner working model is adapted and changed over time as a result of new experiences in the world. Drawing on the principles identified by Bowlby and Ainsworth, a more complex model of attachment theory, adult attachment, developed from romantic partner and couples research. This more complex model better describes teaching relationships. While the teacher–student relationship is a dyadic one and therefore carries some of the common attributes of all dyads, it is not the same as a romantic dyad, about which most of the literature exists.

Adult attachment theory builds onto the original theory the concept of dyadic or reciprocal attachments between people. Romantic dyads, couples, are said to exist when each member of the dyad is both care seeker and caregiver, with the roles alternating depending on individual needs at any particular time. Although Bowlby wrote about attachment as lasting from the "cradle to the grave" (1982), it was Hazan and Shaver (1987, 1990) who reconceptualised Bowlby's theory, hypothesising that romantic love may be a new attachment process, similar to a primary attachment, but built from the inner working models and the shared experiences of the protagonists. They employed a simple technique of writing brief romantic descriptions to match Ainsworth and colleagues' (1978) three categories of childhood attachment: *secure*, *avoidant* and *anxious/ambivalent*.

Participants in their study were asked to read the three descriptors and decide which one best described them. They also gathered data relating to the experiences of romantic love and correlated it with the attachment profiles. They hypothesised that the internal working models formed in childhood would affect the quality of the romantic attachments in adult life. They reported three key findings. First, they discovered that the prevalence of adult attachment styles matched childhood prevalence, indicating that attachment style and inner working models, once formed, are robust and relatively stable. Second, they found that "the three kinds of adults differ predictably in the way they experience romantic love" (Hazan & Shaver, 1987, p. 511). Their third important finding was that "attachment style is related in theoretically meaningful ways to mental models of self and social relationships and to relationship experiences with parents" (Hazan & Shaver, 1987, p. 511). Their simple measure, three brief descriptions of secure, avoidant and anxious/ ambivalent attachment, had high concordance with the adult attachment interview (AAI). The AAI remains the gold standard for measurement of attachment styles of parents to predict the attachment style of their children (Brennan et al., 1998).

Adult attachment: from a three category to a four category model

Despite the significant development to the concepts of attachment, Hazan and Shaver (1987) were not convinced of the psychometric accuracy of their model and continued to research it. Their concerns related to the two orthogonal dimensions of attachment identified by Ainsworth and colleagues (1978): Anxiety about close relationships, and Avoidance of intimacy (moving toward, moving away or not moving) that result from that anxiety.[1] Orthogonal dimensions do not lead psychometrically to three distinct categories but four. So a four rather than three category model was proposed by Bartholomew (1990) by further delineating the avoidance domain of the three category model into two conceptually distinct categories; namely *dismissing* and *fearful*, with each quadrant representing differing levels of anxiety and avoidance behaviours. The four category model also incorporated the rarer insecure/disorganised attachment style that had originally been suggested by Bowlby. The four quadrants are named *secure* (low anxiety and low avoidance), *preoccupied* (high anxiety and low avoidance), *dismissing* (low anxiety and high avoidance) and *fearful* (high anxiety and high avoidance). The model was tested and supported psychometrically by Bartholomew and Horowitz (1991). This model received a good deal of support from adult attachment researchers and virtually replaced its three-category predecessor (Bartholomew, 1994; Bartholomew & Horowitz, 1991; Bartholomew & Shaver, 1998; Brennan et al., 1998; Fraley et al., 2000). An adapted form of the model appears in Figure 2.1. Table 2.1 shows the relationship between the quadrants and the key features of each.

Bartholomew (1990) also extended Ainsworth and colleagues' original model by conceptually overlaying the inner model of self with the anxiety axis and inner model of other onto the avoidance axis (see Figure 2.1). This development provided

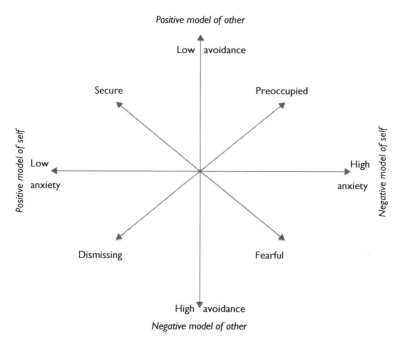

Figure 2.1 Four quadrant model of adult attachment (adapted from Bartholomew, 1990).

Table 2.1 Model of adult attachment developed by Bartholomew (1990) and confirmed by Bartholomew and Horowitz (1991)

		Model of self (Dependence)	
		Positive (Low)	*Negative (High)*
Model of other	*Positive*	*Secure*	*Preoccupied*
(Avoidance)	(Low)	Comfortable with intimacy and autonomy	Preoccupied with relationships
	Negative	*Dismissing*	*Fearful*
	(High)	Dismissing of intimacy Counter–dependent	Fearful of intimacy Socially avoidant

a conceptual depth that had been missing with the previous model and a clearer psychometric fit between the dimensions. This model continues to be refined and has provoked extensive commentary in the literature (see for example, Cummings, 2003; Edelstein & Shaver, 2004; Fraley & Shaver, 2000; Fraley et al., 2000; Sibley, Fischer et al., 2005; Sroufe, 2003; Waters & Beauchaine, 2003). By applying this model, an individual's perceptions of relationships and relating behaviours could be linked empirically to levels of anxiety about, and avoidance of, intimacy and dependency in relationships. These descriptions reveal important information about the type of behaviours teachers, students and school leaders engage in, both positive and negative, as they build and maintain classroom and staffroom relationships. So let us now look at general descriptions of the categories.

The four adult attachment styles

Secure

This category defines people who have a healthy and balanced view of self and others. They are happy to be interdependent. They have low anxiety regarding relationships and do not avoid intimacy. They are placed in the top left quadrant of the figure (Figure 2.1). They have a sense of their own "worthiness (loveability)" and expect others to be "accepting and responsive" (Bartholomew & Horowitz, 1991, p. 227). Securely attached people are also significantly more curious than their insecurely attached counterparts.

Preoccupied

Preoccupied adults feel less worthy than the secure person, but retain a positive view of others. They score highly on anxiety over close relationships and low on avoidance of others. This places them in the top right hand quadrant of the attachment figure (Figure 2.1). They tend to accept themselves only if they are accepted by a trusted and valued "other". This creates a problem because experience has taught them not to trust others, despite wanting to. So they become preoccupied with gaining the acceptance of others to feel good about themselves. This lowers their curiosity about the world around them, as they must remain focused on the opinions of others. It is a confused state often leading to anger and controlling behaviours directed at the very people they seek care from, because they find it difficult to distinguish between genuine responses and those they feel they have cajoled from others (Bartholomew & Horowitz, 1991). Allen and colleagues (2005) described the relentless and exhausting nature of this category:

> Coupled with excessive dependency in continually feeling *let down and disappointment* as well as a *fear of rejection and abandonment.* ... Worse yet, as evident in themes of *ambivalence* and *anger*, the relationship itself is a prominent source of the very distress it fails to regulate. Coping by *coercive behavior* intended to elicit responsiveness from the attachment figure inevitably promotes rejection and escalates fears of abandonment.
>
> (Allen et al., 2005, p. 67 emphasis in the original)

Dismissing

The typical behaviour of members of this attachment style group has been described as obsessively or compulsively self-reliant (Bowlby, 1980). They are placed in the bottom left quadrant of the attachment grid. A score high on avoidance of close relationships but low on anxiety about them suggests that these people may be less in touch with their feelings about relationships than others (Bartholomew & Horowitz, 1991). Having an inner working model that denies attachment needs is more likely to create emotional dissonance when witnessing those needs in others. The person with a dismissing attachment style is likely to be seen by others as remote and unavailable emotionally. It has been found that these people are less likely to respond to talking therapies that rely on the development of a working relationship as they are unlikely to be able to adequately form and maintain them (Crittenden & Ainsworth, 1989; Holmes, 1994b). Teachers with this attachment style would be very likely to find it difficult to form and maintain working relationships with their students and colleagues as they would find it very difficult to trust them. School leaders with this style would find delegation of responsibility stressful, for the same reasons.

Fearful

People who report high scores on both anxiety and avoidance tend to both feel unworthy of love and carry a negative expectation of others' opinion of them. They protect themselves from these painful feelings by avoiding close contact, for their experience tells them that close contact will bring the rejection they fear. They consider others to be untrustworthy and/or rejecting. Yet they want the approval of others: a constant dilemma for the fearful individual (Bartholomew & Horowitz, 1991). In that sense they are not too dissimilar from the preoccupied individual as they share the right side of the grid, but rather than clinging to a significant other they tend to hover at a distance.

Nonattachment

The final category that needs examination, nonattachment, initially appears conceptually difficult. However, it is important to know the difference between an attachment relationship, as described above, and a nonattachment relationship. The subtle differences may have important correlates in terms of classroom relationships. By conducting interviews with experts in the field, Allen and colleagues (2005) were able to distinguish between attachment and nonattachment aspects of relationships. The differences are often difficult to determine. One of the interesting findings they reported was the difficulty of distinguishing between dismissing behaviour and genuine nonattachment.

An important issue to keep in mind when examining school relationships from an attachment perspective is the length of time each member of the dyad spends in contact with each other. Typically teacher–student relationships in primary school last only for one year. Secondary students on the other hand are likely to interact with the same teachers over a number of years, but for much less time each week than they spent with their primary teachers. In both cases the duration of contact may not be long enough meet the strict criteria for an attachment relationship, which takes approximately three years to fully form in both childhood and adult form. However, the emotional investment in the relationship from both parties may produce attachment behaviours as they try to connect meaningfully with each other. In that sense the teacher–student relationship might be conceived as either the first year of the formation of an attachment bond or a nonattachment relationship. What is important is whether or not the attachment behavioural system becomes activated for students, teachers or both.

Attachment needs become elusive

Without a corrective emotional experience that increases the level of felt security, the insecure adult will often unconsciously disguise attachment needs by using a defence mechanism to either repress or sublimate them. This is done in many and often subtle ways. For example, by somatasising[2] the need for emotional care, such as the development of constant low-grade flu symptoms, allowing the legitimate attention of others because one is 'sick' (Skynner & Cleese, 1993) an individual can gain the care she seeks without having to consciously address the fear of rejection: "I am sick, therefore I can accept care in this circumstance, but if I am not sick I don't deserve to be cared for." There are as many ways to disguise attachment needs as there are to disguise any other psychological needs. The disguises are often implemented unconsciously to prevent or at least reduce emotional dissonance.

Adult attachment: from a categorical to a continuous model

Further refining of self-report measures led to the reconceptualising of adult attachment styles from a categorical to a continuous model, where the behavioural repertoire is shaped by context as well as patterns of attachment. This important development was suggested by Shaver, Fraley and their colleagues, who found evidence of differing behavioural responses dependent on circumstances (Fraley & Shaver, 2000; Fraley & Spieker, 2003; Fraley et al., 2000). They argued that complex behaviour is dependent on many variables and that it is overly simplistic to use a categorical taxonomy for classification. They point out that relationships are bidirectional and accordingly each person's behaviour tends in some degree to modify the other's as the two parties are in relationship.

The developments in the conceptualisation of attachment styles in adulthood continue as the theoretical perspective is adopted by more researchers and more widely applied. At present the controversy about the borders between attachment categories is solved if attachment style(s) are conceived as continuous and movement between the dimensions is mediated by experience. Despite these arguments there are eminent practitioners who have argued powerfully for the retention of Ainsworth's categories (Sroufe, 2003).

Stability and change of attachment styles

Smith, Murphy and Coats (1999) conducted a meta-analysis of the literature on the stability and change of inner working models and attachment styles. They determined that there is a general trend toward agreement among researchers in the field. However, there are still areas of disagreement, particularly about the ability of romantic relationships to mediate the inner working models formed in early childhood. They provide evidence for more complex and multiple conceptualisations of adult attachment style:

> people have mental representations (including memories, affective reactions, skills and strategies, etc.) of various different types of relationships, applicable both to people in general and to specific relationship partners. These representations may have different levels of accessibility depending on their recency and frequency of activation ... and more than one may affect responses in ongoing or newly formed relationships. However, one would expect relationship-specific representations to have stronger effects than general ones on behaviors and feelings in a particular relationship.
>
> (Smith et al., 1999, p. 95)

Their review has important implications for the conceptualisation of the teacher–student relationship as an attachment bond formed in specific circumstances for a specific purpose. For teachers, the context in which they work has a powerful influence on who they are professionally and therefore personally. This suggests that the evidence for a continuous model of attachment is the most useful. However for discussion purposes the categories remain useful descriptors even if somewhat oversimplified.

The teacher–student relationship: teachers as alloattachment figures

Applying the principles of adult attachment to the teacher–student relationship reframes the way they can be viewed. Kesner (2000) cautions that while all attachment relationships are close relationships the reverse is not always true. He also reminds the reader that Bowlby (1984) pointed out that children form attachments to significant adults other than their parents, and that "Perhaps there is no other nonfamilial adult that is more significant in a child's life than his or her teacher" (Kesner, 2000, p. 134).

The powerful attachment bond some students feel toward the teacher, as a significant "other" in their life, is also felt by the teacher. This is true for many people closely connected to each individual child. Hrdy (2009) describes this powerfully in the concept of allomothers, who share care of infants in about half of all primate species including humans. However, this reciprocal attachment bond implies that the teacher also has needs in the relationship. The reciprocal attachment between teacher and student, which we might label alloattachment, has an attribute unique to the school setting. The teacher also needs students to show a level of dependence, so that she can construct and maintain a professional identity: there can be no teacher without students, no leader without followers.

Attachment and professional identity[3]

The teacher *needs* at least one student to form a working relationship with to maintain the professional identity of *teacher*. The professional identity, carried by the teacher, cannot exist without the conception by that teacher of at least one student and the relationship that exists between herself and the student. However, the dyad is not a simple one because of uneven distribution of power for each of the roles, along with the legalities and responsibilities that are not equally shared in the teacher–student relationship. This suggests that the teacher–student dyad is a unique one. A further unique complication to this dyad is that while the teacher depends on a relationship with students to maintain a professional identity, this is not the case for the students. This makes the teacher a care seeker from the students, thus placing the student in the role of caregiver, a role that some students may not be ready or willing to perform. A student can exist, and learn, with or without the presence of a teacher. In fact much of teachers' work is concerned with becoming redundant by producing active, independent, resourceful students who will flourish on their own. But this of course carries with it an implicit separation from the student, one that the teacher might consider difficult to embrace.

Consequently, the relationship between the teacher and the student provides the underpinning of a professional identity for the teacher, a learning identity for the students and a professional working relationship for both. When this is viewed through the adult attachment lens the students acquire a great deal of power in the relationship; due to unconscious processes perhaps but powerful never the less. A threat of separation from the class may come from an altercation in the classroom between the teacher and a difficult student who is well liked by her classmates. This can be unconsciously interpreted by the teacher as a threat to the teacher's proximity to the group as a whole, raising the level of separation anxiety in relation to the attachment object, the class. The anxiety then instigates attachment behaviours including anger and separation protest behaviours to arrest the perceived distancing.

The logic of this suggests that the roles of caregiver and care seeker are carried by both parties in the classroom. In addition to the role of care seeker, the teacher also maintains the role of caregiver to the students, by being older and wiser and charged with the legal and moral responsibility for each of the students under her care. The maintenance of these dual roles complicates the attachment behavioural system in operation for both teacher and student in the classroom context.

Attachment to students: individually, the class collectively or both?

A further complication when using the dyadic attachment lens to view classroom relationships is what constitutes the dyad when there is one teacher and many students involved in the classroom situation? Does the teacher form a dyad with each student individually or is some variant of attachment or alloattachment operating in the classroom with the group? It appears that the answer is both. There are multiple dyads in the classroom: teacher to individual students; student to student dyads; and teacher to the group as an alloindividual.

Addressing this issue from a different perspective, Loughran (2006) pointed out that the nexus between theory and practice in education is due in part to different thinking approaches of the researcher and teacher. His findings are that the researcher is often concerned with the individual student whereas the teacher often thinks of the whole class as a single unit. This is because teachers first need to manage the class. Only then can they can deal with the individuals, even though the class is made up of individuals. This is important in terms of how teachers view both classes and individual students.

Applying the attachment lens, it seems that the whole class rather than individual students becomes the attachment object for some teachers. What is unclear is whether the individuals in the class become aspects of a single attachment object for the teacher and/or parallel attachment objects in their own right. Some students are perceived as favourites and others avoided but it is the class as a whole that the teacher seeks or avoids for the maintenance of a professional identity. This type of thinking by the teacher, whether unconscious or consciously conceived, or perhaps a mixture of both, accounts for the language that many teachers use when describing their work. They often speak about a class as a single unit.

Teachers are often heard talking about their classes as a whole, but using the language of an individual. "I have 8F this afternoon", "Can you look after 9C today?", "I think I had a breakthrough with 10B this morning", "I've got 8D today. I hope they're in a good mood", "I'm sick of 9F treating me like that", "I love Grade 3". This may point to an internal working model of the class as representative of an individual, with each of the class members representing an aspect of the collective personality.

Attachment to groups was researched by Smith, Murphy and Coats (1999) who reported that group attachment, as distinct from relationship attachments and group identification, "predicts several important outcomes, including emotions concerning the group, time and activities shared with a group, social support, collective self-esteem, and ways of resolving conflict" (Smith et al., 1999, p. 77). They suggested that adults have multiple inner working models that vary in accessibility due to past relational experiences. These models include multiple models of group membership and affiliation.

For example a person may see themselves as a good team player or a loner, and groups as "warmly accepting or as likely to coerce or reject the self". These patterns of expectation are likely to be context specific and operate on the two dimensions of attachment to individuals: *group attachment anxiety* and *avoidance* (Smith et al., 1999, p. 96). This has significant implications for viewing the teacher–student relationship.

Teachers who score high on anxiety and low on avoidance would be vulnerable emotionally, when confronted with the stressful moments in the classroom, that are also ambiguous. All teachers confront these situations regularly. Teachers who have high levels of avoidance would also be vulnerable, albeit in a different way, through defensive exclusion preventing them from reacting reflexively, and more likely to be overly rule bound and rigid, particularly when dealing with misbehaving students. This has been empirically tested in situations other than classrooms by a number of researchers who have noted changes in attention and memory formation and retrieval that relate specifically to attachment avoidance functioning (Edelstein, 2006; Edelstein & Shaver, 2004; Fraley & Shaver, 1997). The questions that become important for pre-service teachers and school leaders in the light of this context are:

- Is there something in teachers' developmental history that makes teaching attractive as a career, or does something else attract people to the profession?
- Are new (and experienced) teachers aware of this? And, does this make them vulnerable to the trials and tribulations of the job or more resilient?

These questions take us into the realm of unconscious motivation.

Attachment and unconscious motivation to teach: strength, vulnerability or both?

As early as 1963, before the publication of the first volume of Melges and Bowlby's (1969) attachment trilogy, Wright and Sherman (1963) presented arguments that "teacher types are determined, to a large extent, by identification with parents and former teachers" (p. 67). They considered the differing impacts of parents and former teachers on the development of a new teacher. Parents were found to provide moral and intellectual discipline while former teachers provided the primary source of sympathy. This led them to conclude that teachers "think and act in the classroom in ways closely related to those of their former teachers" (Wright & Sherman, 1963, p. 67) and, that this was not a consciously adopted style but developed unconsciously. They employed strongly emotive language, suggesting that the relationship between teacher and student is a form of love, needed by both teacher and student. This language has since fallen into disuse in the educational discourse, perhaps in reaction to its strength and suggestive elements. Attachment theory, which was being developed at the same time as Wright and Sherman researched teacher–student relationships, also directly addresses the concepts of love. In describing different types of teachers Wright and Sherman (1963) presented rich descriptions of the secure and insecure teacher that could have been used to explicate attachment theory, without knowledge of Bowlby's theory. In the following passage the secure teacher is described first, followed by a description of an insecure teacher in search of a corrective emotional experience:

> We propose that for one type of loving teacher her behavior is a means of keeping the love of the earliest mother image she remembers. She remembers that her mother was loving in the first stage and that giving in was rewarded with love in the second. She identifies with the loving, supportive mother by repeating and thus preserving this valued image. This dependency is satisfying to her, for what is most important is the love that she had and which she now keeps by embodying it in her own behavior. There is another type of

loving teacher – one who was deprived of the rewards of love in childhood. She succumbed to her mother's demands out of the fear of punishment rather than the prospect of reward. This teacher's behavior is guided by her desire to make up for her loss. In contrast to the first kind of loving teacher, she loves her pupils not only in order to be loved by them, but also to gain the vicarious restitutional gratification of providing children with the love which was once deprived her.

(Wright & Sherman, 1963, p. 71)

Restitutional gratification, care seeking or corrective emotional experience, it is this need which makes some teachers vulnerable to perceived rejection by students. Given that the relationship teachers seek from students is partly one of care, it is arguable that some teachers may enter the profession partly motivated by an unconscious desire for corrective emotional experiences, through the formation of new attachments to their students. In a study designed to explore this it was reported that teachers who remain in the profession for at least five years do appear to gain the sort of corrective emotional experiences that they sought by joining the profession (Riley, 2009c).

Reparative experiences: the corrective relational experience

It is logical to infer that the internal working model plays a role in the choice of career. An insecurely attached person may be attracted to the teaching profession as a result of a positive experience of teachers as a student, or the promise of having students to attach to. Both offer the chance of a corrective relational experience for the teacher. If these wishes are an unconscious form of perceptual defence they may be seeking the positive aspects of the experience but are not prepared to accept the reality of life in the classroom as a whole. They may be unconsciously seeking only care from students and/or superiors and avoid opportunities to provide care. For some insecurely attached teachers, even if care is offered they may be unable to receive it either through organisational and professional constraints or perceptual defence. This would leave the teacher vulnerable to separation anxiety within the classroom and set the conditions in which separation protest and aggressive responding are more likely to occur towards students.

In the next section I attempt to describe the general characteristics of a teacher with each of the attachment styles as they might present to students. Some of the attributes are over described to give the reader a sense of the character of each of the styles. In any individual however, much more complexity would be observed.

Potential characteristics of the secure teacher

Teachers are best able to serve students when they themselves have been adequately served.

(Sergiovanni, 2005, p. 101)

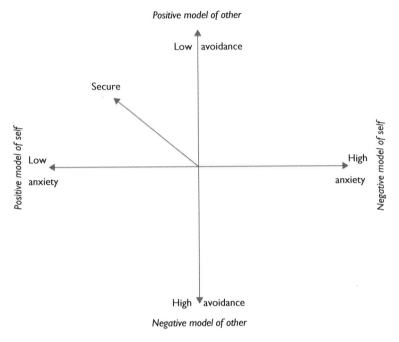

Figure 2.2 Secure attachment (adapted from Bartholomew, 1990).

In the classroom the secure teacher's interest is mainly focused on understanding her students. She is happy to depend on them and have them depend on her. If this trust is broken and the teacher is let down by a student she is more likely to see it as an aberration rather than the norm; it disconfirms her inner working model of others and perhaps drives an investigation into how she can improve the delivery of the information, or the quality of the interaction, so that the student gains understanding and therefore pleasure from the learning experience along with an increased curiosity about the world. This teacher uses the experience to shape and improve her own practice. She seeks to have her internal working model confirmed and does so in ways that benefit the students, the teacher and the relationship between them. Also, as suggested by Wright and Sherman (1963) teachers who feel attached to their students can share much more in the joy of their students' achievement than can nonattached teachers. This has been demonstrated experimentally by Royzman and Rozin (2006, p. 82) using undergraduate psychology students. They suggest that "compared with sympathy symhedonia[4] is inherently more contingent on prior emotional attachment to its targets".

Potential characteristics of the preoccupied teacher

In the classroom the preoccupied teacher may appear to be inconsistent in her treatment of students, over valuing some and devaluing others. The students held

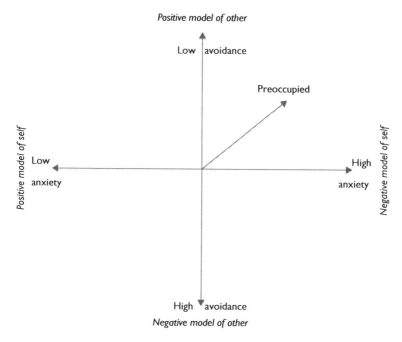

Figure 2.3 Preoccupied attachment (adapted from Bartholomew, 1990).

in high regard may be able to do no wrong in the eyes of the preoccupied teacher, while others appear to do nothing right. The teacher could not afford, in attachment terms, to lose favour with students she deemed special, for instance those who appeared to influence other students either positively or negatively toward the teacher. This might lead to over involvement with preferred students. Bartholomew and Horowitz (1991) found evidence that the preoccupied type is overly expressive emotionally, inclined to inappropriate self-disclosure and care giving. They are also overly concerned with control of relationships. Therefore the attraction of teaching as a means of satisfying many of these needs may have a bearing on the motivation to join the profession. The need for control is satisfied by having the legal responsibility for a class of students and the associated authority that comes with it.

The preoccupied teacher can choose who she would like to be close to and may engineer many opportunities for closeness to preferred students. However, if students reject the closeness, raising separation anxiety in the teacher, as many students with a dismissing or fearful type would, the teacher may find herself displaying separation protest behaviours to those students. The preoccupied type may be more attracted to teaching than the other types. Possibly it could be because they perceive that they will get the rewards of students liking them while remaining largely in control of the relationship, thus reducing the anxiety associated with being liked.

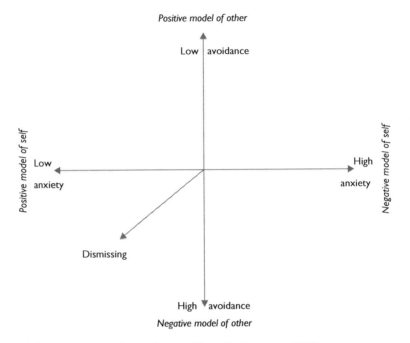

Figure 2.4 Dismissing attachment (adapted from Bartholomew, 1990).

Potential characteristics of the dismissing teacher

While not likely to be attracted to teaching in large numbers due to the forced proximity and interaction with a large number of people, the dismissing teacher may be the type of teacher who tends to "stay on the case" of certain students, always catching them behaving badly and always failing to catch them doing well or being socially proactive (R. Lewis, 2006). If the teacher were to catch the bad student doing good things this would increase her emotional dissonance and therefore challenge the inner working model. To maintain the avoidant attachment she must remain emotionally and symbolically, if not physically, distant from the student(s). However, this is likely to increase the chances of separation anxiety, or even protest, in the students. They may attempt to regain emotional proximity to the teacher to satisfy their attachment needs. This in turn increases the teacher's level of anxiety about the level of intimacy and might lead to increased chances of the teacher misbehaving to remain distant from students who wish to be close.

It might be expected that the dismissing teacher may suffer from more classroom discipline issues as the students try to attach to her. The dismissing teacher's efforts to remain distant emotionally from students would suggest a reaction of separation protest from the students, who may act out in ways that force closer contact with the teacher as caregiver. Like Harlow's monkeys, described in Chapter 8, the students may learn to cling harder to a dismissing teacher, provoking an angry response from

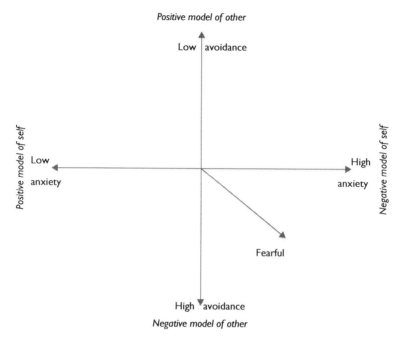

Figure 2.5 Fearful attachment (adapted from Bartholomew, 1990).

the teacher. Thus the cycle of abuse identified by Harlow (1958) may be played out at a lower level of intensity in some classrooms with a dismissing teacher in charge.

Potential characteristics of the fearful teacher

Teachers who exhibit avoidant attachment patterns, both *dismissing* and/or *fearful*, the bottom quadrants of the grid, may find themselves in a heightened state of attachment arousal most of the time. For the fearful teacher, proximity is both sought and avoided at the same time. This creates a number of unique difficulties in a classroom situation where physical proximity is forced upon all. The fearful teacher experiences an increased sense of unworthiness when compared to the other attachment styles. She may feel less able than her peers in her professional capability and is also likely to fear that significant others, such as colleagues, students and parents, will find this out and become negatively disposed toward her as a result (Bartholomew, 1994; Bartholomew & Horowitz, 1991). This makes the fearful teacher more vulnerable to the expectations of others and she would have greater difficulty in managing the competing demands of the people that she deals with daily, including in particular her immediate superiors. Yet, this would also suggest that the immediate superiors have a significant role in the fearful teacher's professional identity. Support by the principal and other superordinates may significantly lessen feelings of inadequacy for the fearful teacher, unlike the dismissing teacher who would not place much value on the opinions of others. Therefore, felt support for the fearful teacher is more likely to create a professional secure base and a chance of a corrective emotional experience with both the leadership and students as she feels supported and encouraged to try new ways of dealing with students. The corresponding reduction in separation anxiety could then allow more emotional freedom in the classroom: less gatekeeping of the teacher's feelings. This consequently promotes flexibility in responding to students and frees emotional energy for application to the tasks of teaching rather than defensive and self-protective behaviours aimed at increasing the emotional distance from students and paradoxically increasing separation anxiety.

Summary

Attachment theory has been a useful tool for the study of relationships for many years. When applied to classroom and staffroom relationships, it helps to explain the variance in classroom behaviour by teachers, students and school leaders when other factors are accounted for. It also explains why some teachers, despite their best intentions, may become aggressive with students: through the mechanism of separation protest. The theory predicts that the teachers who care deeply about their students may be most at risk emotionally: vulnerable to rejection by those students. All teachers are rejected by some students some of the time. The secure teacher sees rejection either as a positive move toward independence from students, as a challenge to do better in maintaining the relationship or some combination of the two. She does not see rejection as a threat to her own security, which lies outside the classroom.

On the other hand the insecure teacher, who may have unconsciously elevated the class to secure base status, is likely to see rejection by these students as confirming her deepest, but unarticulated fear; that she is not worthy of students', or anybody's, real affection. She fears that when the students discover her true self they are likely to reject her just as others have done before. The anxiety this creates has to be reduced by any means necessary and separation protest is the mechanism humans turn to. However, in the classroom setting protest behaviours by teachers increase the sense of insecurity within the students, creating a vicious circle from which no one benefits. Rather than bringing the students closer the separation protests are likely to significantly harm the relationship with many students. The worst case scenario is that the protest behaviours by the teacher drive a wedge between her and the students, eventually leading to despair and detachment in both teacher and students.

As outlined earlier, separation protest behaviours are usually aggressive. With few notable exceptions (see in particular, Sava, 2002; Sutton & Wheatley, 2003) most research into classroom aggression has concentrated on student-to-student, or student-to-teacher aggression. This bulk of the research literature is built on the assumption that teachers, as rational professionals, deal with students, including the aggressive and irrational ones, efficaciously and effectively, at nearly all times given the circumstances, training and experience. This is a persistent but erroneous assumption (Cukier, 1990; Lewis et al., 2005; Poenaru & Sava, 1998; Sava, 2002; Sutton & Wheatley, 2003).

Classroom behaviour by all participants is an emotional experience; not simply a rational display by teachers and an increasingly rational set of behaviours displayed by students as they become acculturated to the system of education, through contact with the rational teachers. A more accurate description of the reality of classroom life is that highly charged emotional bonds are forged between teachers and students that go well beyond the rational, conscious mind. Deep attachments are formed between teachers and students, with favourites and those who must be endured identified by teachers and students alike. Like all relationships, classroom and staffroom relationships are a complex mix of needs, wants, motivations and drives to affiliate, belong, grow and develop. As an example of this, most people can easily identify a teacher that had a profound impact on them, either positively or negatively. The memory of the teacher is usually an emotional one based on how that teacher made them feel rather than what was said.

Paying attention to teachers' adult attachment styles offers a significant opportunity to predict and intervene if needed to improve their student management style. Recent advances in the study of adult attachment, in particular dyadic attachment relationships, suggest that teachers' attachment needs might have a large impact on the classroom environment via the emotional scaffolding they construct for teacher–student and therefore student–student relationships. Most teachers I have spoken to report instances of behaving in ways that might place them in any quadrant of the attachment grid depending on the situation. Although they are more likely to stay in a particular quadrant in most of their relationships, circumstances dictate their response and can invoke both positive and negative change. This lends support to the idea that the attachment styles are best viewed as continuous rather than fixed taxonomies. It also confirms that the context in which we all operate is an important determinant in our behaviour. The next chapter looks at the context of teaching, including the human context, in more depth.

Chapter 3

The emotionality of teaching

This chapter explores the context in which teaching and the teacher–student relationship take place. In trying to capture some of the common essence of classroom context inevitably some aspects will be overlooked in search of the more ubiquitous contexts. To aid this investigation a number of factors are dealt with separately in the chapter which are actually inseparable in reality. In that sense this review may appear to have a number of beginnings or perspectives on teaching contexts but my hope is that readers will be able to put the pieces together and construct the whole by reference to their own experience. The aim is to identify and describe the common factors that the literature suggests have the greatest effect on classroom and staffroom relationships.

In the context of the classroom, the teacher's previous experiences, through repeated interactions with her teachers, form the scaffold for her responses to students. In much the same way that people parent the way they were parented (Cassidy & Shaver, 1999; Roisman et al., 2004; Sroufe, 2005; Yates et al., 2003), teachers tend to teach the way they were taught. As this kind of patterning is strongly persistent, cycles of teacher behaviour, including aggression, may be passed on from one generation of teachers to the next in the same way that healthy security or abuse and neglect are usually passed on within families through intergenerational transfer.

Attachment theory suggests that we have all learnt to form and maintain relationships by our accumulated experience of relationships. The important idea is that the inner working models help us to predict others' behaviours. Our initial approach to new relationships is therefore shaped through previous experience, including teachers' approaches to classroom and staffroom relationships. Every new teacher carries predictive expectations of how teaching relationships work into a professional internal working model from their accumulated experience. This is a sensitive period in the development of a professional identity, which is at its most malleable at this point. So a teacher's introduction to the profession, during pre-service education, induction, mentoring and support, is crucial in the construction and reconstruction of the professional internal working model and for the initial construction of a professional identity.

The internal working model is a construction for making the world and the people in it safe by making it predictable. It has been known for a long time that many teachers feel unsafe, through a combination of inexperience and professional responsibility, when they first enter the classroom (Fuller, 1969). Unless teachers' internal working models of professional relationships and the connections these have with the personal internal working model are examined and articulated they will remain largely, if not completely, outside of conscious awareness, and therefore less open to active change and growth. This leaves teachers with fewer options when it comes to dealing with relationships that lie outside of their personal experience. The strategies they choose to adopt in such circumstances may not be appropriate for the students they encounter and may also lead to unconscious attempts to avoid what appear to be repetitions of unsuccessful relationships in the past. However, it is extremely difficult for a teacher to avoid a relationship with a student or peers, and this can cause teachers a number of professional and personal difficulties, which will be outlined as this chapter unfolds.

The relationships teachers and students form are unique, complex and different from most other relationships. This is the case with all professional relationships, which have their own idiosyncrasies, formal and informal structures and rhythms. The importance of this unique relationship is an important factor in student achievement (Cochran-Smith, 2005; Onwuegbuzie et al., 2007; Sava, 2002; Vanboven, 2005). Therefore it makes sense for teachers to learn about the unique dynamics of the relationships they form with students. In the same way it also makes sense for school leaders to understand the forces that are driving the professional collegial relationships within schools. By examining the contextual specifics confronting teachers from the more universally human perspective of relationship formation and maintenance, both teachers and school leaders can be better equipped to deal with their professional interactions.

Teachers have feelings too

Teaching is traditionally assumed to be rational and logical. In this conception teachers deal with the cognitive aspects of development and deliver curriculum in the most efficacious manner. Challenging this assumption can arouse strong reactions, particularly if emotions are perceived to be the opposite of reasoned responding. However, it is time for educationalists to incorporate current conceptualising of brain functioning, which now places emotions at the centre of all thought, into the educational discourse and practice. (For a review of neurological research developments and their application to learning see: Bechara et al., 2007; Damasio, 2004; Damasio et al., 2004; Goleman, 1995, 2006; Goleman et al., 1993; Immordino-Yang & Damasio, 2007; Rudrauf & Damasio, 2006.)

To ignore or deny teachers' emotions is to ignore or deny their humanity and therefore their authentic selves in the classroom context. This has important consequences. First, it sets up an educational system where teachers find it difficult to be fully present in class. Consequently, the opportunity to fully engage with their students is also diminished or prevented. Second, this approach leaves teachers vulnerable to the expression of emotion by students and their peers. Teachers may become overwhelmed by strong emotions expressed by students, as they have no training in how to deal with them other than their own experience, which for a beginning teacher is by definition limited. All teachers are expected to behave as though they are "in control" but many, particularly new teachers, may feel that they are not in control, priming them for a fearful response to maintain their personal safety (Sutton & Wheatley, 2003). Third, denying the legitimacy of teachers' emotions during classroom practice is to deny teachers two of the most important tools psychologists use as part of their professional engagement with clients: transference and countertransference.

Briefly, transference and countertransference are the feelings evoked internally in the two participants, client and therapist, during an interaction. With practice, transference and countertransference become a form of expert intuition that many teachers acquire. While some teachers develop and use these skills intuitively, training in the use of emotional response sets, transference and countertransference, as tools for assessing and modifying classroom atmosphere, might serve to increase classroom and staffroom efficacy and engagement. To date this has not been introduced formally into teacher education. Sutton and Wheatley (2003) suggested that educational hierarchies continue to promote cognitive development almost to the exclusion of all else because it is more easily measured, and therefore erroneously thought to be more important in the school context.

It is time to acknowledge the complexity and inherent messiness of the teaching and learning context, and the developments in neuroscience which now place the emotions at the core of the teaching and learning experience, and incorporate them into a more complete understanding of what is actually going on in classrooms between people. Cognitive development is of course vitally important, but it is a relatively thin veneer over our primal being; we interact with the world first through tens of thousands of years of evolutionary development and only then through the constraints of our sophisticated era. As Richard Leakey (2005) so eloquently put it in the *Boston Globe*, "Had humanity not been the interested party, we would have been the fifth great ape."

Attachment theory, far from being a challenge to the current, heavily cognitive, conceptualisation of the educative process, offers many insights that fill gaps in the understanding of the complexity of classroom dynamics. Filling in these important gaps can lead to an expanded lexicon of shared practice. Neuroscientists are advising us to look underneath the cognitions to better understand them, but to do that we need a common language to communicate new discoveries and an enhanced articulation of what we know already. Two of the constructs that operate in every classroom, every day, but remain rarely discussed are emotional labour and emotional scaffolding.

Attachment and emotional labour[1]

One of the powerful aspects of attachment is that it is a two-person psychology or theory of interpersonality. This makes it a very useful lens for studying the complexity of interpersonal relationships in the classroom. The multi-personed classroom environment is similar to other environments described by Hochschild (1983) who coined the term emotional labour to describe the emotional effort involved in presenting a particular emotional stance as part of the work role. She studied the effects of emotional labour on flight attendants, who must always appear to be pleasant, helpful and concerned for air travellers' welfare, not unlike teachers, and debt collectors, who must not. Hochschild documented the significant toll on individuals required to act a certain way as part of their employment, noting that dissonance between the customer's expectations of the worker and what the worker actually felt led to all sorts of long- and short-term problems for the worker. Emotional labour is required in many professions and is a fundamental aspect of the teacher's role.

From kindergarten to the academy teachers are faced with moral and ethical dilemmas when they become privy to sensitive and confidential student information, which must be balanced with organisational imperatives. Information about students' lives will be acquired alongside attempts to interest them in finger-painting, quadratic equations, foreign languages, the school musical and the myriad other activities associated with a rounded education. And many new teachers become distressed by the information they hear from and about students' lives.

Once teachers acquire sensitive information about a student, whether they wanted it or not, questions arise that inevitably test their resolve. Will a tenuous relationship with a student, carefully built over time, be irrevocably damaged if they report what they hear? What would the educational implications be for the student? Who benefits? Who loses? Is this story true or made up to test my reaction? What information, if any, should be reported and to whom? Is there a manual for dealing with these situations? While all this takes place the teacher tries to appear calm and in control, presenting a pleasant face to the world. This is emotional labour. It would be interesting to chart how often teachers are forced, through emotional labour, to relate to students, colleagues and parents in ways that move them a significant distance from their "natural" place on the attachment grid.

Who makes the decisions? The external context of teaching

Teachers have to deal with students, parents, administrators and staff colleagues daily, usually in a timeframe delineated by others. They are expected to behave in a professional and caring manner at all times no matter how they are actually feeling or experiencing the world: the emotional labour of the role (Hochschild, 1983; Johnson et al., 2005; Rafaeli & Sutton, 1987; Taylor, 1998; Zapf et al., 1999). Teachers encounter many external forces that operate to make the profession a stressful one (Johnson, 2006; Johnson et al., 2005), and stress can lead to many adverse outcomes.

The previous chapters outlined attachment-related stress. However, that is only part of the story for teachers. The nature of their professional responsibilities has its own stress-inducing correlates. Therefore, it is necessary to see the attachment forces operating in teachers in the environmental context in which they perform their role. Bowlby (1982) referred to this as the environment of evolutionary adaptedness. This is an important aspect of attachment theory. It acknowledges that the environment each of us inhabits mediates the development of each individual. The environment includes everything the person encounters – people, objects, feelings and so on – which must be adapted to during development. Therefore, impact of motivation, classroom context and teaching ideals versus realities must be considered as they influence the types and quality of relationships that can be formed in the environment of adaptedness that each school context represents.

Unlike other professions, teachers deal with students in groups of 25 or more at a time. This provides unique contexts and challenges, and places particular strains on even the best equipped classroom practitioners. Therefore, in continuing the exploration of the overlapping space that began in Chapter 1, the new conceptual formulation of the role of teacher and the teacher–student relationship will be discussed in light of the context of teaching environments. Teachers face many of the same issues, challenges and dilemmas that counselling psychologists do, but receive little or no formal training in how to deal with "difficult" situations that inevitably arise as part of their work. Whether this is due to oversight, lack of resources or lack of time in a crowded pre-service curriculum, they are left more vulnerable than they need be when dealing with difficult students, and increasingly, difficult parents as well.

Helping teachers who are working in demanding and rapidly changing interpersonal environments to do their best work also helps their students to achieve the best possible educational outcomes. To slightly twist the words of Bowlby when he wrote about helping parents as the most efficient way to support children, it can be equally argued that the best way to help students is to meet the needs of their teachers so that they, in turn, can meet their students' needs. Theorists, policy-makers and unions have often construed this as an industrial issue: salary and conditions. While these are important considerations, albeit outside the scope of this book, the emotional needs of teachers require systematic attention because it has been so under-researched until very recently. The level of stress teachers must cope with is a logical place to begin this exploration.

Stress

Stress and the lack of effective support have been identified as causal factors for physical and psychological problems, across many professions (Johnson et al., 2005; Lazarus & Folkman, 1984; Zapf et al., 1999). Documenting the difficulties that many teachers deal with on a daily basis indicates the background level of stress involved in teaching to be quite high. Kay Wilhelm, Jodie Dewhurst-Savellis and Gordon Parker (2000) reviewed the literature into teachers' perceptions of the sources of professional stress. They identified "student misbehaviour; time spent in teaching-related activities; relations with staff, children and parents; the attitude of students toward learning; and work conditions" as the major stressors (p. 292). These might be labelled frontline relationship stressors.

Relational stress on the frontline: links with emotional labour

All the relational professions and many other occupations have an emotional labour component. However, teachers face unique difficulties because they deal with groups. They have to make hundreds of judgements daily, some of which have significant effects on those in their care, and they can be held accountable legally for those decisions much of the time. Given the nature of these demands, it is not surprising that Johnson and colleagues (2005) reported that teachers' stress levels were one of the highest of the 26 relational occupations they surveyed. Their study measured five dimensions of stress drawn from the work of Roberston Cooper (2002):

1   intrinsic to the job, including factors such as poor physical working conditions, work overload or time pressures;
2   role in the organisation, including role ambiguity and role conflict;
3   career development, including lack of job security and under/over promotion;
4   relationships at work, including poor relationships with your boss or colleagues, an extreme component of which is bullying in the workplace ...; and
5   organisational structure and climate, including little involvement in decision–making and office politics.

(Johnson et al., 1999, p.179)

Teachers produced significantly elevated scores on all five dimensions when compared with other frontline relational professions, placing them in the high stress group.

Accountability and emotional labour

Teachers find themselves accountable to many masters and can often need support from the administration, such as principals, assistant principals and faculty heads, to carry out their role. Interestingly, in the UK Johnson and her colleagues (2005) found school leaders, who have a similar amount of difficult issues to deal with daily, but less frontline exposure than teachers, reported significantly less stress than teachers, albeit still high. The authors suggested that teachers' roles require higher levels of emotional labour than the administration. This may be the reason for the difference in reported stress between the two groups.

Drawing on the work begun by Hochschild (1983) and extended by others (see also Fox & Spector, 2002; Rafaeli & Sutton, 1987; Taylor, 1998; Zapf et al., 1999), it seems that emotional labour leads to emotional dissonance and this is a significant factor in the ability to find meaning and fulfilment from work. Administrators generally agree with the proposition that they need to provide support for teachers to reduce stress, but differ on whether the greatest needs are administrative, technical, academic, psychological or symbolic (Ackerman & Maslin-Ostrowski, 2002; Barth, 2004; Sergiovanni, 2005a, 2005b).

A review of the literature on this issue reveals a common complaint from many teachers: they feel that they do not receive adequate professional or symbolic support from their superiors or the public generally. This is compounded when the societal trends are indicating an erosion of good will for teachers (Ackerman & Mackenzie, 2007). A recent study by Lacey and Gronn (2007) interviewed school leaders in three Australian states: Victoria, Queensland and Tasmania. They reported very high levels of stress that led directly to early exits from the profession among school principals. These findings suggest that there is a significant problem in attracting and maintaining high quality teachers and providing adequate support for them in sustaining their work. Those who go on to school leadership would appear to be paying a considerable emotional price for doing so (Lacey & Gronn, 2007).

Increased public awareness and media reportage of the frailty of human beings invested with the responsibility of caring for vulnerable children only compounds the problems. The exposure of paedophiles and other kinds of predation in the profession makes the public more suspicious of teachers as a group. This is despite the fact that relatively few teachers have been charged with or convicted of offences of this kind (Halliday & Ius, 2009). There is a perception that teachers need more accountability to keep them from transgressing. This is an increasing trend in Western society, with the public demanding access to information about all professionals: doctors, lawyers, clergy and so on. This directly and indirectly impacts on how teachers conduct themselves professionally, and may be a structural variant of emotional labour. The term defensive education is increasingly used in the literature: protecting one's self from legal challenge through changed work practices. The research suggests that this is becoming increasingly important, and increasingly frustrating for teachers (Stewart & Knott, 2002). Defensive education, ironically, may limit the chances of teachers and students developing the kind of relationships that foster better learning, which would reduce the need to be defensive about professional teaching practice.

Teachers also suffer, perhaps more so than other professionals, from the "little-knowledge-is-a-dangerous-thing" syndrome. Everyone who criticises teachers has been in the classroom for a number of years, at least as a student, and may claim authority to comment on the process of teaching and learning as a result of his or her past experience. This is a false claim to authority, because experiencing the classroom in the role of teacher is not the same as being a student. A reading of daily newspapers shows that in general society increasingly demands of its teaching force accountability, pastoral care and academic excellence. Politicians of all persuasions routinely criticise teachers for not upholding standards of literacy and numeracy. There seems to be universal political agreement that the business model should be transferred to education. After all, the argument goes, education is about training workers to keep the economy going. For many teachers these kinds of statements are stressful because they have broader ideals for the role of education, but no real voice to debate this agenda.

Another form of stress teachers face is the unilateral curriculum decisions, devised by politicians and their advisors, but implemented, with or without agreement, by teachers. These increase the stress teachers feel because they underline the perception that they command little control over their professional destiny. It appears that this aspect of teachers' professional stress is similar to those reported in the Whitehall studies, in the UK, among middle ranking public servants (see Batty et al., 2005; Carroll et al., 1997; Carroll et al., 2001; Marmot, 2006; Marmot & Smith, 1997; Roberts et al., 1993). These longitudinal studies revealed that significant health/stress correlates appear to be determined by social rank within big organisations. Powerful inverse correlations were found linking public service rank and health outcomes: the lower the rank the greater the health risk (Marmot, 2006). Lack of control over one's professional destiny was reported to play a significant role in the declining levels of health and wellbeing. The public servants' lack of autonomy is very similar to that experienced in the teaching service.

Teachers' background stress is with them before they even enter the classroom, and floating uneasily in their awareness when they are teaching. Using the frame of attachment to interpret these findings it could be argued that as organisations, schools and the professional bodies who oversee them might do well to find better ways to provide a more secure base for their membership. For without it, teachers and leaders find themselves with limited internal coping resources and are therefore more vulnerable to the inherent stress of the professional roles they carry out, and ultimately more likely to leave as a self-protective measure.

Stress takes its toll

For some teachers, stress contributes to behaving inappropriately in the classroom. Disturbing evidence is accumulating with regard to some teachers' classroom behaviour. Writing about it is widespread in the non-English literature, in France, Romania, Russia and Spain (Sava, 2002). Reports have also appeared in Australia (R. Lewis, 2006), China and Israel (Elbedour et al., 1997; Lewis et al., 2005; Lewis et al., 2008), Poland (Piekarska, 2000), Scotland (Hepburn, 2000; Munn et al., 2004) and Japan (Treml, 2001). There is now a common term in the non-English literature for the students' experience of teacher misbehaviour: *didactogeny*, "a faulty education that harms children" medically, psychologically or educationally (Sava, 2002, p. 1008).

Don Watson (2005) has argued that "bad" teachers change lives to the same extent that "good" teachers do. They do not merely deliver less of the same "thing" that good teachers do. Leaving aside for the moment what good and bad teaching might be, if Watson is right in thinking that good and bad teaching are orthogonal to one another, and I believe he is, it follows that research directed toward helping "bad" teachers improve is equally as important as documenting best practice(s) of "good" teachers; even if only as a harm-minimisation strategy. Yet this does not appear to be happening to any great extent (Donohue et al., 2003; Piekarska, 2000;

Poenaru & Sava, 1998; Sava, 2002). One reason for this may be that researchers who study "bad" teaching practice(s) risk misrepresentation of their work as an attack on teachers. This is not the aim here. Rather this is an overdue examination of all that it means to be a teacher so that all teachers can be adequately supported to do their best work.

Teachers who report becoming aggressive also report classroom management difficulties and diminution of teacher self-esteem (Poenaru & Sava, 1998). Self-report studies conducted in Australia, Israel and China show teacher aggression in primary and secondary schools is common enough to justify comprehensive research aimed at reducing the prevalence (R. Lewis, 2001, 2006; Lewis et al., 2005, 2008; Lewis & Riley 2009). However, research into this area has been largely overlooked in the West and according to Sava (2002) may even be seen as a taboo for many Western researchers. This is no longer a tenable position to take, as governments look to system-wide reform and continued high levels of teacher attrition point to the need to re-examine teaching life in all its manifestations. At a more basic level this gives pause for thought when it is understood how important teacher expectations of students are to student outcomes, which are largely determined by the quality of classroom relationships (Kesner, 2000).

It is widely reported that teacher aggression is a factor in negative peer-to-peer relationships in schools: bullying (Lewis, 2008; Lewis et al., 2005; Natvig et al., 2001; Olweus, 1997; Roland & Galloway, 2002; Tauber, 2007). In an interesting research design, Donohue and colleagues (2003) reported on peer rejection and teacher instruction styles in 14 first grade Californian classrooms. They found that when the teacher's practice was learner-centred rather than teacher-directed, students' empathy was increased and anger decreased. They found fewer behavioural problems with the students in a six-month follow up.

Attachment provides a framework for dealing with complex problems

Sava (2002) conducted a comprehensive review of the literature reporting on the problem of teachers using aggressive techniques to manage students, finding evidence of complex and interrelated variables operating, that are not always immediately apparent, to explain the teachers' behaviour. Attachment theory provides the logic that shows the connections.

The following illustrates how attachment theory explains complex suites of behaviour involved in aggressive behaviour in the classroom by teachers and therefore also offers more efficacious ways of dealing with it. While reflecting on a long career working with teachers in the area of classroom management techniques Ramon Lewis (2006) proposed a paradox that may help to explain why the incidence of teacher aggression is so prevalent and persistent, and why researchers have avoided the area. He identified a subset of teachers who decrease then increase their aggression levels following professional development designed to teach non-aggressive responding toward students.

Immediately following the professional development teachers reported that their classroom management and classroom life had improved generally. However, after the initial improvement, to practice teachers' long-term management strategies tended to fall into one of three distinct groups of roughly equal size. The first group took up the new techniques permanently. A second group took up some of the techniques more or less permanently, but needed to repeat the professional development a number of times before the techniques became habits. The third group had a paradoxical response. These teachers initially lessened their aggression levels, similar to the first group, but then reverted to previous levels of aggression. This appears counter-intuitive. Why would a teacher who has successfully implemented a classroom management strategy that is perceived by teacher and students alike as an improvement to class life then abandon it? The paradox is that some teachers become resistant to using the techniques only after successful implementation of them in their classrooms. In effect they become resistant to reducing their own aggression levels.

The discovery that training teachers to use new techniques has only a brief success for some teachers was confirmed by Ingvarson and colleagues (2005) in an extensive meta analysis of 80 professional development activities with 3,250 teachers. They found that for professional development to have an impact on teachers' classroom practice the professional development needed to include "*active learning* and *reflection on practice* .... The extent to which a professional development program influences knowledge and practice ... is enhanced by the extent to which that program also strengthens the level of *professional community*" (Ingvarson et al., 2005, p. 14). The authors may not be aware of attachment theory but they are in effect presenting evidence for its applicability to professional development. However, this way of working with teachers is radically different from most forms of professional development generally offered and is likely to be resisted by some teachers.

Lewis (2006) supported Poenaru & Sava's (1998) findings that aggressive responding to students lowered teachers' self-esteem. He argued that following the lessening of aggressive responding and subsequent reversion to previous aggressive behaviours the teachers perceived their practice as less effective than before the intervention. Not surprisingly, this resulted in decreased levels of self-efficacy and self-esteem. The question posed by this observation is what factors are involved in teachers' aggression surfacing, subsiding and resurfacing? Attachment theory offers a plausible explanation.

Suppose that the teachers were not responding so much to the techniques but the person (in this case Lewis) who was demonstrating them. The sense of "felt security" would have been stronger for the teachers if they perceived a connection with the person delivering the training. Lewis would have been perceived as an expert in classroom discipline, who offers the security of having successfully dealt with difficult students in the past. His suggestions for dealing with difficult students are therefore more than a simple list of techniques to be followed. They represent a vehicle for survival in the classroom through connection to a "secure base". While Lewis remained in contact with the teachers offering support, hints and guidance, they in turn felt less anxiety and increased confidence in managing students. Once the techniques were in place however, Lewis moved to another school, repeating the process. It was only after his withdrawal that the reversions to more aggressive responding began to take place.

Without Lewis in proximity as the secure base to turn to in times of need, these teachers first lost confidence. Eventually the skills provided during the professional development to handle the class effectively were abandoned and reversion to older behaviours occurred. A secure base allows for risk taking and provides more than skill. Removing it becomes too much for the insecure teachers to bear and the resulting stress activates the attachment behavioural system which in the absence of a secure base figure leads to aggressive behaviour as a reaction to increased anxiety. The problem for the teacher is that this runs counter to logic, and the teachers know it. The result is lowering of their self-esteem, so a negative cycle of behaviour is reinforced.

It is self-evident that teachers who do not feel skilled in handling various classroom situations are more likely to behave inappropriately than those who remain confident in their ability to cope. While teacher misbehaviour and its profound effects on students are beginning to be reported in the literature (See Hyman & Snook, 1999; Lewis & Riley, 2009; Lewis et al., 2008; Poenaru & Sava, 1998; Riley et al., 2009; Sava, 2002) it is the effects on teachers themselves that are more worrying when viewed through the lens of attachment. These teachers are in need of more support than they feel they receive. Therefore to reduce counterproductive teacher behaviour, providing support for teachers needs to be rethought, or the cycle of aggression is likely to be passed on to the next generation of teachers. This is the new millennium challenge for school leadership.

Aggression to preserve the inner working model

Returning to Lewis' paradox, teacher aggression born of attachment difficulties and emotional dissonance probably points to unconscious motivation to become a teacher as something to be considered. Teachers seeking corrective emotional experiences by joining the profession have to confront the emotional dissonance of a new way of relating. It is likely that improving classroom relationships through new techniques for managing students may also inadvertently cause emotional dissonance for some teachers, when their inner working model of self and other are inadvertently challenged by pro-social classroom behaviour. For some teachers, despite an unconscious wish to have these experiences and adjust their inner working model over time, the emotional dissonance that this process would inevitably cause may be too much to experience: hence they leave to lessen the dissonance and preserve their internal working model intact and the world predictable enough for them to feel safe within it. Other teachers may revert to aggressive responding in an attempt to lessen the dissonance by changing the students' manner of responding to them, which also preserves their inner working model in its current state, but will necessarily alter the students' models of student–teacher relationships.

Shared internal working models: persuasion, manipulation and aggression

In attachment theory the concept of shared internal working models is crucial to understanding and explaining classroom interactions, including teachers' behaviour. Recall that the development of the internal working model is largely complete for the child by the age of three years. At this time the child has developed the architecture of reflective function (Knox, 2003, 2004). Both Knox and Fonagy and colleagues (Fonagy & Target, 1997, 2005) argue that the ability to understand one's internal working model as a separate model from the internal working model of others indicates that the child is able to internalise multiple, separate internal models and that this is the basis upon which the child begins to negotiate shared goals with attachment figures, including teachers when she arrives at school. This also has the potential to cause distress, as there will always be times when the two models do not align, causing an increase in separation anxiety and therefore increasing the likelihood of separation protest behaviours.

As the child grows up negotiation with attachment figures during times of misalignment of internal working models is one mechanism that enables the models to be modified. The perceived discrepancy in the models also motivates the child to change the caregiver's working model so that it more closely aligns with the child's. When the student–teacher relationship is one of care seeking and care giving – the adult attachment model – the misalignment of models becomes a challenge for both students and teachers as they attempt to change the others' worldview. However, this can be either a positive or negative process, depending on the child's relational history.

Fonagy suggests that a child who has not received recognisable but modified images of her affective states, through her parent's responses to her, may fail to develop an intrapsychic awareness of mind and so to develop a sense of psychological separateness (Fonagy 2001, p. 172). In this situation emotions and even words themselves are not used or experienced as communications but as coercive manipulations, which force other people to do things rather than conveying one's own mental state to them to respond to as they choose (Knox, 2004, p. 13).

This is obviously an extreme example, but it does make the point clearly that the relationships played out in classrooms can be dysfunctional and harmful for all concerned. By becoming aware of the dangers inherent in the process of educating, teachers can be far better protected from many of those risks, and this would also help to inoculate their students from that kind of relational harm.

Understanding shared working models is the basis of understanding adult attachment. Negotiation of shared working models allows the child to interact with multiple attachment and nonattachment figures and this developmental process once begun is carried on until the grave (Bowlby, 1982). Therefore, the need to share internal working models with the people we need to care for us and care about is a process that can very quickly induce separation anxiety. The level of perceived overlap of internal working models directly relates to the level of separation anxiety as people negotiate shared experience.

Extending shared working models to school relationships increases the complexity considerably. Points of contact and points of departure will be many. A metaphor might be a cascade or perhaps flow of internal working models to explain the multiple relationships that exist in any complex multi-peopled environment such as a school. When the multiple relationships that are the foundation of any complex organisation are conceptualised in this way the need for mediated flow of internal working models from one secure base to the next becomes apparent. The hierarchical model of schools with multiple parent figures structurally promotes dependency, both up and down the line of security, for the teachers.

Hierarchies, such as those found in the standard model of schools, also promote defensive rather than flexible functioning (Diamond, 1986). However, rather than hindering growth within the organisation as Diamond suggested, the dependency also affords the teacher the chance for a corrective emotional experience from her relationship with both superordinates and students. Teachers who are trying to negotiate the flow of secure bases via the sharing of internal working models will be confronted with others whose models of self and other differ, possibly dramatically, from their own. Each of these contacts offers teachers an opportunity to adjust their own internal working model or attempt to adjust the other's model through negotiation, manipulation or aggression if the differences create sufficient separation anxiety for the teacher. This may account for both the prevalence and level of teacher misbehaviour, as they unconsciously seek a corrective emotional experience while defending against their possibility.

Attachment behaviours in adults only appear in times of stress

One of the difficulties encountered when researching the effects of the attachment behavioural system on teachers' classroom behaviour is that by adulthood the intensity of attachment behaviours are reduced and they only appear intermittently, during times of stress or crisis (Ainsworth, 1989). Despite this, attachment needs do not disappear and all teachers, just like all students, have a continuing need for a secure base from which to explore and a safe haven to withdraw to in times of stress. Kesner (2000) reported that the childhood attachment experiences of pre-service student teachers accounted for some of the variance in the quality of teacher–student relationships during their practicum. He noted some methodological difficulties, not the least of which was a difficulty with accuracy of childhood memories, as these may become biased by current relational practices. He went on to report, "It is possible that these issues [discipline and relationships with peers] have a significant role in the internal model of child–teacher relationships" (Kesner, 2000, p. 145).

A further difficulty is determining motivational factors. As attachment forces are largely unconscious they are likely to be involved in the motivation to become a teacher, which brings us back to the difficulties associated with unconscious motivation; difficult to assess, even more difficult to measure, but never the less important to examine. So let us now look at unconscious motivation from a slightly different perspective.

Unconscious motivation

Popper and Mayseless (2003) conducted a detailed search of the psychological literature on "good parenting" and transformative leadership, reasoning that the links were very strong, but largely ignored in the research on leadership. They argued that the attachments formed between leaders and subordinates mirror those of parent–child relationships. It is certainly conceivable that teachers, wishing for long-term emotional security through contact with students, actually receive the corrective emotional experiences through relationships with their leaders as surrogate parents. Leader(s) therefore provide the secure base for the teacher rather than students. However, none of the literature cited reported the effects that these relationships with subordinates have on leaders from an adult attachment perspective. This is an interesting oversight given that leaders need followers just as teachers need students and are equally vulnerable to rejection from them. The parallels with teaching might also be considered relevant for this argument, as all teachers are leaders of their classes. Hargraves and Fink (2006) along with others (Ackerman & Maslin-Ostrowski, 2002; Barth, 2004; Sergiovanni, 2005) have suggested that there is much evidence to show that "good" teachers are indistinguishable from transformative leaders.

Popper and Mayseless (2003) cited evidence from a number of studies demonstrating that motivation in followers comes from feeling a secure base is present: they found that the ability to produce a secure base for followers was one of the hallmarks of the transformative leader. Other qualities detailed by the authors were the ability to remain calm in a crisis: not to lose sight of the higher ideals of the organisation at the time when one might be excused for doing so, and remaining empathic and attuned to followers, while coping with the crisis. These are the attributes of the securely attached person. The authors reviewed the evidence that demonstrated long-lasting effects on the followers, as opposed to charismatic leaders who were also good in a crisis but the positive effects of their actions were found to decay quickly with the passage of time:

> we argue that the need of followers for a sense of security in their relationships is not restricted to crisis situations. Moreover, dependency on leaders for protection and guidance does not automatically entail self-loss and regressive dependency. Rather, this "dependency" might be a key for the capacity of followers becoming able to reach needs at higher levels, such as self-actualization.
>
> (Popper & Mayseless, 2003, p. 46)

This leads directly to the question of whether the teacher/leader is in a dyadic or a dependency relationship with her peers or students, or whether the teacher–student relationship is in fact a true attachment relationship:

> There are many similarities between the child–parent relationship and the child–teacher relationship. … Children may look to the teacher for the same sort of "emotional security" that characterizes the sensitive, responsive, and socially supportive caregiving of the parent.
>
> (Kesner, 2000, p. 134)

However, the insecure child may avoid seeking comfort due to past experiences of loss and/or unavailable attachment figures. She may choose instead to punish the perceived caregiver substitute, the teacher, for being in that role. The important question to ponder is whether some teachers might also seek, avoid or punish, albeit in a more sophisticated manner, the same sort of emotional security from their students, to maintain their professional identity.

Providing a secure base through professional development

Earlier I reported a study conducted by Lewis (2006) who worked with self-identified aggressive teachers, delivering professional development to address the problem. The teachers reported motivation to change their management style, and indeed did so for a limited time following his intervention. By taking teachers' motivation into account, the reversion to old patterns of aggressive behaviour suggests that the conscious motivation for change may be mediated by an unconscious motive to remain the same. It may be that the consciously implemented behavioural change creates both emotional labour and emotional dissonance in the teacher that may overwhelm her (Johnson et al., 2005). This explains why success, in lessening aggressive responses in the classroom, may be an outcome too difficult for some teachers to experience emotionally, and raises the question: might pre-service teachers benefit from activities designed to bring unconscious motivation to consciousness and thereby deal with the emotional dissonance more directly, before they enter the classroom?

Bringing unconscious motivation to consciousness

While unconscious motivation is difficult to explore methodologically, and therefore is a somewhat controversial path to follow, it is likely to provide a rich area of research and new interventions to combat the continuing problem of early career teacher attrition, which is addressed in the following sections. If the need for a corrective emotional experience produces strong motivation to become a teacher, it follows that unless corrections begin early, teaching will rapidly become too difficult to continue with.

By addressing teacher behaviour, in all its manifestations, using attachment theory as a new conceptual framework, lessening the prevalence and intensity of misbehaviour may be possible. If underlying psychological processes are driving the teachers to misbehave, interventions aimed at helping teachers to understand their own processes offer the chance for fundamental and lasting change in their behaviour by better understanding their whole motivation, not simply the rational aspects. "As Kuhn has emphasised, any novel conceptual framework is difficult to grasp, especially so for those long familiar with a previous one" (Bowlby, 1988a, p. 26). Working with teachers to develop an awareness of their unconscious motivation naturally leads to emotion work, attunement and thus to attachment theory as the framework on which the emotions are understood by individuals internally. Some suggestions for how this might be done will be offered later in the book.

Unchallenged assumptions

The vast majority of educational research into the practices of teachers is aimed at defining and refining the best of these practices. This approach does not appear to have solved the problem of teachers behaving aggressively or high levels of early career attrition. The unchallenged assumption that has until recently permeated the English literature on classroom management is that unhealthy classrooms may only lack some of the elements of healthy ones. If this assumption is wrong, researchers need to identify the differences between the classrooms where teacher behaviour is likely to produce negative outcomes for both students and the teachers themselves and those that appear to be inoculated against it.

Summary

All the literature reviewed regarding leadership and teacher–student relationships takes a linear view of attachment: a uni-directional, caregiver to care seeker bond. However, this conceptualisation is likely to be too simple. In the first section, arguments were presented to reconceptualise the teacher–student relationship as a dyadic one and by inference the leader–follower relationship also, albeit with differing levels of power attributed to leaders, teachers and students. Logically, teachers' relationships with their superordinates are also reciprocal dyads. These arguments support the postulate that there may be a flow of secure bases operating in schools, perhaps in all organisations that depend on internal relationships. The dual role that teachers take on with the job, caregiver and care seeker to both their students and their superiors, places them in a unique context of complex reciprocal relationships. The emotional correlates of such a position and the emotional labour requirements of the varying contexts are only beginning to be explored.

One of the recurring themes of the book, unconscious motivation to join the teaching profession, was examined from two different perspectives. Modifying teacher education to facilitate pre-service teachers' understanding of their own emotional response sets offers the hope of breaking the cycle of negative transfer to the next generation of students. Teacher educators would need to draw from aspects of counselling training to facilitate the building of the teachers' resilience first, through self-awareness. This does not occur in teacher education at present, except informally, and the failure to provide these kinds of insights leaves teachers vulnerable to repeating the cycles of behaviour they learned in the classroom as students rather than altering learned behaviours through the uncovering of their triggers.

While each of the psychological conceptual explanations for teacher behaviour offers useful perspectives, Knox (2003) has cogently argued that attachment theory is the most plausible underlying theory of interpersonal relationships. She outlines the development of individuals through attachment theory and logically draws together all of the major psychological theoretical explanations as various elements of the same overall account.

Attachment theory provides logical explanations for teachers' positive and negative behaviours, and the aggression that teachers display in the classroom, as a fundamental aspect of human relating. The important aspects of the theory in relation to this are the concepts of the secure base, separation protest, the environment of adaptedness and collective inner working models. This conceptualisation leads to the likelihood that some teachers are unconsciously motivated to enter the profession to find a corrective emotional experience, a secure base, from the job though either:

1   a long-term relationship with a leader or leadership team in a school,
2   multiple interactions with students or
3   some combination of 1 and 2.

In the next section the research into teachers' attachment styles is presented and discussed.

Part II

Researching teachers' attachments

This section of the book is directed toward the discovery of new ways to help children throughout their schooling, derived from attachment theory. The premise is that the best way to support students is to properly support their teachers. This is the logical extension of Bowlby's (1988) clinical work. He suggested that the correct support for parents gives children the best start in life. So exploring the relationship patterns of teachers is the focus of the next chapter. These patterns result from each teacher's "here and now", her relational history, organisational culture and the particular teaching context.

Chapter 4

Does time in the classroom effect attachment style? Does attachment style effect time in the classroom?

Teachers' attachment styles

A cohort model or natural groups design (Shaughnessy & Zechmeister, 1994), was adopted for this investigation. Data was collected from all pre-service teachers at a single university in their final year of study before qualifying. A comparison sample was drawn from a single year cohort of experienced teachers undertaking further educational studies at Masters level. These samples were selected for four reasons. The first was practicality: I had access to both groups. The second was that the sampling method, using all students from a cohort, was likely to be more representative of the variation in motivation across and between both groups. Third, the universities selected for the pre-service and experienced cohorts contained both primary (elementary) and secondary teachers, allowing valid comparisons. The fourth reason was that all participants were currently education students at a university. Therefore any variance in anxiety that might be attributed to study would be equally distributed between the groups. The minimum criterion for experience was set at five years in the teaching profession, which all the Masters students had achieved. Early career attrition data suggests that teachers who last beyond five years are likely to stay teaching for long periods (Brookfield, 1995), and that therefore the differences between the two groups should have emerged.

Self-report measures of attachment, using a likert scale questionnaire format, allowed the use of descriptive and inferential statistics, and discriminant function analysis for the various teaching levels: pre-service, experienced, primary, secondary, gender and age. Groups of these combinations of the teaching types were compared using multivariate analysis of variance (MANOVA) and effect sizes were calculated. This method is the most efficient way to identify trends and make inferences about the underlying motivation between the groups. The questionnaire assessing attachment style helped to determine whether attachment style was associated with motivating a decision to undertake a teaching career. The statistics were reported in detail in *Teaching and Teacher Education* (Riley, 2009a).[1] My aim here is to present a summary then flesh out the issues that the results of the study raised.

Usefulness of self-report measures of attachment for teachers

The questionnaire that was used, the *Experience of Close Relationships* (ECR) (Brennan et al., 1998) is overly sensitive to placing respondents into the insecure attachment categories. Population studies show 30–40% of all people are insecurely attached. The ECR shows a significantly higher proportion as insecurely attached, but it is very robust at differentiating between them, which proved to be useful, as you will see below.

The findings

The following summary outlines the differences between the various types of teachers who participated in the original study:

- *Pre-service and experienced teachers:* Experienced teachers were significantly less avoidant of intimacy than pre-service teachers, accounting for 7.92% of the variance. Experienced teachers' levels of anxiety about close relationships were significantly lower than pre-service teachers, accounting for 12.85% of the variance.
- *Primary and secondary teachers:* Pre-service primary teachers were significantly less avoidant than pre-service secondary teachers, but this only accounted for 2.05% of the variance. No significant difference was found for level of anxiety. No significant differences were found for experienced primary versus experienced secondary teachers, suggesting that experience is perhaps more powerful than level (primary versus secondary).
- *Male and female teachers:* Female primary teachers were significantly less avoidant of close relationships than female secondary teachers. Gender also interacted with the experience and age groups.
- *Age group:* This was a significant variable for level of avoidance but not for level of anxiety. However, it interacted with experience and gender. Young teachers and older male teachers are significantly less avoidant than their peers. Young experienced females and males of all ages reported lower levels of anxiety. This approached statistical significance. This data may indicate that there may be critical periods for receiving corrective emotional experiences for female teachers, with younger females at greater advantage.

The interesting finding supporting the hypothesis that attachment is a useful theory to examine teachers' motivations was that all of the 307 participants in the study were insecurely attached, using the sorting method developed by Brennan, Clarke and Shaver (1998). The whole sample was distributed between only two of the four dimensions shown in Chapter 2, Figure 2.1. Most teachers (80.8%) were found to be in the fearful category, with the remaining 19.2% preoccupied. Many interesting differences between the various types of teachers (experienced versus pre-service, primary versus secondary, age and gender) were also found. In terms

of corrective emotional experiences, the strongest difference between the participants was level of experience.

The more experienced teachers reported significantly lower levels of both separation anxiety and avoidance of intimacy. There are two possible explanations that
can be drawn from this data. The first is that the experienced teachers' professional
or life experience had reduced their insecurity. The second is that the more insecure teachers who began teaching with the experienced teachers had left the
profession and therefore were not sampled.[2] This finding raised many questions,
and confirmed that attachment anxiety and avoidance levels were significantly different when time in the classroom was the discriminating criterion. So the first
question posed in the chapter title was partially answered in the affirmative.

The question that time spent in a classroom as a teacher is likely to lessen the
level of both anxiety for and avoidance of, close relationships produced mixed
results. The reported data indicate that primary teachers' attachment profiles are
different from secondary teachers initially. They appear to be both less anxious and
less avoidant of close relationships. Once they gain experience this gap becomes
larger for females but significantly larger for males. Secondary female teachers do
not change their levels of avoidance of intimacy with experience, despite reporting
lesser levels of anxiety about close relationships. Given that the two dimensions of
attachment are orthogonal, this seems to represent a change in attachment style
over time.

What may have been uncovered by the categorical data analysis is that the people
who choose to work as teachers are more likely to have insecure attachment histories, particularly fearful and preoccupied, than the general population. It is logical
to assume that a dismissing individual would be less attracted to professions that
demand interaction with many people. It is also likely that insecure preoccupied
teachers might be considered to be at an increased risk of aggressive responding as
a management technique when their attachment behavioural system becomes activated in the classroom. Using Brennan and colleagues' (1998) weightings this could
be as much as 20% of teachers. These findings are important for school leadership
teams as they plan the provision of support for teachers.

Using Brennan and colleagues' (1998) discriminant function weightings, both
pre-service and experienced teachers were categorised as either preoccupied or
fearful. This may indicate that teachers form a distinct subgroup of the population when categorised in attachment terms, a finding that needs more exploration.
Given that the current thinking about attachment categories suggests that they are
less useful than dimensional attributions, the categories do offer a shorthand way of
conceptualising patterns of behaviour displayed by teachers.

If some teachers are seeking corrective emotional experiences through attachment bonds with students, a number of aspects of their aggressive behaviour are
theoretically explained. An insecurely attached teacher, who may be consciously or
unconsciously looking for students to provide a corrective emotional experience
through attachment to her, is vulnerable to rejection by those students. Therefore,
the threat of, or actual rejection by students may be an experience likely to activate

the attachment behavioural system in the teacher (Bowlby, 1982). This would inevitably lead to protest behaviours directed at students to reduce the separation anxiety caused by the actual (or perceived) rejection. The kind of self-reported aggressive behaviours that appear in the literature – yelling, sarcasm, humiliation and punishing the whole class for individual misdemeanours – are typical of protest behaviours.

The results reported provide two strong indications. The first indicator was that teachers are not a homogeneous population, and the second was that they are certainly not representative of the population as a whole, at least in attachment terms. Teachers are a unique subset of the population and this has many implications for future research into those who make up the profession.

The results provided by the MANOVA comparing teacher types support the hypothesis that some primary teachers may be getting corrective emotional experiences from their work setting that their secondary colleagues do not appear to receive. Two potential inferences can be drawn from this finding. The first is that secondary teachers, perhaps unlike their primary colleagues, do not seek to enter the profession for a corrective emotional experience. The second inference is that secondary teachers deal with many more students for briefer periods and this does not afford the amount of contact needed for corrective experience from students. Therefore, secondary teachers' levels of both anxiety about relationships and their avoidance of them as a result do not change over time.

Pre-service secondary teachers report more anxiety about relationships than their experienced counterparts. This is not a surprising finding given the context of the two groups. The experienced group know they can survive and even thrive in the classroom. They have done so for at least five years. The pre-service group are far from certain about their own survival, because they have not been tested yet. They are full of Francis Fuller's (1969) concerns about self. However, the difference in levels of attachment anxiety between pre-service and experienced secondary teachers is not statistically significant, as it is with primary teachers. This is an interesting finding given that time in the classroom was the biggest single difference in attachment style between the two groups. This shows that the biggest increases in attachment security, or decreases in insecurity, occur with primary teachers. An explanation for this may be deduced from the nature of their work.

Secondary teachers spend up to 95% less contact time with their students than their primary colleagues. They also have to deal with many more students in any given week. This structural difference in the teaching role may contribute to the prevention of the building of relationships at a deep enough level to provide the corrective emotional experiences that the primary teachers seem to be experiencing. However, unlike most primary teachers, secondary teachers do have the chance to work with the same students over a number of years. This helps to explain why experience, not teacher type, was the biggest single difference between the teachers.

The average primary teacher spends most of each working day with approximately the same 25 students. Secondary teachers, on the other hand, are likely to have up to 200 students in groups of 25 for short periods, a small number of times each week. Primary teachers are also generalists. They deal with students in many differing situations, being solely responsible for much of the curriculum delivery. Secondary teachers, on the other hand, see their students usually for a very limited number of subjects; for example the average secondary teacher only interacts with students for Mathematics and Science or English and History. Therefore, primary rather than secondary teachers are more likely to get to know their students in ways that can foster a deeper emotional connection with them as a function of both the quantity and quality of the time spent together, and the variety of activities they engage in. The depth and complexity of these classroom relationships may be providing more opportunities for corrective emotional experiences for the teacher as well as the students. Further research to determine whether there is a time-order relationship between years of experience and level of relationship anxiety might shed some light on this.

Pre-service teachers' feelings of anger toward students

With regard to the levels of angry feelings directed toward students, there are two interesting findings. The incidence of angry feelings about students reported by pre-service primary teachers was high, with only 17% pre-service teachers reporting that they had never felt angry with students during teaching practicum. These teachers had only experienced six weeks' contact with students at the time they completed the questionnaire, although some may have previously worked with children in other settings. None of the teachers had acted on the angry feelings when surveyed, but it is safe to assume that in the future, unless the teachers work through the issues that caused the anger, some will. This is consistent with the literature on insecure attachment and aggressive behaviour in children (Appleyard et al., 2005; Egeland et al., 1993; Roisman et al., 2004; Sroufe, 2005) and adult romantic attachments (Baldwin et al., 1993; Hazan & Shaver, 1987; Mikulincer & Goodman, 2006; Perel, 2007; Scharfe & Bartholomew, 1994; Simpson & Rholes, 1998). What is yet to be determined is whether the levels of avoidance of intimacy or anxiety about close relationships can in some way predict success in the classroom for teachers.

It is not clear whether the findings suggest that anxiety is more important than avoidance in determining harmonious classroom relationships, yet it does appear that they do not contribute equally. More investigation was needed to determine the extent to which the attachment styles of teachers predict their daily classroom practice. This is reported in Chapter 5.

Surveying both pre-service and experienced teachers demonstrated that teachers who choose either primary or secondary teaching as their career while similar are recognisably different from one another, and this is reflected in their attachment profiles. This finding makes sense intuitively, and also reflects my experience working with each of the groups over a number of years. The differences appear to be greater during their pre-service education. Levels of anxiety about intimacy and dependency differed considerably between the groups (primary versus secondary, male versus female, experienced versus pre-service, and age group). This has important implications for pre-service education and on-going professional development. The kinds of female primary teachers who go on to further study with an eye to eventual school leadership may be yet another subset of the teaching population that differ in their attachment profiles, but the relatively small sample sizes of experienced teachers suggest caution when considering the implications. With that proviso, it is interesting to note the differences in anxiety for males compared to females in the primary cohort. There is a significant drop in male primary teachers' levels of anxiety but an increase in their avoidance of close relationships. This raises the question: is their anxiety level lowered because of increased avoidance as a result of their classroom experiences? After all, male teachers are routinely advised not to get too close to their students in a defensive legal protection of the teacher from allegations of inappropriate behaviour. This data may be a reflection of that rather than a significant difference in gendered responses to students. This also needs further exploration through qualitative and quantitative methodologies.

The evidence supports the hypothesis that attachment is likely to affect to some degree the choice of teaching career type, most likely unconsciously. The attachment styles the teachers reported may be more representative of people attracted to the helping professions in general and not limited simply to teachers. This suggests that education about how relationships work, or even intensive guided personal reflection, may be a useful addition to both the initial education and ongoing professional development of all rather than some helping professionals, as is the case at present.

The research reported provides strong support for the assertion that helping teachers, and perhaps other helping professionals, to understand the boundaries of self and other, by examining their relational history, will provide useful, perhaps essential pre-service learning. People who choose a career based on a hope or wish to become close to others might increase their chances of forming and sustaining relationships that will nurture and sustain them via this type of training: true dyadic benefit. After all, people who receive enjoyment and emotional nourishment from their work are likely to stay in that work and be of greater benefit to the people they work with. It may even go some way to address the significant attrition rates that beset the teaching profession.

These findings are preliminary and exploratory and should be read with some caution. The sample size for experienced teachers was not large enough to make any more substantial claim than that there appears to be a case for further exploration with a larger sample. It should be noted, however, that the qualitative data reported in the next chapter also lend support to these findings.

Although attachment research with teachers is in its infancy, two other large cohort studies confirming attachment as a significant element in teacher motivation, behaviour and misbehaviour have been reported (Riley, Lewis, and Brew, 2010; Riley, Watt & Richardson, 2009), and data being collected in China and Israel, but not yet fully analysed, also shows that once the concepts are explained to teachers attachment is seen as a significant motivator for teacher behaviour, by the teachers themselves.

The results of the quantitative investigation and subsequent studies have indicated that attachment is an important aspect of classroom life, but this does not document how teachers experience it. So research designed to investigate how attachment affected classroom relationships was undertaken. What emerged was a series of six psychoanalytically informed in-depth interviews, based on brief integrated therapy with a present-past-future progression. This is described in detail in the next chapter.

Chapter 5

Contextual Insight-Navigated Discussion

The qualitative investigation

Contextual Insight-Navigated Discussion was designed as a combined intervention and research process. As attachment is an important predictor of teacher behaviour, then teachers' experience of attachment(s) to students is likely to mirror their own developmental attachments. Bringing these to light is therefore a crucial ingredient in developing an understanding their emotional reactions to students and colleagues. So this involved working with teachers who had become aggressive with students. My aim was to help them discover how their relationship history, including attachment style, impacted on their perception and therefore management of classroom relationships. Given that attachment styles are not fixed, albeit stable, the question was whether teachers could change their management style as a result of the new insights about themselves, rather than learning a new series of techniques.

The focus was on general differences between secure and insecure attachment styles and individual histories of attachment, rather than between the differing types of insecure attachment. Interviews were conducted using a form developed from brief integrated psychotherapy (Macnab, 1991a; Teyber, 2006), time limited therapy (Brown, 2002; Levenson, 2004; Mann, 1981, 1991; Molnos, 1995) and case story methodology (Ackerman & Maslin-Ostrowski, 2002; Bateson, 1991; Carter, 1999).

While the quantitative data suggested general trends that could be inferred, it could not capture individual experience. Attachment experiences are by definition individually interpreted. Hence qualitative methods were needed to explore teachers' individual experience. During a series of six one-hour one-to-one interviews with a number of teachers I explored the meaning they each derived from their experience of teaching along with a developmental and attachment history.

As a researcher-educator I was concerned to document the part these played in the formation and maintenance of their current classroom management: both effective and ineffective. By reflecting on their professional work in the context of their personal circumstances and developmental history, teachers' experience of meaning in the classroom could be more fully understood: by the individuals and by me. Once this was achieved the conditions for change would be in place for each teacher. From then it would be up to the teachers to determine their futures: in the light of the new information and insights, would they want to change, and if so how?

The aim of the interviews was to traverse a set pathway for each teacher, with two of the six sessions set aside for each of the following three areas. Starting with a full description of the present (context, environment, career), moving to the past (developmental history, work history) and finally to the future: what they now chose to do with this information and insights (setting and striving toward realistic goals for the future). We were in effect using a brief form of psychoanalysis as an investigative tool. The technicalities of this method are explained in Chapter 8.

The psychodynamic interview method

This was chiefly designed to identify whether and how the attachment behavioural system is involved in classroom management difficulties. A variety of data was gathered and examined to create the most coherent representation of the attachment experiences of teachers experiencing difficulties in the classroom. As the attachment style of a teacher is an important predictor of her classroom behaviour, a teacher's developmental attachments are most likely to provide important information about how she relates to students. To date this had not been researched directly, although a basis for such thinking has been suggested by the exploration of the similarities between leadership and parenting using an attachment perspective. This research has been almost exclusively confined to unidirectional attachment (the early childhood model), with the leader conceptualised as caregiver and subordinates as care seekers (Popper, 2004; Popper & Mayseless, 2003; Popper et al., 2000). However, this is beginning to change (Mikulincer et al., 2009).

The focus was on the teachers' attachment experiences rather than identification of the differing types of insecure attachment. The specific difficulties of each teacher vary with differing forms of insecure attachment, personal experience, developmental history and teaching context. Therefore my focus remained on helping teachers who were experiencing those difficulties. If attachment contributed, both positively and negatively, to classroom management, the aim of the discussions was to assist teachers to gain a better understanding of their own internal working model of self and other, and apply the insights to improve their practice.

As described in Chapter 2, adult attachment theorists are now suggesting that all people may be capable of being identified as insecurely attached to particular others in particular contexts (Fraley & Shaver, 2000; Fraley & Spieker, 2003; Fraley et al., 2000). Therefore, understanding the context in which teachers become vulnerable to separation protest, and other forms negative behaviour, is an important first step in lessening the chances of it occurring. A broad view of context is taken: the context of person, the context of environment and the context of interaction.

The first difficulty to overcome was that adult attachment behaviours are more complex and subtle than those of children (Bowlby, 1988a). The second difficulty was one of discrimination of motivations. While attachment appears to be a significant factor in self-reports of teacher aggression, many other factors also contribute to complex behaviour patterns such as those involved in classroom management. The interaction of all the variables may be more important than the attachment style of the teacher. Thus richer, more detailed information needed to be gathered from individuals to gain as complete a picture as possible of a representative sample of teachers experiencing difficulties with student management. Teachers who participated in this phase of the study had either resorted to aggressive management techniques or displayed aggressive behaviour toward students, mainly yelling at students in anger and/or frustration. Recall that Roffman (2004) described anger as an "in-relation-to phenomenon" (p. 164). So exploring the anger and frustration began the work.

A complementary beginning point was drawn from the work of Kegan and Lahey (2001), who suggested focusing on people's internal languages in a developmental way, beginning with complaints, as a way to highlight strongly held, but perhaps not clearly articulated commitments. This helped to begin the focus on the present. And the teachers had many complaints about their current professional lives.

For each teacher in the sample, the unique situation of the individual was discussed during six hours of interview using the present-past-future format. The structure and content of the interviews are outlined next and some representative cases are presented. The case vignettes are drawn from my work with teachers experiencing classroom management difficulties and aggression.

CIND: the basic structure

Contextual Insight-Navigated Discussion (CIND) employs the methods of brief integrated psychotherapy with a time limitation and an educational contextual focus.[1] The time limitation is a fixed series of sessions, and a fixed time for each session. This is explained to the teacher at the outset of the process. Therefore an important element of the whole process is to begin with the end in mind. This immediately raises the *iatrogenic anxiety*[2] of the teacher and places them in "adult" (fixed, progressing, future focussed) rather than "child" (endless) time (Mann, 1981). Many neurotic behaviours are defensive attempts to keep a person feeling safe in child time (Brown, 2002; Molnos, 1995). Other structures of the sessions are also fixed. The series of discussions is always six by one hour. Each session has meetings of a specific and distinct focus that builds on the previous sessions and adds new content to deepen the understandings gained. The structure of each session is outlined below (see Table 5.1).

For teachers experiencing difficulties with classroom management, CIND enables exploration of their relationship styles, and draws out and develops teachers' insights into how they might modify them to improve their classroom practice. For the individual, this developing understanding is used to examine positive and negative professional relationships and why they differ. This is done within sessions, and in homework tasks, through the use of mentalisation and reflective

Table 5.1 Contextual Insight-Navigated Discussion 6-Session Outline

Session number	Time focus	Attachment focus	Change focus	Discussion content	Language focus
1	Present	Separation anxiety	Defensive restructuring	Context of environment	From blame to personal responsibility
2		Interpersonal processes		Context of person	Diagnosing the immunity to change
3	Past	Unconscious influences	Cognitive restructuring	Antecedent elements	Disturbing the immunity to change
4		Inner working models		Challenging the habits of mind	
5	Future	Intersubjectivity	Affective restructuring	Goal setting	From prizes and praising to on-going regard
6		Existential anxiety		Goal tracking	

function, which is akin to a sophisticated form of empathy (for a detailed review of these concepts see, Fonagy et al., 2002; Fonagy & Target, 1997; Knox, 2004; R. Lewis, 2006; Twemlow et al., 2005a, 2005b).

The acronym CIND (pronounced *k*IND) has been chosen deliberately to underscore both the orientation and the aim of the conversation taking place. The teachers who agreed to work with me had reported sometimes becoming aggressive in the classroom, and were therefore professionally and personally vulnerable. It was a big step for them to agree to do the work that CIND requires.

Trying to unlock the mysteries of another's unconscious motivation for entering the profession is not an easy task. It is necessary to gain a great deal of information from the participant and to use the transference and counter-transference to assess the conversations held with them. Determining the effect of attachment on motivation to teach, and its role in classroom management difficulties, is therefore a subtle undertaking. It may be that hopes for a corrective emotional experience have never been consciously entertained, even fleetingly. The wish for a corrective emotional experience, if and when it does exist, may remain totally unconscious. It could be that the motivation to teach has nothing to do with attachment even for teachers who later become aggressive with their students. Therefore remaining open to other possibilities during the discussions is paramount.

The basic principles of CIND as a brief, time-limited investigation

Based on the dynamic principles outlined by Marmor (1979) that when a person improves her functioning this leads to heightened self-esteem and positive feedback from the environment which helps the process continue, the advantage of

CIND is that the model ensures all the elements are examined, in a structured way, so that information used both by the facilitator and the teacher is not avoided or lost through neglect or defence against important aspects of theory or practice, while leaving open the possibilities for flexibly discussing the teacher's concerns. The preparation for each encounter is an important aspect of the work by both parties and promotes both growth and flexibility in the teacher by looking for the identification of triggers, feelings and strategies for coping with the environment in which she has decided to place herself (Macnab, 1991b).

The model is, as much as a semi-structured interview can be, person-centred. The fundamental core condition of all brief psychotherapies is the working alliance formed between the protagonists. This idea is based on the work of Carl Rogers (Rogers, 1951, 1989) and frequently acknowledged by current theorists, even those espousing cognitive behaviour therapy, traditionally opposed to the person-centred approach (Josefowitz & Myran, 2006). Brief, integrated therapeutic models sit in contrast to the eclectic techniques sometimes employed by psychologists in the counselling environment that result from intuitions regarding the client's needs and desired outcomes, which can have a hit or miss quality. A structured integration of the different theoretical perspectives of psychology provides the opportunity for the teacher-participant to explore her unconscious functioning through an exploration of her core professional anxiety. This involves three tasks identified by Eisold (2000, p. 62):

1   the task of identifying the unknown, that which needs to become known …
2   the role of anxiety as the guardian, so to speak, of that which is being kept unknown, and
3   the creation of the mental reflective space required for its emergence.

The structure of the sessions also offers a kind of mental checklist that aids in both parties staying attuned and sticking to the issues, particularly when the discussion becomes difficult emotionally. This guards against the risk of the facilitator/mentor unconsciously seeking to avoid difficult areas, by offering "procedural awareness, and therapeutic accountability" (Macnab, 1991b, p. 3).

The elements of CIND

Context

The importance of context to therapeutic change was described by Macnab (1991b). For a long time context was discounted in psychotherapy, however this meant that very important information relating to the energy of the client was either discounted or avoided all together, leaving a gap where rich information could have been utilised. The context of a classroom is very different to the context of a staffroom or household. The rich information that can be gained by examining teachers' outer context is important for understanding how they function within that specific set of conditions. Macnab (1991b) emphasises that context also refers to the human context: in this case teachers' inner as well as outer life. The meaning that teachers draw from their experience is an important part of the context in which they live their personal and professional lives:

> It places early emphasis on personality strengths and the practice of managing anxiety and demoralization; on the analytic process of examining connections and directions; on cognitive reconstruction and the re-establishing of the person's capacity and potential for making decisions for the better function, health, well-being and the directions for their life.
>
> (Macnab, 1991b, p. 13)

Exploration of dyadic attachment

The structure of CIND involves, first, developing a trust in the working alliance by the teacher; taking a psychological and developmental history of relationships experienced; using genograms (McGoldrick et al., 1999) to plot relationship styles and structures of the teacher and her family of origin. This technique has been found by many researchers to be a crucial factor in the facilitation of change (Egan, 2002; Geldard & Geldard, 2005; L. Lewis, 2006; Rogers, 1951, 1989, 1990; Scaturo, 2002; Sultanoff, 2003); and finally to use the information gained through the process to imagine and plot new ways of functioning in the classroom.

Crucial to an understanding of the attachment relationships of the teachers is identifying patterns of functioning from the teachers' family of origin (FOO): functioning and dysfunctioning. Teachers discover who they are deep down, and how they relate in the classroom when they reflect about how their FOO functioned together as a unit (Egan, 2002; Geldard & Geldard, 2005; Larner, 2001; Macnab, 1991b). This involves revisiting relationship dynamics learned in childhood through reflection and mentalisation. In a structured way the teacher is encouraged to look for her own patterns of classroom behaviour that were learned in childhood.

Rather than viewing these behaviours as being instigated by students, and therefore beyond a teacher's control, the dynamics of the situation are brought to the surface. Some of these learned behaviours may have been quite appropriate for a young child to exhibit, but not be appropriate for classroom practice. The teacher learns that behaviours have become habits through repeated use, but that all habits can be discarded and replaced by something more appropriate. Indeed, the idea of flexibly responding to the classroom milieu, as opposed to rigid rule or habit following, or worse unmediated reacting to situations in the classroom, is a feature of the discussions.

The level(s) of closeness within the FOO and perhaps of the family of procreation (FOP) also, are very important. This is referred to as "boundaries" in the literature (Corey, 2005). Teachers are encouraged to explore any barriers to closeness that existed in their FOO. How the messages regarding appropriate and inappropriate closeness are conveyed within the FOO and FOP are also explored.

Patterns of family attachment relationships – including: acceptable or reinforced behaviours in the teacher's FOO and FOP; parental relationships; sibling relationships; and intergenerational relationships that point toward transmission of attachment style within the extended family – are discussed and the teachers are gently encouraged to discover insights about how this functioning may be repeating itself in their classrooms. After identifying a pattern of family functioning, questions such as "do any of your students' behaviours remind you of these functioning patterns?" help the teacher to make links between habituated behaviour and current functioning.

This part of the discussion is designed to map the teacher's internal working model and identify patterns of behaviour that may surface inappropriately in the classroom, particularly during periods of heightened stress and anxiety. The anxiety may be construed as separation anxiety and lead to activation of the attachment behavioural system. These patterns become available to the teacher through insights and reflective function promoted by the discussion (Fonagy & Target, 1997; Knox, 2004). In turn this raises the teacher's sensitivity to these cues and aids a better understanding of the inner working model, along with the similarities and differences of the inner working models of those students who seem to provoke heightened, and perhaps inappropriate, responses in the teacher. In effect, this new information sensitises the teacher to the nuances of the classroom environment with the self as the key element of this sensitivity.

If this new knowledge, gained through insights, is useful it should have the effect of protecting the teacher from reacting unconsciously to students through raised awareness of the interpersonal dynamics in the classroom. This intrapersonal knowledge protects the teacher by allowing a more reasoned approach to classroom management, by diminishing anxiety. Armed with this new knowledge the teacher is able to learn more about new ways of relating to students. The discussion technique also assists teachers in coming to their own conclusions about how their past may be interfering with present functioning and to explore new and more efficacious ways to promote self and other emotional protection in the classroom.

Exploration of vulnerability

Teachers who persistently behave aggressively in the classroom may be doing so because of a perceived vulnerability that they feel needs protecting by adopting what Scheinkman and Fishbane (2004) have termed survival positions. The authors argued that this form of dysfunctionality becomes repetitive. The vulnerability they refer to is:

> a sensitivity that individuals bring from their past histories or current contexts in their lives to the intimacy of their relationships. Like injuries that remain sensitive to the touch, when vulnerabilities are triggered by the dynamics of the couple's [or the teacher–student] relationship, they produce intense reactivity and pain.
>
> (Scheinkman & Fishbane, 2004, p. 281)

While the authors were discussing the vulnerabilities of adult couples who seek therapy for their difficulties, it is logical to predict that the same vulnerabilities are carried into all relationships, albeit at differing levels of intensity depending on the closeness of the relationships involved. Therefore, vulnerabilities are present in the teacher–student dyad, and the teacher–leader dyad. If these vulnerabilities are constructed around the attachment system and previous failures to assuage the pain of actual or perceived separations, then the vulnerabilities and the associated pain may also surface in classroom situations.

During the CIND one of the variables searched for is the amount and extent of vulnerability that teachers experience as a natural part of their work. For example, it may be that the teachers exhibiting signs of reverting to old behaviour patterns are locked into a vulnerability cycle where they view the classroom situation as a direct threat to their professional identity, thereby keeping them in a high state of emotional arousal as the (perceived) threat is constant: proximity to students, which is both needed and feared. This may or may not relate to their attachment style. Determining the difference between positive nonattachment and a form of insecure attachment will be an important decision in the process as it evolves (Allen et al., 2005).

The potential differences in teachers' vulnerability based on positive non-attachment and attachment relationships are also interesting in light of Ainsworth's and Bretherton's discussions with Bowlby of the activation of the attachment system. Bowlby originally conceived the attachment system as taxonomic: to be either on or off. However, following Ainsworth's (1985) and Bretherton's (1985) work on the attachment activation system, Bowlby adjusted the theory to incorporate the continuous activation of the attachment system, operating as a kind of monitor of person–environment interactions, mostly in the background but ready to guide the system in a situation of (perceived) threat, and therefore more in line with a physiological homeostatic system (Main, 1999).

Survival positions are adopted to protect the self from feelings of vulnerability (Scheinkman & Fishbane, 2004, p. 282). They persist if they have proven useful. "In the moment of threat, the individual experiences survival strategies as having protective value. Like a shield, survival strategies are put in place to give a sense of safety and control. … Survival positions are often adopted before they can be put into words and certainly before they can be evaluated critically" (Scheinkman & Fishbane, 2004, p. 283), providing confirmation of the tendency to repeat the cycle of aggression outlined in Chapter 3, and perhaps an alternative description of an important aspect of the inner working model.

The difficulty for the researcher investigating vulnerabilities as precursors to teacher aggression is that they are usually unconscious and therefore unavailable for self-report examination. They must be elicited slowly and often by inference in the CIND. This has the potential to create methodological difficulties due to multiple interpretations of the teachers' statements. This part of the research relies on the investigator's ability, on the one hand, to distinguish between transference and counter transference; and, on the other to, separate his wish to find an effect worth reporting. This leaves the investigator open to potential bias. Therefore the vulnerability does not lie solely with the teacher but is also a factor for the investigator to grapple with.

Pring (2000) has described the need to respect the dignity and privacy of those who participate in educational research. Therefore the first decision to be made was where to conduct the discussions, as the venue would influence the level of trust built between the researcher and the teacher-participants. A neutral space was employed and no direct recording of the discussions took place. For record keeping purposes the researcher summarised the discussion at the end of the session, and made any necessary clarifications in consultation with the teacher. The researcher then made notes of the discussion after the session. At the commencement of the next session the previous session was summarised from the notes and the conversation began from there. On occasion, this involved further amendment to the notes of record so that the teacher-participant was satisfied that she had been correctly heard, and understood and that the notes were a valid account of the interaction, even if some of the detail of the session was lost due to the recording techniques. Given that the underlying dimensions of behaviour is the focus of the research, a loss of small detail may have actually been a benefit because the major issues discussed in each session remained unencumbered by extraneous detail.

A further consideration was that teachers who perceived that they were in some way under pressure from their school administration would be less likely to be forthcoming with difficult or sensitive information about both themselves and their classroom relationships (Busher, 2002). Without an honest attempt by the teacher to bring information to light the teacher is unlikely to benefit from the process and the research loses any claim to validity. Participants need to feel that they can be as open and honest as possible and that the researcher will protect this information from any unnecessary disclosure. Therefore the information collected in the interviews is disguised to protect the relationship between the researcher and participant-teacher and to protect the teacher from misuse of the information by an administrative authority.

The use of story

> One of the dominant contemporary themes across a number of specialty areas is that human knowledge is storied – that is, much of what we know and understand is embedded in stories.
>
> (Carter, 1999, p. 171)

CIND uses story to recast teachers' experience if they have become trapped in a constraining narrative, and as a way of imagining different futures:

> story is not simply an alternative way of expressing or illustrating propositional knowledge, but rather an idiom that tells something very different. In addition, story can be a staging ground for human self-enactment, "a panorama of what is possible, because it is not hedged in either by the limitations or the

considerations that determine the institutionalized organization with in which human life otherwise takes its course" (Iser, 1996, p. 19). Story can transport us, in other words, not only to experiences we have not had but to insights that cannot be expressed in conventional discourse.

(Carter, 1999, p. 170)

Advantages of this methodology

The key advantage of this methodology is that the teacher can implement new knowledge immediately. The investigator gains understanding of the issues for the teacher and is perhaps able to make broader connections to other teachers, while the individual teachers gain a deeper understanding of their own intersubjective processes in dealing with students, colleagues and superordinates. In regarding the praxis as the cure (E. Levenson, 2001), the teacher's insights become the change in the teacher's practice: immediate and solid (see also, Brown, 2002; Gibney, 2003; H. Levenson, 2004; Macnab, 1991a; Mann, 1981, 1991; Teyber, 2006).

CIND is similar to expressive psychotherapy, with "less emphasis on reconstructing childhood events … than occurs in psychoanalysis and more focus on current functioning" (Sadock & Sadock, 2003, p. 928). Another similarity lies with the investigator being equally divided between supporting the vulnerable client and extending her ability to go deeper into herself, so both may better understand the processes that surround and inhabit their functioning.

Contextual Insight-Navigated Discussions with teachers

After working with many teachers using the CIND methodology I selected five representative cases from teachers who agreed to have the content of the interviews reported. All identifying information has been removed and in some cases disguised to preserve the anonymity of the participant teachers. The cases describe the application of Contextual Insight-Navigated Discussion (CIND) for teachers experiencing difficulties in maintaining classroom discipline and therefore the safety and wellbeing of the students under their care.

Teacher 1: Ted – Primary

Ted was a 25-year-old teacher in his first year at his current school, having commenced there during the second term. He had previously worked as a casual relief teacher on contracts lasting between one to three terms in three other schools. He taught a Grade 6 class for 80% of the week, and the remainder as a specialist Information and Communications Technology (ICT) teacher to all students from Grade 3 and above.

Ted described himself variously as "happy-go-lucky", "easy-going" and someone who "doesn't get ruffled easily". He said he did "yell and scream" at the students, but explained, "it's all an act". He believed all the senior school staff used fear to control the students. Personally, Ted saw students as highly competitive, often ranking each other on all sorts of measures, both academic and nonacademic that he thought trivial. He reported finding much student behaviour "difficult to understand".

When questioned about his reasons for attending the sessions, Ted reflected that he "never lost control of the class" but feared that he "might soon". He also reported that he did not "like to be authoritarian in the class," but felt compelled to "because that's what students and teachers expect". He did mention one other member of staff, who did not behave in an authoritarian way and saw this teacher as a potential role model.

Relevant history

Ted had been brought up in a close, extended but "extremely cold" family of origin, who valued intellectual pursuits over all others. He described his father and uncle as particularly cold. During sessions he came to see himself as having similar qualities to both of these relatives. Having previously derogated such behaviour, he determined to change this aspect of his personality that he did not like in others. His paternal uncle was viewed by that side of the family as the source of a great deal of family distress. Ted's uncle experienced a deep religious conversion at the age of 14 and had since spent most of his spare time trying to convert others. This involved many separations from the family and home life as he travelled to "spread the word". This had caused a great deal of conflict within the family. The uncle also had a conflicted relationship with his brother, Ted's father. The two had rarely spoken since their early teens, following the uncle's religious conversion.

When discussing his parents Ted thought that they must have reached "some kind of understanding" about the marriage. They no longer fought as they had done for much of Ted's early childhood. However, his parents now appeared to live separate lives, even when doing things together, such as travelling to functions in separate cars because otherwise "he would always make her late; which she couldn't stand".

Ted described his father as very a bright professional who was always very quiet, remote, socially awkward in most situations, and passively aggressive toward his wife. When the family dined out at restaurants, his father usually brought a book to read at the table rather than engage in conversation with his family. He spent all his spare time at home on the computer, which he found relaxing and stimulating. This was his only real point of contact with others. He discussed his computer projects rather than personal matters with family.

Ted's mother was described as opposite to his father: "very vocal, likes to chit chat, controlling". He found it very frustrating, when growing up, that his mother would never ask for something to be done for her, but would complain "long and hard" that it had not been done after the event, and it seemed no amount of discussion from any member of the family could persuade her to ask for things to be done in a timely fashion and therefore reduce her need to complain to the family. The result of this was that the immediate family had resigned themselves to being whinged at constantly, and "basically ignored her when she whinged".

Ted found his older sister to be "intelligent, loud and controlling". Her relationship with their maternal grandmother had been highly conflicted for as long as Ted could remember. The maternal grandmother, who Ted described as "evil personified", and a "perpetual complainer who whacked you for no reason", had highly conflicted relationships with all of her family of origin over money. However, Ted had never been privy to the details.

Insights

In describing his family of origin, Ted gained insight into learned patterns of interacting with others (Bartholomew & Horowitz, 1991; Corey, 2005; Teyber, 2006). He became aware that he was often striving for complete quiet from his students, rather than accepting that a low level of noise was the norm, not the exception, in most classrooms he had experienced. He realised that this related directly to his family's pattern of interaction where silence was expected. He determined that he would refocus his expectations regarding class rules. He had originally devised a comprehensive list of rules that the students were expected to learn. The students would often forget the rules and he would find himself whinging at them in the manner of his mother's admonishment of her family when jobs were not done. This insight was used to reflect on his classroom practice.

This produced the insight that general principles of behaviour rather than specific rules gave Ted the chance to negotiate rules with students before they broke them. He also realised that pointing out a student's previous agreement to a class rule could be used to control student misbehaviour without resorting to yelling. Ted realised that he may have unconscionsly developed many detailed rules to produce student transgressions. He found he was constantly pointing them out to students, becoming like his mother in the classroom; the constant whinger that everyone ignored. Being ignored by students led to arguments with them, and aggressive responses to lessen the separation anxiety, so that he would not be ignored. But the behaviour he sought to reduce, being ignored, was replaced with student dislike of him, which increased separation anxiety. Rather than fix his unconscious wish to become closer to students the distance was increased and the spiral of bad behaviour continued.

The chance to stop behaving this way became a powerful motivation for Ted. He was now able to set his agenda consciously and consistently for the class and change his expectations of the students to something more appropriate to their developmental stage.

Increasing Ted's understanding that expectations in relationship patterns are formed through the continual experiencing of relationships, the inner working model (Ainsworth, 1969; Bowlby, 1975, 1982) was the most important intervention. He was encouraged to gain insight into faulty perceptions and expectations (Ellis, 2000) he had developed for his students as a result of his experience of family relationships. He reported that these insights considerably lessened his anxiety in the classroom, and that he was able to spend more time on planning interesting and challenging lessons for his students.

Ted's insights led to a lessening of anxiety with regard to control of the class. He became willing to allow a low level of talk in the classroom. He negotiated a code of behavioural principles for the classroom with students, rather than the previous long list of rules. Through this change he gained agreement for acceptable behaviour from students before any trouble began. Following the implementation of these changes, he reported a reduction in aggressive behaviours by students and a reduction in his aggressive responses to aberrant student behaviour. This was confirmed by his Principal. Ted stated that he was more relaxed and comfortable in the classroom and felt he had more realistic expectations of the students under his care.

Teacher 2: Pat – Primary

Pat was a 42-year-old primary teacher in her third year teaching after a 15-year break from it. She had taught at five other primary schools, one in the country, and taken an extended sabbatical from the profession when her own children were young. They were now school age and attended a school she had taught in previously. Pat taught a composite grade for most of each week and ran an elective programme for the older students the rest of the time. She reported that the size of the school caused difficulties with pastoral care. To address this they had recently been restructured into a series of mini schools across two campuses "to create a more caring community". She believed that this had been good for students but not staff, and that the junior staff, including herself, were regarded as "second-class citizens" by the teachers on the senior campus, despite the fact that she worked on both campuses.

Pat presented with anxiety and feelings of disempowerment over dealing with her colleagues, but particularly in staff meetings where she felt bullied and ostracised. The anxiety led to aggressive behaviours directed toward students; mainly yelling angrily. She reported no difficulties with classroom management. However, some parents had insisted their children be moved to other classes. At the first meeting Pat said she felt her emotional resources were "spent", but did not report or display symptoms of depression.

Pat described herself as extremely caring of others "just like my mother. I always put others first". She reported "yelling and screaming" at the students, but explained, "they know I only do it when I'm upset". She had also cried in front of students, stating, "If I am upset, the students should know it". She described the school culture as "toxic" and "poisonous" and her belief that many of the senior school staff used fear to control the junior staff and bullied people, "including parents, to get what they wanted". She reported that this group organised staff meetings to suit their own ends and not those of the school generally, and she felt intimidated when speaking to them about professional issues concerning her class because "they didn't care".

When questioned about her reasons for attending, Pat reflected that she "needed to find ways to get her message across to the others, and I don't want to feel bullied by them". She also disliked being "bossy in the class", but felt compelled to "in some parts of the programme, like music classes, everyone has to do everything at the same time".

Relevant history

Pat described being brought up in "nutty" family of origin. The focus of the family was "looking out for dad", who had suffered a severe trauma in World War II, which he would never discuss. On his return from the war, her father had joined the public service. However, he was forced to retire on medical grounds in his early 40s, as his behaviour became increasingly erratic: alternating between aggression, depression and suicidal ideation that generally prevented normal daily functioning. He had not worked since and spent most of his time within the family home. Pat's father disliked the noise his children made and would often punish them aggressively when they were what he considered too noisy. So Pat and her siblings had to be "overly quiet in the house" for "all the time I can remember growing up". The family rarely had visitors and the children were not encouraged to bring friends home from school.

On at least six occasions, "but there might have been more", her father had attempted suicide in the marital bedroom. These incidents were vividly recounted, with rich detail as Pat described the noise and confusion of ambulances and the talk of the paramedics as they dealt with her father. Despite the serious nature of the attempts on his life, Pat's father remains alive and now lives independently, approaching his 90s. When Pat's mother died suddenly her father had became independent and all attempts to end his life ceased.

Pat described her mother as "the most amazing woman in the world": someone "who could get along with anybody", but "always put family first", often at great personal sacrifice. She described her mother has having "overcome a tragic child-hood". During her teens, Pat's mother's older sister had been killed in a car accident on the same day that her brother, a soldier, was declared missing in action, sending her own mother, Pat's grandmother, into a severe depression "that was undiagnosed in those days". Very little else was known about her maternal grandparents but Pat reported, "Mum just got on with things and never let too much get her down". She reported feeling very close to her mother and her unexpected death had been an immense shock for the whole family: "Nearly ten years later, I still think about her every day, and probably always will". She described her mother as "her best friend" and still felt "her loss terribly". After marrying in her late 20s Pat initially miscarried twice. She described the first miscarriage as bringing her even "closer to mum". Three successful pregnancies followed.

Pat's older sister had "a very hard life". Having stayed with a violent partner for 15 years, "at the time she separated from him it turned out that her oldest had ADHD.[3] It's probably related. She's a closed book now".

The teacher's own marriage lasted four years: He "turned out to be hopeless at everything". She reported that they were in the final phase of a "bitter financial separation that has gone on for years" and that "the lawyers were likely to get all the money". She hoped that she would now be able "to get on with [her] life".

Insights

In describing her family of origin, Pat gained insight into learned patterns of interacting with others. She became aware that her need to be heard, and her reluctance to speak up in meetings, resulted from a childhood spent "having to be so quiet". She also gained the insight that she had not been able to practice and therefore improve her ability to engage in professional dialogue with colleagues. Many of these discussions involved some level of professional dispute over the allocation of scarce resources within the school. Pat came to understand that she longed for the sort of care from her colleagues that she missed receiving from her mother, but that this was an unlikely prospect. A further insight was her acknowledgement that her marriage breakdown had left her emotionally labile. She determined to "let go" of the wish for her colleagues to look after her emotional needs, and of her hope that her professional relationships would improve without the need for her to change her own behaviour. She decided that the way to reduce her anxiety over dealing with colleagues was to concentrate on pre-planning her contributions at meetings. Previously she had waited until frustration or anger rose to levels strong enough to provide the impetus to "speak up in meetings", resulting in overly emotional outbursts, often followed by sullen silences. Presenting well-reasoned arguments rather than asking her colleagues to "just believe her", induced more considered responses from them that reinforced her decision to continue her new approach to meetings.

The painful recognition that she was displacing unmet needs for love and support by caring for others was more difficult to come to terms with. She vacillated between coming to an understanding that by assuming her mother's role of "carer" for her father, she could pretend to remain close to her mother and keep things "how they used to be", and defending against this knowledge. She also reported great sadness that caring for her father after her mother's death had also caused some tension with her siblings, who wanted to place him in a nursing home. Losing the support of her sisters was something that appeared too difficult to experience and remained defended throughout the sessions.

Pat reported that the insights that surfaced during and between the CIND sessions considerably lessened her anxiety in the classroom, and that she was less intimidated by her colleagues. She reported that the school culture remained "poisonous, but I'm doing my best to change it, but I can't do it on my own". Pat found a lessening of anxiety when speaking up with colleagues during staff meetings. She also reported becoming "less emotional" with the students. She planned to build more positive relationships with other colleagues and refresh her teaching by taking on a different role, deciding to apply for this the following year. She reported that while this was "scary, because I'm moving into the unknown" it was also a source of professional excitement.

Teacher 3: Thomas – Secondary

Thomas was a 30-year-old secondary teacher in his third year at his current school. He had previously worked in two other schools on single year contracts, neither of which were renewed. He taught Year 7 and 8 Science, Year 9 Mathematics and Year 11 Chemistry. Like all of his colleagues he was also responsible for a number of students in a pastoral care role as an advocate. Most weeks saw complaints about his performance reported to the Principal by students, colleagues or parents, and sometimes all three.

Thomas presented with anxiety over loss of classroom control stemming from what he thought were difficulties in "planning and time management". He labelled himself "a serial procrastinator". He also reported aggressive behaviours directed toward students; in particular sarcasm. However, this would lead to yelling angrily if it did not restore order quickly. Both these approaches led to on-going difficulties with classroom management as students responded in kind.

Thomas appeared extremely nervous at our first meeting. After taking his seat he picked up the chair and moved it back from its position to the wall, more than doubling the distance between us. He spent most of the first session stroking his beard and moustache in what appeared to be self-soothing actions. He described himself as "easy-going" which did not appear congruent with his behaviour. He reported that he did "yell and scream" at the students, but explained that, "they know I'm joking". He went on to describe the differences he saw in his students, "I like Year 7 and Year 11, but not in between". He reported that he liked "girls who get on with their work" and "I don't like girls who seem to be on another planet. They only talk about make-up and boys". For most of the session he seemed pre-occupied with matters other than those we were discussing. He constantly changed the subject. He averted his gaze often, and appeared distracted easily by thoughts and musings provoked by ideas raised in the conversation. He reported that he played squash and football locally with some of the boys he taught and that this had been both good and bad for his relationships with them. Good, because they were able to see him "in a different light" and bad because "they become overly familiar" or used the change of roles to their advantage in "wrecking his classes", by calling out during class about incidents at a weekend game or calling out during the game about class incidents.

Initially he outlined the types of student he found frustrating. He stated that he rarely became angry with students but he reported avoiding dealing with diffi-cult students on many occasions. The avoidance followed unsuccessful one-to-one talks with students where he would outline the change in behaviour he required. "If they don't do it I try not to notice, unless they hit each other". He reported that some students "seem to have competitions as to who can do the least amount of work" and "they try to ruin my lessons". He discussed the differences between his Year 9 classes. One of these had "eight keen students who are keen to get on with their work, which seems to be a critical number". The other had four students "bent on wrecking the class".

Thomas talked about both the keen students and those bent on wrecking the class in the same way: from a position of powerlessness. He appeared to have resigned himself to surviving whatever type of students came his way. He gave no sign that he thought of the process of teaching and learning as either an opportunity for growth or reciprocal. He acknowledged that it was common for some students to seek attention from their teachers through inappropriate behaviour, but seemed genuinely surprised with the proposition that this could offer him an opportunity to teach the student about appropriate behaviour. He seemed to have assumed that all students acted in a totally calculated and rational manner in their dealings with him, even when behaving inappropriately, which must therefore have been deliberate choice on the students' part. He noted that "good students really don't need teachers much at all, just good activities and the right equipment". He reported that he had been "a successful but lazy student: because of my high IQ, I never needed to study". He reported that he had "not really needed teachers to show me what to do. I was always able to work it out for myself – often more efficiently". He stated he did not "understand many students" and thought that he could benefit from learning about them through these sessions "because that's what students expect of teachers".

Relevant history

Thomas reported that he had been brought up in an "eccentric family" alternating between closeness and distance on many levels. He described himself as the "family favourite", much as a mascot might be described. He described his mother as the most important person in his life, but only spoke of her rarely, spending much more time in conversation about his father and siblings. He described his father in glowing tones as a serial philanderer. His parents had gone through three separations and reunions. Each time his father had left the marital home to pursue an affair after having it "discovered" by his mother, "but she always let him back when it was over". A different woman was involved in each of the affairs. The teacher described his father as "a man of integrity" after conveying this information. When questioned about the incongruity of this he reported that, "I suppose it could look like that, but he stuck to his values". His father travelled a great deal for work, and it appeared that he spent very little time at the family home as a result. Therefore, apart from their mother's reactions or mood state, formal separations and absences through work may have appeared almost indistinguishable to the children. The teacher reported that he formed "a unique bond with his father through a shared dark sense of humour". A shared sense of humour was also a connection for the teacher to his younger sister, and got him out of "many tricky situations".

When his parents separated for the first time his mother decided to return to work and become financially independent. The nature of her employment meant that the parenting role was abdicated to her daughters. Both sisters had "explosive tempers" and clashed often. They also clashed regularly with their mother, who could be equally explosive. Retreat into intellectual pursuits to evade conflict with his siblings provided safety for Thomas. His elder brother also retreated from the intense conflicts through drug use. The ten-year age difference between the two brothers meant that they had very little to do with each other while growing up. Recently his brother had curtailed his destructive drug use, largely as a result of forming a romantic relationship. He was now reporting to the family that he would like to take up social work to help people like himself.

Insights

In describing his family of origin, Thomas gained insight into learned patterns of interacting with others. He reported that he had been very shy as a child. He had found that his connection with people came through helping them with intellectual tasks, and that he had developed an interest in teaching from a young age as a way of making contact with people. He became aware that he was attracted to students who needed his help and also that he was only vaguely interested in students who required help but did not ask for it or those who refused help when he offered it. He found this type of student behaviour very difficult to understand, until he made the connection with his memories of many of his own teachers when he was a student.

He also became aware that he was often withdrawing from his students, mainly in conflict situations. He was also able to see that by taking this course of action he was, in effect, letting the situation escalate to a point where he had to intervene in an even stronger way. When the situation reached this level, his anxiety about his ability to control the class also rose dramatically and he usually resorted to sarcasm in an attempt to control students by demonstrating his intellectual power over them. This was undertaken in the hope that those not directly involved would be impressed by such a display and would remain "onside when he had to be the boss" and he "wouldn't lose face". He was able to state that this was very rarely successful and nearly always led to yelling at students as a show of strength. He readily made the connection that this was a pattern he had developed with his sisters whenever conflict arose that he could not avoid. By letting the situation get out of hand in the classroom before he acted, he felt even less able to effectively control the students than he would have by intervening earlier. Rather than avoiding conflict, he saw that through his inaction he was promoting it. It was not difficult then for him to decide on an early intervention strategy.

Finally the realisation that living on one's wits, and being the class "wise guy, always cracking jokes", which had been a successful strategy as a student, did not make for good teaching practice. He had not yet made the distinction between teaching content and pedagogy. He succeeded as a student by being able to memorise facts easily. Now as teacher, not student, he was required to organise class sets of manipulatives, photocopies, textbooks, student records and all the other paraphernalia associated with teaching practical subjects. Many hours were lost to him, spent in searching for teaching materials on his desk, in cupboards and at his home office. He often resorted to discarding lessons because he could not find the materials he needed to conduct them, resorting instead to textbook lessons which neither he nor the students found satisfying and which increased the chance of student misbehaviour through boredom. This deliberate undermining of his own ability to perform the role of teacher was perhaps the most difficult insight to come to terms with. He could not blame student behaviour for lack of his own organisation. Once acknowledged, this became the positive driver for changing his professional practice. Before our final session he had spent the weekend at school organising his desk so that teaching materials were sorted, categorised and available for immediate use.

Thomas reported that insights gained during sessions led to a lessening of anxiety with regard to classroom management. He became more aware of watching out for changes in student behaviour that may lead to conflict and attempted to intervene early. He also negotiated a code of behavioural principles for the classroom with the students he had the most difficulty with: resetting the agenda for their future interactions. He reported that this had mixed results but had been positive for a few students. He also reported a reduction in his aggressive behaviour. He stated that he was more relaxed and comfortable in the classroom and felt he had more realistic expectations of the students and more dedication to preplanning lessons, referring to the cliché that the best form of student discipline is good curriculum.

Teacher 4: Ben – Primary

Ben was a 51-year-old teacher in his tenth year at his current school. Before this permanent appointment he had worked at a different school every year for the past 15 as a Casual Relief Teacher. He enjoyed this for many years, before it eventually became tiresome. He took the permanent appointment to "make a difference" in a single school. This decision coincided with the death of his father. He moved back into the family home to look after his mother who had become frail, and took a job at the local school. Like many of his previous appointments, this school also had its systemic difficulties; however Ben was happy to let others deal with that side of things, so he might fully concern himself with teaching and learning. After nine years and four changes of Principal, he was offered a new role as a specialist teacher for all year levels. He reported difficulties in communicating with his colleagues, which led to deterioration in his morale and classroom management, and interfered with his potential to bring innovation to the school.

Ben presented as quite anxious. He sat uncomfortably in the chair; spoke very rapidly at high volume, often pausing mid-sentence, making the silences pronounced. Without a question he described his strengths as a teacher as "writing policy and grant applications to help the school", suggesting he was personally responsible for the significant increase in resources at the school since his arrival. He continued by listing his perceived weaknesses. He reported becoming frustrated with the staff politics and factions within the school, "although it is much better now than it has been" and that "I have been known to blow my top", adding that "once it's over, it's over and I move on". On questioning this statement he offered, "I don't hold grudges. I am an optimist who sees the good in people and do not dwell on the negatives. When working with peers, I try to remain focused to achieve expected outcomes and remain so until the job is done. I certainly do not whinge about them behind their backs about perceived failings. I am always encouraging and supportive of colleagues".

Ben liked his new Principal "because he is on my wavelength". After many changes to the leadership of the school this gave Ben hope for the future. He then went on to describe his life outside school and his family of origin. "I never married. Too many other things to do," then after a long pause, "and I moved around a lot".

Relevant history

Ben was the second of four children. He had grown up adoring but fearful of his father who, "like many men of his generation was firm when it came to parenting". He spoke at great length about his father, and their relationship. "My father, like his father before him, had a bad temper, and as a result of experiencing this as a child and adolescent, I am better able to control my own temper and deal with anger". Ben's father was a practical man who worked for most of his life in the public service, but spent the after work hours in "a meticulously clean shed". Ben spent many childhood hours watching his father at work in the shed. He would marvel at all the tools his father could use. "Each tool had its own a space on the shadow board: he never put a tool back after using it until he'd cleaned it." His father's preference was to work alone, but his son always wanted to help him. On the rare occasions that his father would ask for help, few if any instructions were given, it invariably called for fine hand-eye coordination, and a mistake would usually be made.[4] The more mistakes he made, the less he was invited to help. "Dad was not a very good teacher and he didn't like to be helped. He was a perfectionist and a wizard at everything. He didn't suffer fools. He used to say to me, son, I've made all the same mistakes as you … but I only made them once!"

With great sadness, Ben reported that during the last weeks of his father's life "Dad told me he regretted that I hadn't followed his footsteps more closely into his chosen career. If only I'd known that when I was beginning my career I would have. I loved doing what Dad did. I thought he didn't want me to, because I was too clumsy". At this point Ben became very still and quiet. After a long pause he said "I wouldn't be a teacher if I'd known". Ben stated that he loved going into the shed now because it is like being with his father in their "spirit of place", adding, "he was really innovative, way ahead of his time. He made us eat omega 3 in the 1970s!" This statement led to observations of students' diet and possible correlations with many behavioural difficulties.

Ben described his mother as "the family adhesive tape", laughing at his own description. Fifteen years younger than her husband, she was the caregiver, the nurturer. As children the siblings spent quite a lot of time with their mother's side of the family and all became close to their cousins. They "still get together a few times a year". His father's family on the other hand were never seen, due to a significant falling out between Ben's father and uncle when in their early 30s, after which the two never spoke again. While Ben rarely saw much of any other family members from his father's side, the content of the sessions were full of details of that side of the family rather than his experiences with his mother's family.

Insights

Ben presented with anxiety over staff politics that were impacting on his ability to communicate his ideas for innovation to his colleagues. The frustration and anxiety associated with an inability to communicate effectively led to aggressive behaviours directed toward colleagues and students. For students this was experienced as yelling angrily, with staff it was a combination of yelling, sarcasm and derogation, leading to further communication difficulties. He now felt that his colleagues were deliberately avoiding him, escalating his feelings of separation anxiety, which in turn led to more aggressive behaviour during staff meetings.

In describing his family of origin, Ben gained insight into learned patterns of interacting with others and he realised that he was much more like his father than he had previously believed. His short temper, inability to accept help from others and coming to quick, decisive and often negative judgements about others were identified as underlying causes to his communication problems. He also came to understand that he, like his father, expected other people to know what he was thinking without communicating it to them. He reflected that this stemmed perhaps from the difficulty he had in articulating some words. This led to more communication difficulties as others tried to finish sentences for him, "but said the wrong things", leading to a blunt correction from him. He determined that he should shift his focus from the details of his communication, which had been a constant annoyance in dealing with others to "the big picture," stating "that's what's really important isn't it? Some details don't matter".

Ben reported that insights gained during sessions led to a lessening of anxiety when dealing with his colleagues, but he remained sceptical about how his change in approach would affect others, reporting that he could see "no evidence of a change in his relationships" after a week of implementing his new approach. Ben's Principal stated that Ben had appeared much calmer in the classroom since the sessions had started and he had not heard a single report of him raising his voice to either staff or students during the six weeks of sessions.

Teacher 5: Terry – Secondary

Terry presented with anger and frustration, partly through student disrespect, but mainly due to perceived inconsistent behaviour by colleagues regarding policies, particularly school discipline. This led to aggressive behaviour directed at students and staff, in particular sarcasm, derogatory labelling and yelling angrily. Rather than remedying the situation, Terry was either avoided by both students and colleagues, or challenged aggressively by some students, which led to on-going difficulties with classroom management. The students who reacted to the aggressive behaviours by responding likewise were often suspended. Terry had considered leaving the profession as a result.

Terry presented as the quintessential knockabout Aussie male: 33 years old, tough, no nonsense, with a ready supply of one-line jokes for every situation. He was in his second year at his current school having previously worked at a few other schools on single-year contracts. Prior to teaching he had held a number of positions after completing a science degree, "none of which suited". In his late 20s he joined the public service doing some youth work and stayed in that role for three years, before "deciding to teach", stating that "if he was going to do any good [for people] he'd have to get in early, while you can mould them". Like many rural high school teachers Terry's duties were broad, teaching senior classes in Chemistry and Mathematics and junior Science. Terry lived alone, slightly out of the town and his preference was to remain private outside of school: not easy in a small community. However, he had joined his local community club branch upon arriving in the town, ensuring the locals would see him as not just a teacher.

He described teaching as "a lonely job", and felt that he was under constant surveillance when teaching, which he found disconcerting, saying "you're always being watched – 40 eyes, 7 brains". These types of derogations were a constant element of his dialogue. He reported many small confrontations with colleagues over inconsistent implementation of school policies. He became particularly animated when reporting the inconsistency of his colleagues in preventing the use of ipods and mobile phones in class. When asked whether he knew about other schools that had embraced the new technology, he responded by saying he too thought it was a good idea, "but rules are rules" and "whether you agree with them or not, they have to be followed".

Terry was "very frustrated" with a colleague who "took teaching equipment from trolleys" he had prepared without informing him, so that when Terry got to class without the correct equipment he looked unprepared and had to adapt lessons. He also spoke of his frustration that even after challenging the teacher about this in a meeting the behaviour had not ceased. He reported that he had been in many schools with "hypocritical staff" noting, "the school employs two mothers a day to clean up the staffroom so that teachers can be messy. They are pigs in the staffroom and then tell the students to clean up rubbish".

Terry's major frustration with both colleagues and students was reserved for school uniforms: "The school has a uniform policy that is not policed by many teachers and therefore students flout the rules". He reported that he was not supported by his Principal in matters of uniform transgressions, describing him as "weak and spineless", citing a number of complaints he had lodged that had not been acted on. When questioned about his classroom management Terry reflected that he "never lost control of the class" and "was never likely to". By the end of the session his level of agitation had become quite marked and his skin tone had coloured considerably. He stated that all teachers should be respected by their students, therefore he demanded respect from them. In the next sentence he described students as "dumb" and "stupid". Possibly noticing my reaction to the inconsistency he offered; "but they can't help being dumb, you just have to do the best you can with them. Life is shit. You just have to make the most of what you've got."

Relevant history

The fourth of seven children from "a typical Catholic family", most of whom are not much more than a year apart in age, Terry recounted a severe childhood, punctuated by violent episodes from his father and siblings, stating "Most of us got hit three or four times a year … and when he hit you he didn't hold back. It only stopped when [oldest brother] Michael fought back as a 15 year old". He described his mother as a "liar, like the old mother in [the television programme] *Everybody Loves Raymond*, always nagging". His mother had a very hostile relationship with her elder sister for much of their lives, but the two formed an "allegiance" with each other after their brother left the priesthood, renouncing his vows after 30 years' service. He then married one of his parishioners. His actions split the family. Two of his sisters have not spoken to him since. The remaining sister, the teacher's maternal aunt, a long-serving nun, defied her two older sisters and remained in touch with the "black sheep".

Terry reported that he was like his father in his quickness to react, but "I'm much better at keeping it under control now". He reported that his colleagues' behaviour rather than his students' was the source of his frustration, however, "the kids are sometimes on the receiving end when it's not their fault, which I know is not fair". He described his colleagues as "dumb, lazy, undermining and thoughtless". He described teaching as a calling rather than a job and saw it as his role to teach kids about life, which meant "giving them firm and consistent boundaries". This was the source of many conflicts with his colleagues, many of whom were described as "too gutless to follow through on staff decisions. They let their teammates down". Terry described himself as a lazy student who had always had to struggle to get on, and said he saw himself in many of the students. "They need a lot of direction from me".

Insights

In describing his family of origin, the teacher gained insight into learned patterns of interacting with others. He was quick to react defensively to any perceived threat, and tried to keep his world as ordered as possible so that it felt predictable. He related this way of acting in the world to his father's violent outbursts, which "always came without warning", were very frightening, and "were over as quickly as they started". He became aware that he was often striving for control of his students so that they too would be totally predictable and therefore non-threatening. He agreed that this was impossible to ask of any group of people or himself. He determined to negotiate more reasonable codes of behaviour with his students, noting "this did seem to work" when he tried it. He determined that he would refocus his expectations regarding class rules, by simplifying them into higher order constructs, or class values.

With regard to his colleagues, he determined that he would genuinely question their behaviours rather than sit in judgement on them. He would try to help them see the inconsistencies in their own behaviour by "pretending not to understand" the distinction between their behaviour and espoused views. When he was gently encouraged to use the same techniques on himself, he grinned broadly and said, "you got me!" Subsequently he reported that this had been a good piece of advice, stating "I now know what *do unto others* ... was getting at."

Terry reported that insights gained during sessions led to a lessening of anger and frustration with regard to control of the class, but not yet with his colleagues. He reported becoming less concerned with "off-task talk" in class if students remained generally on task, reasoning that he might learn useful information about his students through listening to these discussions. He also reported a reduction in aggressive behaviours by students, which he attributed to this change in management. He stated that he was more relaxed and comfortable in the classroom and felt he had more realistic expectations of the students. However, his frustration when rules were breached remained high and appeared to prime him for strong reactions, including aggressive behaviour. Terry remained critical of individual colleagues who did not enforce student dress code rules. He saw this as undermining his authority with students and teachers' authority in general. He also stated his belief that it would take a lot more effort to get his colleagues to change their behaviour but he was willing to persist, at least for the foreseeable future.

Summary

It is a privilege to be allowed into another's life in such a way as CIND offers. All of the teachers demonstrated courage by taking part. During the sessions I was able to form a therapeutic alliance with each of the teachers except Ben and Pat, who remained pleasant, polite and distant throughout the course of sessions; each also missed Session 4 at the allotted time and had to reschedule a week later, leaving a two week gap. In each case this appeared to be a defensive retreat.

Intergenerational patterns of behaviour as inherited attachment style

In attachment terms each of the teachers displayed insecurely rather than securely attached behaviour and their histories confirmed this. In each case, the attachment history of the teachers demonstrated an intergenerational pattern of insecure attachment and in one case could have been classed as chronic neglect of the teacher by his parents, particularly during the formative years when the internal working model is constructed.

The teachers who undertook CIND all had parental relationships that were manipulative in some way, rather than warm and loving. Each appeared to be typical members of their extended family and each could draw links to other family members they resembled emotionally. An intergenerational pattern of behaving within their family of origin had been passed on to them and through CIND they were able to make the connections between these patterns and their relational style in the classroom. It was not difficult to draw the conclusion that the inner working models of the teachers were such that they distrusted others (all cases) and distrusted themselves (most cases) once they had described their own history and that of their extended family. That these people were all attracted to the teaching profession, in light of their attachment history, offers support for the hypothesis that they had perhaps been yearning for a stronger connection with people and may have been unconsciously motivated to enter teaching to satisfy this relational need. However, once they entered the profession, rather than receiving the corrective experience they sought, each typically behaved in their professional role in a manner that reproduced familial responding.

Through their actions in the classroom, these teachers defensively denied themselves the chance of the corrective experience they unconsciously sought. Usually this was accomplished by creating emotional distance from their students. In all cases the teachers reported becoming terribly frustrated by certain students they taught.

During the CIND most developed insights that the students they had difficulty with in some way represented a model of familial relating and that this had unconsciously moved them to repeat behaviours learned while growing up rather than flexibly responding to the classroom environment and the students. In each case the teachers' genograms pointed out patterns of conflict or distance that the teachers saw as reflective of their typical way of responding in the classroom. This was often the most powerful moment in the course of CIND: the construction of the genogram took place during Session 3. It is placed at that part of the process so that a working alliance has had time to develop, allowing for a deeper exploration of familial patterning for the teacher than would be achieved if it were commenced too early in the course of sessions.

Parental characteristics

Each of the parental relationships experienced by the teachers as they grew up were characterised by unequal distribution of power, with one parent dominating the emotional life of the family. The typical presentation of family history was a dichotomous one: an over-controlling mother or father, who appeared not to trust their offspring to grow up, and equally distrusted their partner to parent. Therefore the over-controlling parent used constant surveillance and frequent intervention to prevent them from acting inappropriately.

In contrast to this the other parental figure remained remote and ineffectual as parent and partner, often the source of derogation within the family. In each case the ineffectual parent seemed to be regarded by the dominant parent as equivalent to one of the children (often a naughty child) rather than a partner in the parenting experience. The amount of legitimate power the ineffectual parent was able to exert on the family was negligible. Therefore they often exercised power in a passive-aggressive manner and some also encouraged their children to behave likewise. The underlying message transmitted to the child (now teacher) by this way of relating was not to trust either of their parents for security or their own feelings and intuitions when it came to relationships.

A question of trust

Each of the teachers interviewed had suffered many experiences of their trust in others being betrayed, very often with serious emotional consequences. Deep down each believed that trusting others would usually lead to personal damage and distress. This behavioural pattern was often exhibited by the teachers in the classroom: a constant theme was reflected in the statement "If I'm not careful to keep them in line, they [the students] won't do any work". Most of the teachers perceived fear as the most effective way to control the students: fear of poor marks, fear of the teacher's anger, fear of punishments, fear in all its forms. Having experienced this type of "control" in their family, they each felt it was their turn to take on that powerful role. Freud called this behaviour "identification with the aggressor". The result was that the teachers simply could not trust students to behave in a sensible way, if left to their own devices. They did not believe their students to be in any way curious about the lessons they presented and assumed that most people, including all of their students, only responded to external force to control their base desires.

In conceiving their students in this way most of the teachers resorted to behaviours for controlling students they had experienced growing up, despite having described them as stultifying and claustrophobic. It was only at this point in the CIND discussion that the teachers made the connections between their relational style in the classroom and their childhood family experiences. This was often a painful insight and one that was tentatively reached. In some cases the clear evidence that their students were indeed curious, self-motivated and independent learners was acknowledged. Most had reported witnessing their students behaving well and showing curiosity many times, as they interacted with teachers or each other in different contexts. However, in the early part of the discussion the teachers were typically unable to satisfactorily explain this behaviour in their students, and it proved easier for them to simply ignore the evidence or alternatively "blame" themselves as incompetent teachers who could "never come up with such interesting lessons". This was consistent with insecure attachment.

The model of self that was reported by each of the teachers, as unworthy of real attention by students, produced thoughts that any real interest shown in them by their students should to be read with suspicion. Witnessing the students behaving in a way that challenged the teachers' inner working models created an emotional dissonance that could not be tolerated for more than a short period. This is a plausible explanation for the effects of Lewis' (2008) discovery of teachers who revert to habitual practices after professional development.

Using CIND

In the past five years I have worked with many teachers using the CIND model. The interviews presented have been carefully chosen to reflect typical rather than extraordinary cases. They have been mainly males and mainly primary teachers. In all cases the success of the model has been demonstrated anecdotally: initially by teacher self-report and confirmed by their supervisors, in most cases by the Principal or Assistant Principal. Five of the teachers completed the sessions five years ago and the recent reports on their progress are that they are continuing to: sustain less aggressive practices in the classroom; appear not to get so flustered or frustrated by the normal ebb and flow of classroom life, such as interruptions and less than ideal timetables; and are dealing with the acute difficult situations with students, parents and colleagues that arise from time to time more appropriately and calmly. Generally the classroom "tone" has been significantly improved.

While the patterns of relating for each case displayed common themes, the variation between the stories presented by each of the teachers is a powerful reminder that each of us has a unique story and developmental history. After working with many teachers using the CIND framework I feel that a teacher who has shared, and deeply reflected on, his or her personal story is far better equipped to deal with students in all their manifestations, particularly with difficult students. By their own admission, and the reports of their direct superiors, the time taken to articulate and comprehend their personal narrative in a shared situation, such as CIND, offered valuable insights to the teachers who took part and led directly to the implementation of new ways of dealing with students. These did not have to be taught to the teachers as techniques, but rather became a function of who they were.

The sessions were also valuable for me, as a researcher, confirming that attachment processes are crucial to human relating even when the relationship is not an attachment per se. It is therefore logical to infer that teachers who understand the mechanisms involved in the attachment behavioural system are able to predict student behaviour more accurately and are therefore better equipped to manage classes. Those who also understand their own processes, including personal triggers for security and insecurity, are even better equipped, but this can only be achieved through deep reflection on the significant events of one's personal life in relation to the professional one.

The CIND model is an easily adapted structure. The following chapter describes how it was used as a mentoring aid, providing support for new school leaders, who face similar issues of transition to new teachers. The success of the model in mentoring new school leaders suggests that CIND may have potential for addressing the pressing issue of early career teacher exits from the profession, particularly if they are caused to some degree by the failure of the role to provide corrective emotional experiences that new teachers might be wishing for when they enter the profession.

Chapter 6

CIND mentoring

Supporting transitions and early career retentions[1]

Walking out or working through: learning about relationships the hard way

A tenet of this book is that that all schools can and should become places that foster security, and therefore curiosity, and that this will happen when two fundamental conditions are met. The first is that teachers and leaders understand the concept of a secure base at a deep level. Second, this knowledge is actively used to create structures that facilitate the emergence of security for each other and for students. From that notion I imagined security flowing like water throughout the school. If one imagines the school as a delta, security flows from the main river, the Principal or leadership team as parent surrogate, and branches out in streams that further divide within the school community.

The delta represents the myriad relationships in the school: collegial, teacher–student, student–student. In a secure base school security flows and distributes widely. If the Principal is a secure base for the teachers, the main river will be strong enough to prevent small blockages that develop lower down. They will either be swept away or circumvented. Adequate support for teachers allows them to reach their potential and facilitate the best learning experiences for students. This ensures that the flow of security within the school as a whole, the delta, will be maximised. However, if the main branch of the river, the leadership, begins to dry up the delta suffers first. Small flows in narrow regions become blocked first as the delta quickly dries. This may be a way of measuring the health of leadership within schools. By studying the quality of the delta relationships inferences could be drawn about the level of felt security regarding the leadership team, and therefore the health of the organisation as a whole. It may be that deficits in the background level of security flowing within the school delta could easily result in the various forms of self-reported teacher aggression discussed in the previous chapters.

Extending this notion to teachers is logical when concepts of adult attachment operate between students and teachers. Many teachers struggle to do their best for students, often in very trying circumstances. Therefore, as was outlined in Chapters 2 and 3, it should not come as a surprise that some teachers have difficulty in dealing with the emotional aspects of their work. Teachers have had very little professional training in the emotions relating to interpersonal relationships. The education they have received consists mainly of: modelling of teacher–student relationships (where they have been students); discussions with supervising teachers; trial and error during the teaching practicum; and learning on the job, which as Darling-Hammond (2010) found is a sink or swim process, with the former occurring most often when the training is inadequate or under-resourced. Clearly this could be improved, but the question is how? What is clear from the literature is that teachers who are inadequately prepared for the emotional aspects of teaching are more vulnerable to all sorts of difficulties in maintaining self-control (Ashkanasy & Daus, 2002; Brown, 2002; Chan, 2003; Goleman, 2006). If this is not present in schools then many new teachers will find the job too difficult and leave early.

The alarming level of early career attrition underlines the importance of this issue. The almost universally consistent levels of attrition among early career teachers suggest that something fundamental is missing from both pre-service education and ongoing support for early career teachers. As stated previously, when teachers move into classrooms it is their ability to form and maintain relationships with students, sometimes in difficult circumstances, that will form a large measure of their success or failure as professionals; this is an important measure of teacher competence, and certainly has a significant bearing on teacher wellbeing. It will also be a significant factor in their decision to stay in the profession. Teachers who stay teaching repay the money invested in their education through service and reduced need to attract and educate replacements; the return on investment grows over time. Teachers who leave early ensure increased waste of scarce resources through the cost of replacement; the return on investment stops. Continuous training of replacement teachers is a significantly higher cost to the community than adequately training teachers in the first place.

Increased investment in teacher education targeted at helping students acquire some of the skills taught to counselling psychologists would ensure that new teachers start their careers far better prepared for the reality of life in the classroom from their first day on the job. They would not be left in difficult classroom situations with little or no theoretical or practical support. This would see more of them enjoy their initial experiences and therefore stay in the profession. The net saving for increased spending on teacher education by government would run into many millions of dollars, even if attrition was reduced by only 10%.

If something fundamental has to change, and it is difficult to argue that it does not, schooling could be improved by incorporating more emotion work, including helping teachers understand who they are and who they are dealing with at a human level. The proposition that the secure base from which to launch a career is the missing factor for many new teachers is certainly worth considering.

One of the interesting patterns of early career teacher attrition across the world is that very similar figures have been reported. This suggests that the issues causing many young teachers to leave early have perhaps more to do with the human condition than national or cultural issues. The US estimates that approximately 2,000,000 extra teachers will be needed to cover early career attrition over the next 10 years

(Center for Innovative Thought, 2006; Education Commission of the United States, 2000). The UK (Ewing & Smith, 2003; Rudow, 1999), and Europe (Kyriacou, 2001; Santavirta et al., 2007) report similar levels of attrition, although in all cases the actual figure is difficult to determine accurately because no single agency is responsible for collecting the figures and, more importantly, accounting for them.

Take the example of Australia. In 2006, just over 25,000 new students began an "initial teacher training" education course (DEEWR, 2007). Nearly half of these students were needed to fill positions vacated by teachers with less than five years' experience. Subsequently, these new teachers are following their predecessors out of the profession at the same rate. About a quarter lasted only one year. Then they too had to be replaced. Apart from the obvious drain on scarce funds, high levels of attrition represent a more fundamental crisis in education at all levels, not just teacher education.

While financial disparity with other professions remains a significant issue, pre-service teachers know that they are not going to be richly rewarded financially before they apply for their courses. Yet they still apply. Something is still attracting them to the profession, but the levels of attrition suggest that initial expectations are not being adequately met. When this data is examined with reference to attachment mechanisms, explanations involving perceptual defence and defensive exclusion make sense. The teacher who is attracted to the role for a corrective emotional experience then works assiduously to ensure it does not happen. Like clients entering psychotherapy, the wish to change (engaging the therapist and presenting for treatment, or becoming a teacher to gain positive experiences of relationships) is almost always accompanied by unconscious resistance to actually changing (see Brown, 2002; Diamond, 1986). The anxiety of a different and less predictable future that change creates causes the resistance to reduce the anxiety. However, the wish to change was also a result of anxiety: a now intolerable situation for the teacher. The emotional exhaustion that such a continual defence propagates explains the early onset of depersonalisation and other burnout effects that some teachers suffer (Pillay et al., 2005).

Unlike the therapy session where a trained counsellor is there to guide and hold a safe space while the client works through the presenting issues, the teacher seeking a similar outcome cannot create it without help. If she is lucky enough to have a class full of securely attached students and a secure base leader, the corrective emotional experiences can begin and are accepted with increasing pleasure. Attachment theory shows that the organism, in this case the teacher, will adapt to a new context, but will also try to change the environment of evolutionary adaptedness. The teacher's inner working model tries to recreate the relational conditions she knows from previous experience, but hoped would somehow change by entering the classroom. Success in creating a predictable world makes the classroom a place too difficult to manage and enjoyment is lost.

Making the world a safe and predictable place, even if unhappy, is a set goal of attachment. But without a secure base, the teacher only succeeds in recreating her insecure way of relating to students that she sought to avoid by becoming a teacher.

The resultant unhappiness of this situation may be unconsciously blamed on the students, who might then be punished for causing the teacher's internal distress. This in turn creates "difficult students" who feel unsafe with the teacher, a no-win situation. Clearly, if this is the case early interventions are needed to ensure the emotional safety of teachers and students alike. Reconsidering the approach to educating and supporting new teachers in people and self-management skills can inoculate them somewhat from the stressors of the profession that lead to both the early exit and the depersonalising relationships of significant numbers who remain. This is where CIND can also be effective.

Recent research suggests that pre-service teachers expect that the rewards of the job will come from the relationships they form with their students along with the chance to have a significant impact on the lives of young people (Riley, 2009a, 2009c). For many teachers this is exactly what they experience when they join the profession. And, despite the low salary relative to other professions, they stay in the job because of the rewarding and important nature of the work. However, many new teachers report that they are under-prepared for the difficulties associated with life in many classrooms. Unless they chance upon a skilled mentor who is able to guide and protect them as they begin their careers, these new teachers are very likely to find the emotional aspects of the job overwhelming, and thus to contribute to the high rates of attrition. CIND was adapted to a mentoring structure and the model was taught to experienced Principals who then used the model to mentor newly appointed and aspirant school leaders.

Similar to the teachers from Chapter 5, the new leaders who were being mentored using CIND felt quite vulnerable in their new roles. While leadership in a school has many similarities with teaching in attachment terms, it is also very different from teaching, as anyone who has made the transition will attest. And new leaders are by definition incompetent, until they gain experience. The new leaders, while confident about their teaching, feel exposed and vulnerable as they move from the relative comfort of the classroom into the new and unexplored territory of leadership with adults. They are also aware that they are not dissimilar from beginning teachers who have yet to be tested, and naturally feel anxious about this state of affairs. The mentor/facilitator must remain fully aware of the difficult material they are asking their protégés to describe or run the risk of alienating them and diminishing their potential. Also, when attempting to help people restructure or let go of unconscious defences that have been built up over many years, proceeding gently and carefully is the only ethical approach to take.

A second series of vignettes are presented to capture the flavour of this different use of CIND. The basic structure of the interviews remained the same, but the content varied for a focus on mentoring. The vignettes are drawn from a group of teachers who are clearly high achievers in schools. They had been promoted to senior leadership positions and were offered mentoring to help them take the step forward. For CIND to be successfully implemented the basic principles remain fixed: for people to grow, they need to make an honest assessment of their present circumstance, their past influences on their present situation, and where they would like to go next in light of their new understandings. This sounds simple, but knowing oneself is a lifetime's work.

For protégés, like the teachers in the previous chapter, CIND also focuses on the relationship styles, but emphasises how the new leaders work with the adults who report to them rather than students. In both formats the structure of the CIND sessions are based on the premise that relationship differences and difficulties are a function of the dyad. So understanding self in the context of others is what needs exploration. There are some other important details in the adaptation of the model to a mentoring structure. These are outlined below.

The successful mentoring of new school leaders by their experienced colleagues involves two busy professionals seeking time to conduct enough mentoring conferences to facilitate protégé growth. This alone can be a significant impediment to success of the relationship. If there is a perception from either party that time is not well spent when they do meet, the relationship is unlikely to survive. Yet time can be wasted and significant issues overlooked or avoided without a robust structure to frame the mentoring relationship, along with the ability of the mentor to quickly build a strong working relationship with the protégé (Awaya et al., 2003). With these obstacles in mind, two theories of interpersonal relationships were adapted to design a programme in Victoria, Australia for teaching experienced school leaders the craft of mentorship. In this chapter, the initial delivery of the programme is reported and evaluated.

The idea of mentor as protector is drawn from the French root of the word "*protéger*, to protect" (Roberts, 2000, p. 148). The support provided by the mentor, as the *secure base* (Bowlby, 1978, 1988a) for the protégé, allows the examination of the individual's own "problem frame" from within (Stammers, 1992, p. 77). Framing obstacles to growth internally allows the protégé to identify and come to terms with the skills and attributes needed for successful leadership.

Mentoring has long been used as a vehicle for educating aspirant leaders in many types of organisations and the benefits of successful mentoring have been widely reported (Ehrich et al., 2004). However, within the education sector internationally, outcomes of mentoring programmes vary widely. A meta-analysis of the mentoring literature by Ehrich and colleagues (2004) identified three significant impediments to success: insufficient time; the mentor's lack of professional expertise; and personality mismatches. The authors indicated that lack of professional expertise placed a considerable emotional burden on mentors and that this deficit magnified their reluctance to accept new protégés.

Considerable effort has been spent investigating the efficacy of different mentoring approaches and subsequent outcomes for protégés (Ehrich et al., 2004; Mertz, 2004). However, with one notable exception (Smith, 2007) little research has been conducted into two significant aspects of the mentoring process that the literature identifies as problematic:

1   The efficacy of specific training for experienced school leaders to become expert mentors before they undertake a mentoring role, and

2   The outcomes of the mentoring process for experienced school leaders when they have received training.

Experienced school principals (mentors) who could quickly form a strong working alliance with protégés (assistant principals and other aspirant leaders), and articulate the working processes of relationships and solution-focused helping, would increase the likelihood of accurate problem identification and therefore correct, rather than expedient solution generation by their protégés. Outlining the process of relationship formation and maintenance to mentors would increase their ability to understand the protégé's situation, and articulate the human processes involved in achieving leadership goals. Mentors who consciously adopted specific relational skills such as open questioning and active listening techniques would be more likely to help protégés clarify the issues that *they* deemed most important for their development as leaders. This hypothesis was generated from the literature related to evidence-based, time-limited counselling, specifically the work of Brown (2002), Egan (2002), Macnab (1991a), Mann (1991) and Molnos (1995).

Mentors were taught how to facilitate significant and sometimes difficult conversations with their protégé using the CIND structure. Mentoring conversations are relatively easy to facilitate when everything is going well; any experienced Principal would be able to undertake such a role without specific training. However, the skills of managing difficult conversations can and should be learned by mentors as they allow the mentors some comfort in knowing they are prepared when sticky situations arise.

Just as the context in which mentors work is important, so are the attitudes and perceptions of both the mentors and protégés. It is easy in a mentoring situation to have an unequal distribution of power. This is particularly true in an education system that is already hierarchical in nature. So it was important to alert the mentors to this and provide a structure for equal power sharing. The programme design was therefore conceived as a protégé-centred stance (Rogers, 1990; Rogers, Kirschenbaum, & Henderson, 1989b), which has been shown to be "above average compared with other educational innovations for cognitive and especially affective and behavioral outcomes" in a meta-analysis of 119 studies from 1948–2004 sampling 355,325 students (Cornelius-White, 2007, p. 113).

For mentoring to be effective, it had to be done efficiently, without time wasted on superficialities. This is not easily achieved, especially if the two people do not know each other well, or even at all, before the first meeting. The time-limitation of CIND generates an underlying sense of the importance of progression. As the time together will be limited, neither party should waste it.

Difficult conversations, particularly where some intimate disclosure is involved (e.g. a mistake that caused some sort of embarrassment), are difficult to begin and the protagonists often find it easier to skirt around rather than directly address the central issue. In professional settings these conversations occur with some form of time-limitation (e.g., one of the parties has to leave to attend to another matter). Often the impending end of the meeting triggers the disclosure of the discomforting information that had been previously avoided. In many one-on-one meetings important information is not discussed until the last five minutes because the iatrogenic anxiety induced by the time-limiting process (awareness that the meeting is coming to an end) increases beyond the level of anxiety associated with the self-disclosure and possible feelings of embarrassment or shame that might result. Without the time-limitation the information may never have been disclosed. So, by focusing at the outset on the limited time for mentoring iatrogenic anxiety is used to facilitate progress.

There are of course other factors involved in whether a protégé will reveal important information, in particular, the level of trust afforded to the mentor. Protégés will only reveal sensitive information to a mentor who can withhold judgement while the protégé works through the issue. This is true of all judgements in the mind of the protégé. A mentor quick to judge positively is also likely to be quick with negative judgements in different circumstances. Thus, if negative judgements undermine the level of trust in a relationship, Kegan and Lahey (2001) point out that by implication positive judgements do too. Trust, and therefore judgement, determines the strength of the working alliance that can be formed between the mentor and protégé. And the strength of the working alliance is the best predictor of a successful mentoring relationship (Awaya et al., 2003; Bouquillon et al., 2005; Hargreaves, 2002).

Tools of the trade: the working alliance

The fundamental core condition of all effective mentoring is the working alliance formed between the protagonists. This assumption underpins the development of the programme structure and skills taught to the mentors. As stated above, it is appropriated from the significant corpus of work by Carl Rogers (1951, 1989) and those who followed him, such as Egan (2002), who introduced the ideas of solution-focused helping. The reason the working alliance is crucial in the mentoring setting is that coupled with a structured series of meetings, it provides the opportunity for protégés to safely explore their unconscious functioning through an exploration of their core professional anxiety.

The final measure of an effective mentoring relationship is that it helps to produce well informed, well rounded school leaders. When the protégé performs the leadership role without the need of a mentor, despite the fact that the relationship may continue, the work of the mentor is completed. In this sense it is not unlike a parenting relationship; facilitation of growth in the protégé while "letting her go." Thus effective mentors "empathically fail" their protégé (Winnicott, 1993b, 2002) allowing protégés to gradually take over their long-term leadership direction.

Methods and techniques

The programme where mentors were taught the principles and techniques of CIND was designed to be experiential. The trainee mentors were taught active listening and other skills during professional development sessions. After outlining each skill, the participants practiced in small groups of four that remained together for the whole of the training phase: quad group work. In these sessions each participant took on the role of mentor once, protégé once and observer twice. The quad group provided feedback at the end of each practice session on the specific skill and during the course of the workshops all six sessions of the model were outlined and practiced in vivo. This covered two of the three impediments to successful mentoring identified in the literature: insufficient time, and mentor's skill (Ehrich et al., 2004). The third impediment, personality clashes, was addressed through a partnership protocol that strongly encouraged mentors to select rather than take on an assigned protégé. This would allow them to develop their mentoring skills with a supportive protégé so *their* learning could be the focus. The programme design included skills in creating a strong working alliance in spite of personality differences, but this was to be avoided during the mentors' skill learning phase.

Participation in the training programme consisted of pre and post surveys to determine any change in mentoring capability pre and post involvement, and three days of formal workshops. Initially, participants (experienced school leaders) attended a two-day workshop, after which they began to work independently with a protégé (Assistant Principals looking to take the next step into school leadership and a few leading and expert teachers) using the CIND model. They attended one hour of small group supervision/review (10 to 12 participants) with me during that period. A third workshop was delivered after each participant had completed approximately three of the six mentoring sessions. This professional development opportunity was designed to extend the learning from the first workshop in light of direct experiences with individual protégés.

Participants were also required to reflect on the process individually once they had completed the six sessions with a protégé and submit a 500-word meta-reflection of the process. These data were used for triangulation with other aspects of the programme, to determine its success or otherwise.

CIND mentoring outcomes

Participants

Ninety school principals took part in the course at a Melbourne conference venue and undertook the mentoring sessions at convenient locations across the state (modal age group 50 to 54 years; range 30–55+). Elementary Principals constituted the majority of the cohort (76.6%) with the remainder a mix of secondary (junior college: 12.2%) and P-12 (7.8%) school Principals. The mean level of experience for the participants was 27.59 years. Most (83%) had previously mentored at least one colleague before attending the workshop. Overwhelmingly, the initial survey data showed that the participants had the desire to develop their communication skills, with listening skills rated three times more important than any other single skill.

Data sources

Information was obtained at five different time periods during the programme. Survey data included an initial survey as a condition of entry to the programme (100% response rate); post Workshop 1 (89% response rate); and post Workshop 2 (67% response rate). Qualitative data was collected from all participants via: audio-recorded small group interviews (86% response rate); and participant's written meta-reflections submitted after completing the programme (42% response rate). The variations in response rates were partly due to attrition between the workshops. A number of Principals were unable to attend Workshop 2 for a variety of reasons not associated with the programme itself: some changed jobs, others had to prioritise dual departmental obligations on the day and yet others had to deal with unforeseen crises in their schools involving students, parents or teachers. Also, experience in delivering other programmes has shown that it can be difficult to lure Principals from their schools for extended periods, particularly when attendance at a workshop involves as much as six hours of additional travel each way, even when accommodation is provided.

A mixed-method analysis of participant responses was employed. Numerical and open data were captured from pre and post workshop surveys, transcripts of the small group interviews and participants' meta-reflections submitted at the end of the first mentoring partnership employing the CIND model taught in the workshops. On the whole, participants were very supportive of the programme, with a number reporting it was "the best professional development I have ever done". On a seven-point likert scale ranging from 1 (strongly disagree) to 7 (strongly agree), participants rated the programme as follows (see Table 6.1).

The qualitative data reported in the next section identifies key themes that emerged from analysis of participants' written responses and small group interviews during their engagement with the programme.

Emerging themes

Support provides the conditions for professional growth

The participants' level of experience in school settings allowed for rich conversations to occur during the programme. As each quad group remained intact for the

Table 6.1 Participant evaluation of the mentoring skills workshop

General evaluation questions	Min	Max	Mean	SD
After participating in this workshop I have a better understanding of ways I can develop my mentoring capabilities	3	7	6.22	.819
I feel confident that I know what is expected of me in my work with the protégé	3	7	6.22	.851
My capacity to address the challenges of mentoring has increased through my participation in the workshop	4	7	6.44	.775

whole of the programme group members were able to deepen and strengthen their professional relationships. They were in effect mentoring each other while learning about the process. Having the quad groups pre-arranged by geographic region and keeping them together for the whole of the programme achieved a level of comfort that allowed greater depth in their explorations of the process. They were mirroring the developmental nature of the mentor/protégé relationship, by building trust in each other during the quad group sessions. Participants appreciated the chance to reflect on their mentoring style as they discussed each mentor's progress with their protégés. This added depth to conversations during the workshops and small group supervision.

One participant summed up the effect of the supportive quad group structure: "The opportunity to network, debrief and work collaboratively with my group was very worthwhile. This has given me confidence to really extend myself." A second participant reported that the "greater building of trust" within the group over time allowed her to participate in "richer discussions" that increased her understanding of the CIND model and mentoring generally.

Structure provides security

A common theme that emerged from the small groups and the meta-reflections was that the structure of the mentoring sessions, made transparent at the outset to both mentors and protégés, acted as a "container" – to borrow Winnicott's (2002) term – for both parties in the dyad. The boundaries provided by the structure allowed the mentors to feel secure in conducting sessions without feeling obliged to provide the content. One participant, who had previously mentored many teachers, reported:

> The big difference is structure. ... This is something totally different to the way I have previously conducted any mentoring type meetings. They have usually been ad hoc meetings to discuss specific issues relating to school issues, often with me providing advice or "the answer".

Another found the structure of the sessions aided focus on the protégé's development: "Because I know my protégé very well, it would be easy to become distracted or move away from the focus without a structure to work from".

Emerging challenges

One of the major challenges identified by many of the Principals was described as "that itching, burning desire to give answers". Most identified the ability to "switch off" from the principal role and on to the mentoring role as a significant challenge early on but one that became easier, but not easy, with time and practice. For example, one participant reported:

> I think it's a very different role too [mentoring]. We see ourselves as good teachers, but being a mentor is entirely different. So it's a very new, very big

learning experience, figuring out how to do it and figuring out how to stay a mentor and not the teacher [who says] "yep do this do that".

Another participant said: "the hardest part is holding back opinions and ideas. This is what we get paid to do and to restrain is always difficult." One participant described active listening as "particularly helpful" as a technique for "the holding back of opinions. My inclination is always to suggest my way of doing things so to have the focus on not doing this was really good", but added ruefully, "The strength required to act in this way was a challenge for me."

Wellbeing

Teaching CIND processes as a mentoring aid provided to experienced Principals has been successful in building the skills and confidence to mentor. While the aims were focused on the skill development of the mentors, a surprising finding, albeit preliminary, is that there appears to have been a benefit in terms of the health and wellbeing of both mentors and protégés. By acknowledging the fundamental need for protégés to address the big issues confronting them as beginning school leaders, in a confidential setting with an experienced school leader, the underlying message of the programme was that both mentors and protégés are important people who need, and positively respond to, support. One participant articulated it this way: "Some of my colleagues told me when I got back to school that I looked like I had a whole lot more energy, that I seemed so much happier, that I got obviously so much out of it." The positive effect on wellbeing may be a function of the logistics of the programme rather than the structure of the course. All participants were able to spend at least one night in the hotel where the programme was delivered, most of the remote area participants spent two nights. This kind of pampering, rather than the course of study, could have been the cause of a refreshed look when returning to school.

By providing specific mentoring training to experienced principals, and giving them practice in stepping out of the principal role where they are constantly required to make judgements, and into the mentoring role, adopting a non-judgemental stance, was a significant challenge for the participants in the course. When they were able to do this they reported that it allowed both parties to perform to their capacity and the issues that needed to be addressed were explored in depth rather than superficial solutions searched for. The purpose is that this allows the teachers and students in their schools to perform at their best, because the new leader is fully engaged in the true educative process.

While the results reported are preliminary, they are largely positive. Longer-term follow-up has been planned to investigate whether the initial findings can be sustained over time. What can be argued as a result of the first phase of this project though is that CIND mentoring can enhance school leadership development by helping to develop the capability of the mentors, who then use these skills in their daily leadership work, not just in the mentoring sessions. The mentor assists in the development of the whole person from within, rather than providing a box of tricks.

The benefits of CIND mentoring for new leaders has also been outlined with a perhaps surprising finding of an improvement in wellbeing for the mentors who undertook the training. In terms of attachment this is best summarised as follows: when the conditions of meaningful human relating can be met, the positive effects on both members of the dyad are felt strongly. Human beings are a herding species and we need the company of others to make our lives complete. Schools can provide this opportunity in powerful ways, and this probably contributes to the unconscious motivation of some to stay within its confines, as a teacher. Sadly though, some school cultures seem to prevent or diminish this sort of contact. This must be a constant source frustration for all its members, albeit probably not articulated. CIND, or something akin to it, can assist in uncovering the issues that prevent or diminish human relating so that they can be dealt with more directly.

The sharing of one's personal story is recognised as a significant component of a counsellor's education, but this is not the case for teachers ... as yet. This is a gap in teachers' education that should not be left any longer. CIND offers a chance to tell a story of personal history and imagine a hopeful future that could become a useful addition to the pre-service education of teachers, just as similar techniques are used for counsellors. There is a great deal of overlap between the professions of teaching and counselling. The points of contact between the two seem to be increasing with developments in each of the professions, the sharing of craft knowledge and the increasing pastoral care expected of teachers. Both often end up doing similar work: helping people develop into the best people they can become. Perhaps the next step is to share more of the techniques.

Part III

New directions for practice

Chapter 7

The implications of new knowledge

Old wine in new bottles?

The more things go around the more they come around

There are many different professional development interventions being researched with teachers in an attempt to improve practice. The history of these things tells us that most are likely to have limited success. Like R. Lewis' (2006) discovery of teachers who revert to poor practice after improving, most interventions seem to have a limited lifespan in schools. The contention of this book has been that these failures to improve represent a mismatching of the interventions. They do not take the human reality of teaching into account and therefore do not address the key issues.

Teaching is a messy business, full of guesswork and intuition, hopes and fears, joys and sorrows, laughter and tears, risks and rewards. This is not bad thing, it is just how things are. This is also difficult to articulate to new teachers during their pre-service education and is therefore often avoided. The hope is that teachers move beyond surviving to thriving with students, while their intuition becomes expertise. This approach leaves new teachers vulnerable. However, the messiness is not easily documented, it is learned experientially, and this seems to have troubled many politicians and the educational bureaucrats who serve them. These people seem powerfully attracted to stand-alone curriculum packages, because they sell the idea of something new and complete to voters as educational improvements. But the improvements are never enough. There is always the next programme to promote addressing the next problem. This is because the programme packages usually lack the 3Rs. As Alfred North Whitehead (1929) so beautifully put it, "knowledge doesn't keep any better than fish".

For example, direct observation of teachers at work, with the aim of discovering and perhaps modifying practice, is gaining in popularity. However, what attachment theory can teach us is that this too is unlikely to succeed in improving teacher practice unless it provides increased security for teachers. It is more likely to raise teachers' anxiety and therefore increase insecurity: the intervention is more likely to increase that which it seeks to lessen. There are other problems associated with it too. The change in classroom dynamics that result from either a neutral observer or the installation of video recording equipment defeats the purpose of the exercise.

Also, the reality for the teachers is that they are required to deal with the students without such equipment over the course of their career. Most teachers can put on a good lesson for an observer, whether in the room or remote. They have learned to do this during their pre-service education. What is important is whether a teacher can sustain a positive change in practice. And that requires changing the self.

In psychodynamic terms the details of any act of behaviour is not as important for the teacher to understand as the underlying patterns that created it. This can only be achieved through experiential education. Unless the teacher recognises the personal triggers for her behaviour and experiments with new forms of response to novel situations no sustainable change will take place, no matter the quality of the advice by the observer. Therefore, the expression of vulnerabilities that lie at the heart of teachers' aggressive responding are better dealt with by inference with high levels of support such as CIND, rather than direct observation. It does not help the teacher if a behaviour that is deemed important by the observer has no meaning for the teacher, or conversely, the researcher may misinterpret or exclude an observation that the teacher identifies as crucial.

Questions revisited

Is the teacher–student relationship an attachment relationship?

It is probably more appropriate to ask whether the teacher–student relationship is an attachment relationship or a positive nonattachment relationship. The answer seems to depend on the context, so it is still an open question. In some instances the student–teacher relationship appears to be an attachment while in others it seems more suggestive of positive nonattachment. Further research is needed to clearly identify the differences between attachment and nonattachment in significant relationships such as the teacher–student dyad, and also the collegial relationships formed in schools between teachers, administrators and significant others. It should be noted that perhaps this question is not as important as a variant of it: do attachment styles affect relationships formed between teachers and students, whether they are strictly attachments or not? This is an easier question to answer: yes. Whether teachers form attachments with some or all of their students or not is really not as important as the finding that they behave in ways that are determined as much by their attachment history as their particular context and that this can be a useful self-evaluative tool for a teacher when understood.

Is teacher aggression usefully conceived as an attachment issue?

The data suggests that the attachment style of the teacher is an important factor in her tendency to become aggressive with students. It appears that a teacher's attachment style affects her ability to incorporate teaching strategies that rely on person-centred approaches to relationship building. The kind of professional development offered to teachers identified later as reverting to aggressive behaviours, is based largely on a Rogerian model (Rogers, 1983, 1990). The techniques are well honed and relatively easily applied as long as the teacher has an inner working model that can cope with scaffolding the new information without creating emotional dissonance. Teachers seem to revert to old patterns of behaviour when they are unable to rely on an underlying model of attachment that assumes that they can usually trust the students. For the teachers I worked with the assumption of trust for students could not be made until they had learned about their attachment history and determined to put in place some corrective actions that were not easily done initially but later became easier.

Hart (2007, p. 8) reported similar findings, albeit without reference to attachment theory, and using slightly different language. However, his argument is clearly aligned with the theory of attachment:

> When an individual does not feel the basic sense of belonging that a community engenders, alienation and anxiety rule ... This may leave both students and teachers wary, causing us to expend our energies on self-protection, on closing down rather than opening up. We may keep our distance from one another and the material, positions that are the opposite of those that invite depth. Wariness can also take the form of a lack of civility, and even aggression, which is a violent expression of self-protection.

Do(es) attachment style(s) of the teachers contribute to aggressive behaviour?

The data suggests that attachment is likely to be a significant factor in teacher aggression. It can be claimed with some confidence that attachment processes, particularly separation protest behaviours and defensive exclusion, are present in some teachers at the time they become aggressive with their students. This results from a systems response to stress. These teachers should not be blamed for this as individual bad eggs in a good system, but rather the kinds of processes that attracted them to the profession need to be made more explicit for them, so that they can begin to re-story their classroom engagement. Of course this can only happen if teachers feel they have a secure base in the school leadership who can remain steadfast while they work through the associated issues that are preventing their growth and development as teachers.

Do some people choose teaching unconsciously desiring a corrective emotional experience?

From the evidence reported here it seems that for a significant percentage of teachers sampled, including all who undertook CIND, the answer to this question is yes. It also seems clear that many teachers may be able to gain corrective experiences as a function of their role within schools. It seems that more primary teachers are able to gain these experiences than secondary teachers, perhaps due to the structural differences between the school types and the work roles of teachers within them. It may well be the school structure that prevents secondary teachers from gaining the corrective experiences they might unconsciously be seeking.

The structure of a secondary school may be attractive to a teacher who does not want to form intimate relationships with students and can use the structure to manage proximity to others. However, the lowering of both anxiety and avoidance levels for all teachers as a result of experience in the classroom suggests that despite the structural difficulties some secondary teachers are also able to gain corrective emotional experiences through their contact with students and/or superordinates.

Do some teachers unconsciously wish for students, colleagues and/or superordinates to provide a corrective emotional experience?

In a sense this is almost impossible to answer, and will always be open to challenge by those who believe the psychodynamic approach has no place in education. It is likely that there are many unconscious processes involved in classroom life and we may never be able, or perhaps even want to, explain all that is going on. As Einstein said, "Beethoven's 5th symphony can be accurately explained as a particular set of differential air pressures but what is the point in doing that? It sheds no light on the experience of listening to the music". What matters is that having decided on a profession people who choose teaching as a career should be able to grow. And this should happen alongside their students as a result of their shared classroom experiences. If this does not happen they risk becoming locked in a defensive battle for self-protection with their students that is ultimately unsatisfying for all concerned. When learning happens in a classroom, teachers as well as students should be energised by the experience. Whether that is driven from a conscious or unconscious desire is of little or no practical consequence.

If a corrective emotional experience is not forthcoming, what happens next?

It appears that when the task of teaching is not accompanied by the joys of playing a part in students' growth toward independence, it is a cost many teachers find difficult to experience. Attrition rates and levels of aggression shown toward students may be indicators of just how difficult the job is when it challenges an individual's fundamental understandings of how relationships work. These are areas of concern that need to be addressed in new and creative ways: not more of the same.

Do teachers' attachment styles predict important aspects of teaching styles?

The evidence is that attachment is a significant factor for some teachers and a factor to be accounted for in all teachers. Teachers who are insecurely attached when they enter the profession appear to be quite vulnerable to feelings of perceived rejection by students and therefore they run the risk of retribution directed toward students as a result of separation anxiety and protest. On the other hand, the positive experiences that can be gained from working in a classroom appear to be quite powerful for many teachers. Therefore it seems very likely that attachment style is an important element in the development of a sound professional identity as well as an ingredient in a rewarding and successful career in the teaching profession, perhaps in all of the helping professions.

Is insecure attachment a factor affecting aggressive responding in classrooms?

It appears to be the case that insecure attachment is predictive of aggressive responding in classrooms, it must be stressed, by *some* teachers, at *some* times. This is consistent with the literature on attachment. The links between attachment and aggression are very stable and well researched. The more significant question that has arisen from this investigation is whether a brief integrated therapy such as CIND can alter the professional relational patterning of an insecurely attached teacher so that she gains corrective emotional experiences through the work. The conclusion so far is that for at least some teachers the effects of CIND appear to last for five years, which is good news. However, a teaching career lasts many years. So it is too early to make any definitive claims despite the positive evidence collected to date.

Does the experience of teaching affect teachers differently (primary versus secondary)?

The answer to this question is far from clear. It appears from the evidence that different attachment profiles partly affect the motivation to choose primary over secondary teaching, and vice versa, as a career. However, it is almost impossible to assess the impact of the role differences on those who choose either primary or secondary teaching. There are simply too many variables to consider, most of which are not controllable in the research designs. With that said though, in attachment terms, primary teachers appear to have an advantage in forming relationships that could provide corrective experiences because of the structure of their roles: fewer students for longer periods as opposed to many students for shorter periods. However, as classroom experience is the major factor in reducing insecurity, further research to explore the impact of teaching over time in each of the different settings using mixed methods to uncover the subtleties of the potential differences will perhaps further amplify this issue.

Does the experience of teaching impact on the attachment style of teachers over time?

This question has not been definitively answered to date. Clearly, experienced teachers seem more secure than the inexperienced on the two higher order constructs of attachment: anxiety and avoidance. However, attrition rates in teaching are very high, perhaps skewing the data for experienced teachers toward those who entered the profession with more secure attachment profiles in the first place. If the teacher–student relationship is one of positive nonattachment rather than an attachment relationship, that alone would explain the difference in levels of anxiety of intimacy and dependency and avoidance of intimacy found in this study.

Is avoidance or anxiety the key attachment dimension to understanding teachers' classroom practice?

It seems that avoidance is the more significant dimension of relationship building in classrooms. Anxiety is universal, important but ubiquitous. Avoidance accounts for much more of the variance between the teachers studied so far, both in the surveys and through the CIND process. The interviews revealed that teachers' avoidance strategies were causing them the most trouble. Most wanted to keep significant emotional distance from the students, but many students crave close relationships from their teachers. The more students tried to get close, the more the teachers felt under duress. This eventually led to aggressive responding to keep the students at a distance. This is not unlike the common paradoxical response of clients in therapy who seek help and then resist it until enough trust is established in the relationship to begin restructuring the way they apprehend the world. Unless the counsellor understands the foundation of the client's resistance and "honours it" any progress will be slow. In the same way teachers undertaking their work to gain corrective emotional experiences will also defend against them, and if success-ful, thereby make sure that they do not occur. So, in the following section, the implications for teacher education, professional development and ongoing support for teachers and school leaders are discussed.

Implications for pre-service teacher education

> Clearly, given the amount of turnover in the profession, the claim that traditional teacher preparation programs are the only acceptable way to prepare teachers for American [and international] classrooms rests on shaky assump-tions. ... Equally clearly, given the complex pedagogical challenges of today's classrooms, the argument that just about any reasonably able person can step into the classroom with limited preparation is difficult to accept. It is time to abandon the sterile debate between "traditional" and "alternative" teacher preparation programs to make sure that, no matter how they enter the class-room, new teachers have the grounding they need to do their jobs properly. ... it calls for innovation and new models for preparing future teachers.
>
> (Center for Innovative Thought, 2006, p. 17)

Incorporating the principles of attachment theory into the pre-service education of teachers is a significant challenge both for teacher educators and at a policy level: the way pre-service teacher education is currently conceived. CIND would be a powerful tool in the pre-service phase of teachers' development, directly addressing teachers' need for corrective experience versus their defence against changes to the inner working model needed to achieve it. The obvious point of its application is during pre-service education.

Given that anxiety is ubiquitous in pre-service teachers, acknowledging it provides for examination and reworking of the resulting avoidance strategies that can cause teachers difficulties in the classroom. For some teachers the anxiety, caused by students displaying a differing approach to relationships than they have come to expect from others, triggers avoidance strategies that are implemented unconsciously to protect them from students' challenges to their inner working model. By defending against a new way of relating the teacher prevents the chances of corrective emotional experiences through contact with students.

By restructuring teachers' defending during pre-service education they might just be able to really experience a new form of relating in the classroom free from the anxiety that would have blocked the beneficial relationships from occurring at a deep enough level to facilitate corrective emotional experiences. If experienced teachers' anxiety is reduced by classroom experience, this suggests that pre-service education emphasising relationship building may have long-lasting positive effects on beginning teachers. The evidence reported shows that for some teachers at least the possibility exists that they will receive corrective emotional experiences through the relationships they are able to form with their students and/or colleagues. However, the corrective emotional experiences could be built into their pre-service education through the application of CIND. This would begin the process of becoming aware of their own and others' unconscious needs, and gaining corrective experiences before they reach the classroom. On the evidence gathered so far, this is likely to facilitate stronger classroom relationships from the outset. Education for relationship building, which is not currently practised pre-service, may also hold much potential in lessening aggression by teachers directed toward students, through building their emotional resilience and flexibility.

CIND could be used in a number of ways during pre-service education. Apart from following the model as outlined in Chapters 5 and 6, it could also be used to structure the debriefing sessions that follow each teaching practicum. In this way CIND frames the exploration of the feelings that pre-service teachers experience during their teaching rounds. Alerting pre-service teachers to the idea that they may have unmet and unacknowledged attachment needs that partly motivated their career choice begins the process that can lead to insight-navigated change and reduction in their vulnerability to rejection by students. This then affords them the ability to be flexible, not fearful, in responding to the students they teach. As a consequence they can bring all of their training to bear on the inevitable difficult situations that they will encounter, rather than reverting to old patterns of relationship behaviour. CIND as a discussion model could be incorporated into many other aspects of pre-service education that have traditionally been largely cognitively based.

Refocusing some aspects of pre-service education is likely to be important for the wellbeing of students in classrooms also. It would appear imperative from this research and from much of the literature cited that the problem of teacher aggression is widespread and highly damaging to student wellbeing. The reporting of this is only beginning to address the magnitude of the problem in the West (Sava, 2002).

If teacher aggression is the result of attachment needs remaining unmet or defended against through emotional dissonance, it behoves teacher educators to address this directly as part of the pre-service experience. It is vital for teachers to understand themselves and their emotional strengths and weaknesses as an inoculation against the relational difficulties they will experience in dealing with students they will teach, in particular the insecurely attached students. This is the kind of training that counsellors are given. The contention presented here is that teaching is a form of preventative psychology and therefore the techniques used to train psychologists could and perhaps should be adapted to help teachers deal with their students in a way that is both protective and supportive of all parties. Population studies showing 30–40% of all students are insecurely attached (Brennan et al., 1998) pose problems for teachers who are also insecurely attached. A version of CIND may offer the tools to mitigate the kinds of aggressive responding that is evident in non-English literature.

The potential benefits from this approach may also lead to a reduction in teacher attrition. The cost savings of even a small reduction in attrition rates would more than cover the costs of resourcing the additional training, but is likely to have much greater benefit than simply being cost neutral. The Center for Innovative Thought reported in *Teachers and the Uncertain American Future* (2006) that the teaching profession in the United States "is in crisis" (p. 9). The same is true in the UK and Australia. If attrition rates could be brought down by even a few per cent by incorporating activities such as CIND into pre-service education, the emotional and relationship benefits as well as cost saving would be significant.

The Center for Innovative Thought (2006) was tasked with getting to grips with the teacher shortage crisis across the US. They took a wide-ranging view of the situation and their report is a significant challenge to teacher educators and governments:

> The time has come to adopt a different posture. Teachers deserve respect and an income that reflects their high calling. At the same time, the profession needs to understand that the public is not willing to pay more for more of the same. Some of the traditions that lie at the foundation of the current profession need to be reconsidered. Some teaching jobs are more difficult than others. We should say so.
>
> (Center for Innovative Thought, 2006, p. 17)

To address this issue in teacher education is vital, but we must not do it in a "more of the same" way, which clearly is not working. So let us now turn our attention toward the beginning teacher. What can she tell us about how to change teacher education?

Beginning teachers face a number of difficulties that their more experienced counterparts have achieved some level of competency with, particularly in relation to classroom management and dealing with difficult students. However, factors are emerging which appear to be critical for new teachers. Surprisingly perhaps, burnout is one, becoming an issue of growing importance, and showing up within the first eight months of teaching (Pillay et al., 2005, p. 24). Pillay and colleagues reported a significant association between self-rated wellbeing and self-rated competence, claiming a positive relationship between self-control of inner states and perceived competence. This is an important finding and was confirmed in a study of 315 pre-service and experienced teachers (Riley, 2009a). However, teachers' self-rated competence did not relate to stress and wellbeing levels. Perceived competence may even have a negative impact on students when levels of depersonalisation employed by teachers to cope in the classroom are taken into account (Pillay et al., 2005).

Depersonalisation, defined as "a negative, callous and detatched attitude to people" was reported to be a significant coping mechanism for some teachers (Pillay et al., 2005, p. 24). They suggested that depersonalisation may be a self-protective defence mechanism invoked to minimise the sense of incompetence felt when teachers have to deal "with the more difficult human interactions where the worker lacks sufficient skills to bring the interaction to a successful conclusion" (Pillay et al., 2005, p. 29). They went on to suggest that this issue should be explored further, because teachers were rating their level of competence as satisfactory or above while using depersonalisation strategies for interactions with students. Although not reported on, the teachers were presumably depersonalising colleagues also, as this is not something that is easily switched on and off. This raises the question with regard to self-reported levels of perceived competence: competent for what?

Many exiting teachers, not just beginners, report difficulties with classroom management as reasons to leave. There is very strong evidence from multiple Maslach studies (see for example, Cano-Garcia et al., 2005; Maslach, 1999) that a depersonalising teacher is more likely to have relationship difficulties that eventually result in classroom management difficulties than an empathic teacher, independent of level of pedagogical expertise: a vicious cycle.

Implications for professional development in classroom management and mentoring

Professional development based on the principles of CIND may offer a means of dealing with the current population of aggressive teachers in schools. School psychologists and counsellors could be taught to facilitate CIND in the same way that experienced Principals were taught to use the method reported in Chapter 6: as a train-the-trainer model. This would allow for widespread implementation in schools as they in turn could train the senior teachers who are responsible for mentoring incoming teachers. The mechanism for reaching all new teachers with such a model already exists in many educational systems, where beginning teachers, like beginning psychologists receive professional mentoring from an experienced teacher. If these teacher/mentors were trained to use CIND techniques, they would be able work in new ways with all teachers coming into the profession. They would also be available to work with other colleagues who might be having difficulties with student relationships also. Using this model would ensure that there were at least some CIND trained counsellors and teachers in every school relatively quickly.

Implications for school leadership

The research conducted with teachers supports the emerging literature on leadership conceptualised as good parenting (Popper, 2004; Popper et al., 2004; Popper & Mayseless, 2003; Popper et al., 2000). It is likely that leadership and/or collegial relationships provide corrective experiences for teachers. And, as these relationships are likely to be much longer lasting than teacher–student relationships they offer the opportunity of gradually, and significantly, changing the internal working model of teachers over an extended period of time.

The data reported suggests that relationships teachers are able to form with their colleagues and/or superordinates, rather than their students, may be what provides a corrective emotional experience. A recent nationwide study of the management of student misbehaviour in England, published by Ofsted (ISQ Briefings, 2007) listed a number of common features displayed in classrooms where student misbehaviour was well managed. One of the interesting findings was that the protective factors for students were teachers who had good support from their administration, notably the background level of support offered to them by their Principals. The more visible and supportive the Principal was in the school, the lower the incidence and intensity of student misbehaviour. The report suggested that the teachers who were given this kind of support by their leadership teams were able to respond earlier and more appropriately to students, often effectively nipping inappropriate student behaviour in the bud.

The Ofsted report could be explained in terms of secure base behaviour. When teachers felt they had a secure base, in this case a Principal who would be available and supportive, they could more easily become the secure base for the students; responding early and flexibly addressing the situation at hand, offering emotional scaffolding for the students and modelling the behaviour they were encouraging the students to also display. Thus the teacher becomes the secure base for the student. This then appears to have a flow-on effect to the student-to-student interactions (ISQ Briefings, 2007), much like the delta metaphor outlined in Chapter 6. The result is a lessening of attachment-driven anxiety in the classroom for all members and a resetting of the emotional thermostat so that more time is spent on the learning tasks. The language used in the report is very similar to the language of good parenting literature. The report could easily be renamed: *Teaching from a Secure Base to a Secure Base*.

The implications of this research for school leadership are also important. As the set goal of attachment is "felt security" rather than physical or emotional proximity (Fonagy, 2001) teachers can feel secure when supported by their direct managers, in most cases the leadership team or the Principal of the school. Teachers who feel supported by the Principal will be less threatened by rejection from a student or students as their security can reside with the relationship "felt" from the Principal. This would allow the teacher, as the Ofsted study demonstrated, to be able to respond earlier, more effectively and appropriately with students who were causing difficulties within the class (ISQ Briefings, 2007). Therefore it is very important that leadership teams impart a feeling of security to their subordinates and that they too feel supported by their regional managers so that they perform their role well. This amounts to a flow of security from one secure base to another: a cascade of secure bases.

A recent study by the Australian Education Union revealed "more than three-quarters of Victoria's first-year teachers are employed on short-term contracts" (Smith, 2007). This type of employment practice can only raise the background level of anxiety for teachers increasing the likelihood of fearful-aggressive responding in the classroom. An ongoing job adds to security of beginning teachers, leaving them with more emotional resources to deal with the actual duties of teaching. This is therefore a leadership issue also.

The data reported here also has implications for policy makers. It would appear to be wise to implement and/or adjust induction mentoring programmes for new teachers by ensuring mentor-teachers have at least five years of experience. These teachers are likely to have significantly lower levels of both anxiety and avoidance of close relationships and thus would be better able to form sound relationships with new teachers. Hence they are better placed to begin providing the corrective emotional experiences that some new teachers are seeking.

CIND might also be usefully employed as part of the "due process" mechanism that leaders need to implement when they have to deal with underperforming teachers. As many cases of underperformance relate to classroom management in some way, it is reasonable to assume that underperformance is in many cases attachment related and the teacher would therefore benefit from CIND as remediation strategy. Consequently, it would seem beneficial to include CIND into school leadership training courses, perhaps all leadership training courses related to the helping professions.

Research investigating the combination of leadership, collegial and teacher-student relationships, while complicated in design, offers chances to explore the complexity of the teacher's school experiences. New ways of analysing dyadic information also offer a number of possibilities for discovering meaningful connections between members of school communities (Gonzalez & Griffin, 1997; Kenny et al., 2006). This holds a great deal of promise for the transformation of individual teachers and whole school communities. The leadership, as secure base from which security flows throughout a school, is likely to provide the conditions for many teachers to reduce their unhelpful avoidance strategies and more fully experience the potential joys of classroom relationships by supporting teachers in ways that they need.

Suggestions for future research

There appear to be many positive applications of attachment theory to teaching. Further research aimed at priming security for teachers (such as partial replications, adapted for classrooms, of the studies by Baldwin, 2007; Carnelley & Rowe, 2007; Lemche et al., 2006; Mikulincer et al., 2003; Shaver & Mikulincer, 2002) and recording behavioural, cognitive and affective changes may provide guidance on the best way to induce feelings of security in teachers.

The development of a School Secure-Base Scale that could by used by leaders to gauge the sense of security felt by staff and students would be a useful addition to the existing staff and student attitude surveys currently in use. Finally, CIND appears to be an effective intervention model to help teachers and leaders improve their practice. Its application is resource intensive, being based on six hours of one-to-one conversation. Research directed toward a wider application of CIND, such as training-the-trainer models, might provide more chances for teachers to engage in this kind of reflexive review of their teaching strengths and weaknesses.

New wine in old bottles or old wine in new bottles?

Many techniques offered to teachers for student management are based on having more authentic relationships. This began with Carl Rogers' work (1951, 1961/1989, 1990) and has been developed widely since by many authors. Teachers with reduced attachment scaffolding to incorporate such techniques will be likely to find them a threat to their understanding of how the world works: their inner working model. Incorporating new techniques into professional practice without the insights required to understand at a deeper level what they are changing about their practice appears to be unsustainable. This is what Ramon Lewis (2006) found, despite initial improvement. In effect some teachers could not trust themselves to improve through trial and error of new techniques, styles and curricula.

The most encouraging outcomes of the work presented in this book are that all of the teachers who experienced the CIND process reported that they were operating in a more relaxed and flexible manner, and this was confirmed by their superordinates. For some of these teachers they continue to do so nearly five years after the intervention of CIND. "When one has matured surrounded by implicit disparagement, the undiscovered self is an unexpected resource. Self knowledge is empowering" (Bateson, 1991, p. 5).

What remains to be discovered is whether the CIND model can be incorporated into the initial education and ongoing professional practice of teachers. It seems to work as a restorative and preventative model. CIND might become the vehicle through which pre-service teachers safely lay out their vulnerabilities for examination and re-story their inner working model to form a personal secure base from which to continue to explore what it means to be a teacher, or to slightly amend the words of Carl Rogers, to be that teacher which one truly is.

Conclusions and recommendations

An important series of questions need to be asked of those licensing, registering and employing teachers, the communities in which they work, and the profession itself. In today's climate of increased expectations and accountability, what are acceptable minimum knowledge and skill requirements for teachers? How much should a teacher know about child development, interpersonal skills, classroom management and pedagogical content? These questions have not been adequately answered to date. Some, such as the level of knowledge of child development for secondary school teachers, and interpersonal skill development, have barely been addressed at all, and only informally at best. At the very least, governments and policy makers should provide recognition of the difficult and often psychologically demanding work that teachers do with very little education in interpersonal work, and often limited understanding of the processes of child development. Teachers and teacher professional bodies do not appear to be pushing for this, perhaps because they too lack awareness about the importance of such matters. It is time for psychologists, who have had the benefit of this education, to alert them.

As stated earlier, the "taboo" on this topic first needs to be acknowledged by the wider education and research communities: we must grasp the nettle to weed it out. However, this needs to be done calmly, carefully and compassionately rather than in a "knee jerk" fashion. Logically, addressing the issues must begin at the beginning of pre-service education, where new training regimes need to be put into place. Just as psychologists are made aware early of the dangers of becoming over-involved with clients, so should teachers be made aware of similar dangers concerning students, and this must be done early. The importance of these issues also needs to be acknowledged by the profession through the development and implementation of an extensive code of ethics and comprehensive guidelines that give protection to individual teachers, by providing detailed advice on how to behave in an ethical manner. And such a code is best developed and administered by the profession, not regulators.

Breaking hundred year old habits

The changes to teacher education and professional development are important for the wellbeing of students, as well as teachers. The problem of teacher aggression is widespread and highly damaging to student wellbeing. The assertion I advocate on the basis of this review is that it is vital for teachers to understand themselves and their emotional strengths and weaknesses as an inoculation against the relational difficulties they will surely experience when interacting with students during their professional careers. If we are serious about improving education three significant changes to current practice need to occur. First, governments must provide adequate investment in the initial education and ongoing professional development of teachers. This is not a cost, rather it is an investment in our most precious resource: our children. Second, changes in pre-service teacher education, professional supervision and practice need to be implemented to include dedicated study of the emotions and emotional scaffolding, in particular attachment theory. Finally, a comprehensive code of ethics and detailed guidelines for their implementation, similar to those used by psychologists who also find themselves in emotionally charged environments with vulnerable people, should be developed and adopted by the teaching profession.

These recommendations have far reaching implications as I have outlined above, but they are likely to have multiple benefits in schools. Teachers, like psychologists, work within an intensely human environment with the same pitfalls as the other helping professions. Yet currently they have no formal access to training in the skills required to deal with them. Psychology as a profession addressed this issue, at the end of World War II, when the influx of returning soldiers who needed help instigated the Boulder conference designed to rethink how psychologists were trained and expected to practice (see Baker & Benjamin, 2000; Benjamin, 2000; Petersen, 2007; Peterson, 2000). It is time for the teaching profession to follow suit and do more to protect its members, educators and school leaders. Attachment theory offers many possibilities for rethinking and envisioning how schools should change to cope with the demands of the era in which we find ourselves without losing sight of the fact that each of us are born more into the human condition than any particular era.

Chapter 8

Further into attachment theory

For the reader interested in further applying attachment theory to teaching, I have included some more detail on various aspects covered in the earlier chapters. This chapter contains more technical detail about various aspects of the theory, how they were used to construct the CIND intervention, and the implications of both in relation to the early career exits of too many teachers.

Attachment theory

Like all complex theories of human behaviour, attachment theory is evolving as new information is discovered and its applications are expanded. A number of aspects of attachment theory have already been applied to educational settings. For example, a recent search of the literature on attachment and education revealed over 300 studies reported this century. These were almost entirely concerned with students' attachment profiles and the effect these had on their academic outcomes. One that differed examined teacher burnout (Diaz, 2003). One other interesting study (Beishuizen et al., 2001) examined students' and teachers' perceptions of "good teachers". The authors reported significant differences between primary school students, who described good teachers as competent instructors, but were dependently attached to them, and secondary school students, who described good teachers in relational terms. Their study suggested that good practitioners were those who could establish personal relationships with students. The emphasis on relationships shown by the secondary students and the teachers themselves suggests that both teachers and students view relationships as integral to teaching and learning. It is likely that primary school age children, who work mainly with one teacher on most days, take the relationship so much for granted that they omit identifying it as a factor.

A further consideration is determining which aspects of attachment theory, a vast and broad theory of human development, are the most useful to education. I have argued previously (Riley, 2009a) that as childhood attachment style is set and relatively stable by three years of age, the adult model is a more appropriate one for understanding the relationships that are formed and maintained in school settings.

Adult attachment theory offers more sophisticated explanations for the dynamics of classroom relationships. It is self-evident to any classroom observer that some relationships between teachers and students are strong and robust, others appear fragmented and fragile, and most fall somewhere between these two extremes. Systematic observations and examination of teachers' patterns of relationship building and maintenance reveals important aspects of the underlying differences. Specifically, Bowlby's (1978, 1988a, 1988b) concept of the *secure base*, crucial to understanding attachment processes in the classroom and staffroom, appears to have a wider application than he originally conceived. However, to fully consider how this might be useful to the school setting, the whole of the attachment conceptual framework first needs to be understood. And for that to occur we need to go back to the beginning and build from the ground up, so to speak.

The attachment behavioural system is fundamentally a system of connections between members of a species, including human beings. My dog would argue that attachment also occurs between species. At its core, attachment is one of physical and emotional proximity and proximity seeking. The concepts developed over a number of years after many important contributions by a number of researchers (see Aberbach, 1995; Ainsworth, 1982, 1985, 1989, 1991; Ainsworth, et al., 1978; Bowlby, 1975, 1980, 1982, 1983, 1988a; Bretherton, 1985, 2003; Hrdy, 2009; Main, 1999; Sroufe & Sampson, 2000). Attachment is now understood as a set goal of "felt security" which developed from the earlier conceptualisation of physical distance regulation (Fonagy, 2003a; Waters & Waters, 2006). For teachers to understand how the principles of attachment might explain the complexity of relationships within classrooms, it is necessary to first understand the fundamental principles of attachment that operate within all of us shortly after birth and continue throughout our lifespan. As the attachment behavioural system is largely automatic and stable well before we enter school, outlining the concepts may at first seem unrelated to professional educators' relationships. However, when one understands the whole of attachment theory, and in particular the processes involved in the activation of the behavioural system, the direct links with classroom processes and its importance as an explanatory tool become clear.

History and development of attachment theory: a new model

The theory developed largely from the object relations tradition of psychoanalysis. John Bowlby was interested in bringing a stricter scientific method to the study of development by incorporating the "concepts from evolution theory, ethology, control theory, and cognitive psychology" (Bowlby, 1988a, p. 120). He looked for predictive evidence, rather than the retrospective evidence used by all psychoanalysts at that time. He came to reject the two major stands of psychoanalysis, *object relations theory* promoted by Melanie Klein and her followers (Klein, 1986) and *drive theory* promoted by Anna Freud (1966), daughter of Sigmund, and her supporters (Holder, 2005). This was partly because of his opinion that each discounted the significance of the relationship between the caregiver and the child. He disputed their theories, which he believed were derived from philosophical rather than empirical evidence. Theirs were instinctual models derived from either feeding (Klein) or sexuality (Anna Freud).[1]

However, Bowlby's concerns were manufactured to appear more different from psychoanalytic theory than was actually the case, by both him and his detractors, which helped to fuel the dispute and left neither appearing to hold the intellectual territory (Knox, 2003). This only served to hold back the cause of both theories (Fonagy, 2001). Bowlby's concern with the psychoanalysts' thinking of the time was the lack of scientific support for the instincts proposed by both Klein and Anna Freud and their lack of interest in finding such evidence (Holmes, 1993b).

Originally Bowlby's aim was to unify the two distinct theories of behaviour that impressed him most: ethology – the scientific study of species behaviour, using an evolutionary perspective – and psychoanalysis, in particular to bring psychoanalysis in line with modern psychology "and the commonly accepted criteria of natural science" (Bowlby, 1988a, p. 120). Before completing his training as a psychiatrist, Bowlby worked at a "progressive" school (Holmes, 1993b) similar to A.S. Neill's *Summerhill* (1968/1985), where he found he had the ability to communicate with emotionally disturbed children, noting that each of them had difficulties that seemed related to unhappy and disrupted childhoods.

Like Sigmund Freud's development of psychoanalysis, the development of attachment theory began with concern over early childhood deprivation (Fonagy, 2003a). While at the school he made the decision to train as a psychoanalyst in order to study this deprivation more systematically (Holmes, 1993b). However, in the beginnings lay the point of departure also.

Bowlby's departure from psychoanalytic tradition began with his insistence that the external reality (as opposed to internal drives) that each infant is born into constitute a "key process in the formation of the unconscious internal world" (Knox, 2003, p. 138). This may seem obvious today but was a revolutionary departure from psychoanalytic tradition at the time. Bowlby saw attachment as a primary motivational system for most if not all species (1982) and found what he believed to be solid evidence for its operation and interface with other environmental systems. He was profoundly impressed by the work of two contemporary researchers: Conrad Lorenz and Harry Harlow. Lorenz (1935) demonstrated that for goslings herding behaviour was the result of initial imprinting, not instinct. Harry Harlow and his colleagues' (Harlow, 1958; Harlow & Harlow, 1965; Harlow & Zimmermann, 1959) controversial Rhesus monkey studies saw baby monkeys separated from their biological mothers at birth and reared with the aid of "wire mothers". The extraordinary findings of the Harlow experiments, in which he claimed to have found the nature of love, were that the baby Rhesus monkeys preferred to cling to a fur-covered wire "mother" that could not feed them rather than a lactating wire mother without fur.

The new research medium of film was employed by Harry Harlow, and indirectly helped settle the controversy over attachment. Harlow's studies (Harlow & Harlow, 1965; Harlow & Zimmermann, 1959) powerfully described the distress to Rhesus monkeys brought on by separation from the mother and the inadequacy of a nonresponsive surrogate for psychological development. The most important finding of these studies in relation to the settling of the dispute over the validity of attachment theory was the discovery of the primacy of the attachment bond. Harlow and Zimmerman (1959) demonstrated infants' need for attachment to a secure base figure that was not related to the ingestion of food as had previously been thought. The failure of the surrogate Rhesus monkey mothers to comfort the babies despite the fact that they could adequately feed them was proven by the babies' choice to cling to a fur covered surrogate that did not feed them, even when that "mother" became punishing, via the use of compressed air jets and pins that would randomly frighten or injure the babies. Attachment proved to be and was henceforth regarded as an internal drive equal in power to feeding and sex drives. It was this finding that led Bowlby to realise that:

- attachments, once formed are lasting, and
- attachment is a powerful but not necessarily positive force.

As Lorenz's geese bonded without feeding and the Rhesus monkeys showed feeding without bonding, Bowlby postulated an attachment theory unrelated to feeding which better fitted the biological evidence, but fundamentally challenged the current psychodynamic conception of human development. He saw the primary purpose of attachment as protection from predation and developed attachment as an "epigenetic" model.

An epigenetic/sociobiological model

Epigenesis describes the progression points and possible pathways of the developing organism (Waddington, 1977), but is now more commonly referred to as the sociobiological model (Fonagy, 2003a). When a new infant enters the world several lines of development are possible, each depending on specific interactions of the environment with the organism, such as the diet, quality and amount of sleep, exercise, level of care, safety and so on. This theory lies in contrast to the homuncular model supported by psychoanalytic theorists at the time.

The homuncular model (from *homunculus* or *little man*) describes development as the passing through of preset stages of development that are the same for each member of that species. Bowlby's epigenetic model was more in line with Klein's "positions" but unlike Freud's stages that are fixed and through which all must pass in sequence, regardless of environmental influences (Holmes, 1993b). "Thus 'anxious' attachment, rather than being a 'stage', like the so-called 'oral' stage of development, becomes a possible epigenetic compromise between a child's attachment needs and a parent who is unable fully to meet them" (Holmes, 1993b, pp. 219–220).

Recent developments in neuroscience have confirmed that environmental stimulation does indeed play a pivotal role in the wiring (and rewiring or neural plasticity) of the human brain (Abel & Kandel, 1998; Ramachandran, 2003; Schore, 2001a,

2001b, 2001c). It is now known that the process of brain development continues at least until the early 20s. This discovery has necessitated a dramatic reappraisal of brain development which until recently was thought to have been largely complete by birth and certainly by three years of age (Schwartz & Begley, 2002). Over time, the research begun by Bowlby and later Ainsworth and others has reframed the "nature versus nurture" debate to one of "nature through nurture", or epigenesis/sociobiology. Bowlby believed that humans had a genetically inherited predisposition to form attachments, but that the quality of each attachment is environmentally mediated for each individual. This was a strong theoretical challenge to the psychoanalytic community (Knox, 2003).

In the 1930s a number of clinicians, mostly working independently of each other and not all with humans, were coming to the conclusion that breaks in the bond between the primary caregiver and infant had a negative effect on the development of the infant's personality; the younger the infant, the greater the effect. Separations may occur during the early years of a child's life through events such as a prolonged period of institutional care in a hospital. The multiple disruptions to mother–child bonds caused by World War II and the increase in the number of orphans led to a stepping up of research into this phenomenon.

In 1949 John Bowlby, then a young psychiatrist, was appointed to study the needs of homeless children by the World Health Organisation (Bowlby, 1988a). This appointment allowed Bowlby the unique opportunity to read, and tie together, all of the literature that had been accumulating in disparate repositories. The appointment also enabled him to travel to meet many of the authors from both Europe and the United States who had been studying in the same area. The result, Bowlby's monograph *Maternal Care and Mental Health* (1951), documented the "adverse influences on personality development of inadequate maternal care[2] during early childhood… and made recommendations of how best to avoid, or at least mitigate, the short- and long-term effects" (Bowlby, 1988a, pp. 21–22).

In an interesting parallel, the development of attachment theory saw the psychology of child rearing move significantly toward the emotional and away from the behavioural, beginning in the 1960s. Previously the behaviourists held the power to influence young parents and the damage inflicted on children, and their carers for that matter, under the banner of scientific child rearing practices was tragic. When Bowlby suggested that it was wrong to let babies cry themselves to sleep, indeed that giving attention was not spoiling the child but fostering her development, this not only helped babies but "it also led to practical benefits for parents" (Hrdy, 2009).

In conjunction with others, Bowlby also used the power of film, to show the effects on children of separation from the primary caregiver or attachment figure. Even today the film, *A two-year-old goes to hospital*, commissioned by Bowlby and completed by James Robertson (Bowlby et al., 1952) is a powerful demonstration of the distress suffered through the breaking of an attachment bond.

Undaunted by the criticisms of his psychoanalytic peers regarding his developing theory, Bowlby and a few dedicated colleagues continued to research and gather evidence. But it was not until 1962, when an important publication by Mary Ainsworth appeared reviewing the "extensive and diverse evidence and considered the many issues that had given rise to the controversy", that a more reasoned approach to the study of attachment began (Bowlby, 1988a, p. 23). This controversy came at some cost to Bowlby's reputation as a scientist.

Peter Fonagy (1999b, 2001, 2003b; Fonagy & Target, 2003) has detailed the bitter battles and how Bowlby defended against the attacks by using straw man arguments. In the end he concluded that neither Bowlby nor his critics came out of the dispute well, and that the rifts were prolonged and deepened by the defensive exclusion of sound evidence on both sides of the argument. It is only in recent times that theoretical bridges are being constructed, by carefully piecing together the evidence that has been accumulating separately in the domains of cognitive neuroscience, academic psychology, psychoanalysis and analytical psychology (Dennett, 1995; Fonagy, 2003a; Grossmann, 1995; Knox, 2003). With the addition of Ainsworth's contribution, attachment theory became the theoretical "glue" holding what were previously seen as disparate and competing theories together. The following section covers in more detail the concepts of despair and detachment; fundamental concepts of attachment theory needed to establish this claim.

Despair

The concepts surrounding despair were built from Bowlby's understanding of widows' stages of mourning reported by Marris (1958). Bowlby was able to identify common stages of both healthy and pathological mourning: anger directed toward the self, others and the lost object. In an interesting observation he also noted that mourners tended to exhibit disbelief at the loss, which until then he postulated had been wrongly conceptualised as denial. He also found a tendency for the mourner to "search for the lost person in the hope of a reunion" (Bowlby, 1988a, p. 32) and that this was often but not always unconsciously driven. This led him to the concept of detachment.

Detachment and the connection to mourning

Mourning has also been extensively written about by Colin Murray Parkes (1986) who worked alongside Bowlby at the Tavistock Institute in London. He researched bereavement, loss and the grieving process since the late 1950s. His work was later popularised by Elizabeth Kübler-Ross, whose book *On Death and Dying* (1970) became a best seller. Bowlby pointed out, in the introduction to the second edition of *Bereavement: Studies of Grief in Adult Life* (Parkes, 1986) that the processes of healthy and pathological mourning, identified by Parkes, lie on a continuum of intensity and duration and should not be viewed as distinctly different processes from each other. Parkes outlined the major features of bereavement reactions for most people:

1   A process of realisation, i.e., the way in which the bereaved moves from denial or avoidance of recognition of the loss towards acceptance.

2   An alarm reaction – anxiety, restlessness, and the physiological accompaniments of fear.

3   An urge to search for and to find the lost person in some form.

4   Anger and guilt, including outbursts directed against those who press the bereaved person towards premature acceptance of the loss.

5   Feelings of internal loss of self or mutilation.

6   Identification phenomena – the adoption of traits, mannerisms, or symptoms of the lost person, with or without a sense of that person's presence within the self.

7   Pathological variants of grief, i.e., the reaction may be excessive and prolonged or inhibited and inclined to emerge in distorted form.

(Parkes, 1986, p. 202)

Perceptual defence and unconscious processing

The unconscious has always been a controversial aspect of psychoanalytic theory that many behavioural theorists find difficult to allow philosophically, some denying its existence altogether, the most well known and strident critic being B. F. Skinner (1974). However, in 1991 Dixon and Henley reported powerful experimental support for the unconscious processing of information. They had participants look at images of faces displaying neutral emotional expressions, with a simultaneous presentation of a subliminal word that had either happy or sad connotations. The participants' responses to the faces were found to be influenced by the subliminal word's connotations. They demonstrated a behavioural response to stimuli that the participants were unaware of, providing evidence of unconscious processing leading directly to changes in behaviour in real time.

Many interesting studies have since followed which confirm and extend the findings of Dixon and Henley (Baldwin, 1995, 2007; Baldwin et al., 1996; Banse, 1999; Bartz & Lydon, 2004; Branigan et al., 2005; Carnelley & Rowe, 2007; Desmet & Declercq, 2006; Hazan et al., 2004; Lemche et al., 2006; Mallinckrodt, 2007; Mikulincer et al., 2000; Mikulincer et al., 2001; Mikulincer et al., 2003; Peterson & Park, 2007; Shaver & Mikulincer, 2002). Some studies have directly measured attachment-related internalised experiences and their effects on behaviour (Andersen & Berk, 1998; Green & Campbell, 2000). Mikulincer and colleagues (2002) used priming of a subliminal threat in a lexical decision making task. They reported that "Attachment anxiety heightened accessibility of representations of attachment figures even in neutral contexts, whereas attachment avoidance inhibited this activation when the threat prime was the word separation" (Mikulincer et al., 2002, p. 881). Mikulincer and colleagues (2005) also found that if they experimentally enhanced attachment security this would "facilitate cognitive openness and empathy, strengthen self-transcendent values, and foster tolerance of out-group members" (Mikulincer et al., 2005, p. 817).

Predicting attachment behaviour: the Adult Attachment Interview and self-reports

To understand the intricacies of attachment behaviours in adults and their predictive usefulness in parenting, Mary Main and her colleagues developed the Adult Attachment Interview (AAI) (Bakermans-Kranenburg & IJzendoorn, 1993; Cassidy & Shaver, 1999; George et al., 1984; Main, 1990; Wei-li & Li, 2004). Their work built on the *strange situation test* research, developed by Mary Ainsworth and her colleagues (Ainsworth et al., 1978; Bretherton, 1992). The strange situation test proved to be one of the significant empirical contributions to the development of attachment theory, and was greatly appreciated by Bowlby, who immediately saw its significance to the development of the theory. The strange situation was used to determine the attachment style of infants.

The AAI was developed for use as a predictive test of an unborn infant's attachment style in utero. The aim was to accurately identify mothers with insecure attachment styles and supply corrective measures such as parenting classes so that their babies would have a better chance of secure attachment. The AAI is a comprehensive interview protocol designed to tap prospective mothers' childhood memories. Consisting of a series of open-ended questions, adults are asked to reflect on their memories of attachment relationships from childhood and perceptions of the influence these experiences had on their development (Bretherton, 1992). The AAI was found to predict a baby's future attachment style at three years with 70% accuracy (Bakermans-Kranenburg & IJzendoorn, 1993).

The training in administration and scoring of the assessment is carefully controlled by the developers of the model and has produced an accurate but time and resource consuming instrument. Subsequent research validated the AAI classifications of attachment with Ainsworth's infant classifications (Allen et al., 2005; Bakermans-Kranenburg & IJzendoorn, 1993; Fonagy et al., 1991).

Despite the effectiveness of the AAI the drawbacks remain a significant impediment to widespread use. It is cumbersome: it can only be administered by a trained interviewer, to one person at a time and each interview plus interpretation of the data collected is very time consuming. The AAI has long been considered the gold standard. However, the search for a more efficient means of determining attachment profiles began in the late 1980s, beginning with Hazan and Shaver (1987) who produced the first self-report measure of attachment. Much work went into finding useful and efficient alternatives, particularly self-report measures in light of Hazan and Shaver's work. A number of less cumbersome, perhaps less discriminating, but good enough self-report instruments have been developed and validated since (see for example, Allen et al., 2005; Bakermans-Kranenburg & IJzendoorn, 1993; Bartholomew & Horowitz, 1991; Bartholomew & Shaver, 1998; Brennan et al., 1998; Cassidy & Shaver, 1999; Crowell et al., 2002; Fonagy et al., 1996; Fraley & Shaver, 2000; Fraley et al., 2000; Hazan & Shaver, 1987, 1990, 1994a, 1994b; Hazan & Zeifman, 1999; Kirkpatrick & Hazan, 1994; Knox, 2003; Scharfe & Bartholomew, 1994; Shaver & Brennan, 1992; Shaver & Hazan, 1987; Sibley et al., 2005; Sperling et al., 1996; Stein et al., 1998; Stein et al., 2002; Zhang & Hazan, 2002). While the search continues the development of valid measures allowed large numbers of pre-service and experienced teachers to submit attachment profiles. This would not have been possible with the AAI as the instrument.

Hazan and Shaver's work showed that attachment styles at three years could be used to predict adult attachment styles, confirming Bowlby's prediction that, generally speaking, patterns of behaviour are bestowed on the child from their caregivers, who in turn pass them on to the next generation unless significant counter experiences interrupt the cycle. This is good news for teachers as they have the opportunity to provide significant counter experiences to students, literally changing lives.

Leadership and attachment to organisations

It is useful for teachers to reflect on the relationship they have with their super-ordinates within the organisational structure of the school. Those teachers who are supported by their school leaders will feel they have a secure base from which to conduct their professional role. This has been shown experimentally to increase empathy and caring behaviours (Baldwin, 2007; Mikulincer et al., 2005; Peterson & Park, 2007). Teachers who feel that they cannot rely on their superiors for support are likely to defend against a lack of support in times of need (Lemche et al., 2006; Mikulincer et al., 2000; Mikulincer et al., 2003; Mikulincer et al., 2002). They are more likely to become preoccupied with their own behaviour, to protect them-selves from the behaviour of their superiors. They will feel that they must look after themselves, professionally and personally, in the workplace because they will not receive care from those who might supply it when needed. They are, in effect, insecurely attached to the organisation and are therefore more likely to behave in ways predicted by insecure attachment.

While all sorts of behaviour are possible, this situation is likely to produce rigid rule following which allows the environment to appear safer than they feel it actu-ally is. They have not achieved a secure base within the system and are likely to feel compelled to attempt to construct one for themselves and their students to rigidly follow. The effect of this is for each of the members of the class to be confined to role-playing rather than natural interpersonal interaction. The paradox of this response by the teacher is that it reduces the chances of deepening the relation-ship with students: which would increase the level of felt security for teacher and students alike.

The qualitative investigation that led to CIND

The impetus for the investigation was to discover if the underlying reasons for teachers' self-reported aggression[3] in the classroom were attachment related, and if so, what might be developed by way of professional development to reduce it.

The map of the terrain consisted of object relations conceptions developed by Melanie Klein and others (see Klein, 1986), from which the theory of attachment developed, and Harry Stack Sullivan's practical questioning style (Sullivan, 1954a, 1954b). Sullivan was not simply interested in satisfying his curiosity through probative questions. He was driven to find out what people do to avoid anxiety in interpersonal relations, so that he might help them. Probing questions need careful formation, consideration and refinement. A sharp probe will get further than a dull one. However, a sharp probe pointed in the wrong direction will go further astray. Therefore my methodology needed to include tools for understanding the invisible processes of the highly complex and specialised environment of the classroom, and what might be going awry for teachers within its confines. This led to the adoption of psychoanalysis as an investigative tool. However, this methodology needed to be carefully considered as there are a number of strands that were available for use, and the area has been full of controversy over many years.

Psychoanalysis as an investigative tool

It has been argued that psychoanalysts have often been their own worst enemies (Fonagy, 2001, 2003a; Knox, 2003). Historically they have been slow, perhaps resistant to the incorporation of new knowledge gained from psychology and neuroscience (Knox, 2003). Over the years various factions of psychoanalysts have refused to deal logically with each other as they splintered off into subgroups delineated philosophically rather than empirically (Fonagy, 2001). The defensive positions they took collectively to the undeniable advances in brain science seemed almost anti-intellectual. "The irrational prevailing belief appears to be that hard-won psychoanalytic insight could somehow 'be destroyed' rather than elaborated and enriched by the new methods of inquiry" (Fonagy, 2003c, p. x). This prompted a systematic devaluing of psychoanalysis as both an investigative and an explanatory tool for complex behaviour.

Psychology claimed the intellectual territory and actively sought discovery and application of new knowledge relevant to the understanding of behaviour. Psychologists, particularly academic psychologists whose education had been grounded in behaviourism as a reaction to psychoanalytic enquiry, took a very dim view of psychoanalysis. They maintained that true scientific knowledge could only be gained through a positivist approach, antithetical to psychoanalysts and with "an almost exclusive concern with behaviour" (Fonagy, 2003b, p. xi).

Psychologists failed to acknowledge that reductionist "purposively naïve" approaches to the study of behaviour determining the efficacy of therapeutic interventions "are as easy to explain in terms of psychoanalytic ideas as in terms of behavioural ones" (Fonagy, 2003b, pp. xi, xiii). Psychoanalysts also routinely ignored opportunities to do so. It is only in recent times that any serious attempts to bring the two disciplines together have been attempted, and this has been a cause for concern to some sections of both psychoanalytic and psychological communities, who remain wary of each other's intentions.

The uneasy relationship between attachment theorists and psychoanalysts has also been well documented (Fonagy, 1999b, 2001) and it is only relatively recently that the benefits of bringing the two perspectives together have been seriously addressed (Bretherton, 1998). The restatement of the common core of both theories and the possibilities for extending both by embracing aspects of the other offer many possibilities for broadening and deepening attachment theory. Fonagy (1999c) has suggested that the sophistication of psychoanalytic conceptualisations adds much depth to attachment theory. Addressing this issue, Jean Knox (2003) detailed the points of contact and departure from psychoanalysis, and also documented the overlap of each with analytical psychology in a detailed analysis that appeared long overdue. However, the disputes and pockets of resistance remain in some quarters.

The union of various psychological theories has been accomplished to some extent through the growth of brief, integrated psychotherapy (Gibney, 2003; Macnab, 1991a; Teyber, 2006) and the incorporation of systems thinking into clinical practice (Marmor, 1982, 1983).

This has opened up many opportunities for developing people, through therapy-like undertakings directed toward the future, but looking both forward and backward during the course of the interaction. It is in this context that a modern form of psychoanalysis, one that embraces the recent developments in knowledge derived from neuroscience, control theory and cognitive psychology, combines the complexity and sophistication of a broad spectrum analytical tool with a sharp probe. CIND offers this possibility in a time-limited format that is well suited to time-poor school leaders and teacher educators. Attachment theory provides the bridge and psychoanalysis means to cross it.

Notes

Acknowledgements

1 She preferred everyone to be called "people" and disliked referring to children as students.

Introduction

1 Self-reports of teacher aggression include yelling angrily at students, using sarcasm and humiliation with individual students, and punishing the whole classes for individual misdemeanours when the culprit could not be identified. See Hyman & Snook (1999).
2 *Separation protest* is a fundamental concept of attachment theory. It is explained in detail in Chapter 1.
3 Priming is an important concept in relation to classroom dynamics. It is outlined in more detail in Chapter 2.
4 Not to be mistaken with triangulation in psychotherapy, considered detrimental to the counselling relationship.

1 Attachment theory and the classroom: Overlapping space

1 These terms are for all intents and purposes interchangeable. Each term represents the target of the care seeker's attention when in need of care. Thus a primary caregiver is an attachment object for the care seeker.
2 Chapter 8 reports some interesting experiments carried out on this phenomenon.
3 Attachment style is an alternative term to represent the inner working model.

2 Adult attachment theory and the teacher–student relationship

1 Orthogonal dimensions do not correlate to each other. In this case the levels of either Anxiety or Avoidance reported by an individual do not predict the level of the other dimension, which could be either high or low.
2 The *Diagnostic and Statistical Manual of Mental Disorders* describes the process when a person converts a psychological need into a physical complaint: often employing "colourful, exaggerated terms" (American Psychiatric Association, 2000, p. 486).
3 This section and the next have previously appeared in a slightly different form (see Riley, 2009b). It is reprinted with permission.
4 Sympathy for another's good fortune.

3 The emotionality of teaching

1 Emotional labour is sometimes referred to as emotion work.

4 Does time in the classroom affect attachment style? Does attachment style affect time in the classroom?

1 The information is reprinted with the kind permission of Elsevier.
2 With attrition rates for early career teachers around 45% during the first five years' service this is quite plausible.

5 Contextual Insight-Navigated Discussion

1 The theoretical basis of the technique has been drawn from brief integrated therapy (Akyalcin, 2003; Gergen, 2001; Macnab, 1991a, 1991b; Teyber, 2006), time-limited therapy (Brown, 2002; H. Levenson, 2004; Mann, 1981, 1991; Molnos, 1995) and case story methodology (Ackerman & Maslin-Ostrowski, 2002; Bateson, 1991; Carter, 1999).
2 Iatrogenic anxiety is the anxiety provoked by the process being undertaken by the teacher. Time limitation increases the level of iatrogenic anxiety as a combatant to the anxiety that tries to keep that which should be known from becoming known (for a thorough discussion see, Brown, 2002; Eisold, 2000).
3 Attention Deficit Hyperactivity Disorder.
4 The tasks Ben was asked to perform were made more difficult because of a congenital eye condition that made it difficult to discriminate fine detail. This remained undiagnosed until he reached secondary school. A series of operations in his late adolescence remedied much of the disability, but also left him with what appeared to be a tic, and constant blinking.

6 CIND mentoring: Supporting transitions and early career retentions

1 Some of the material in this chapter was originally published in Riley, 2009b. It is reprinted with the kind permission of the publisher.

8 Further into attachment theory

1 Sigmund Freud had proposed the instinctual drive theory much earlier and the internal politics of the psychoanalytic community meant that it was a brave theorist indeed who challenged this. With attachment theory, Bowlby did just that.
2 Bowlby used the language of the time and at that time it was mostly mothers who were the primary caregivers for infants and children. The theory does not distinguish gender. However it does distinguish between primary and other caregivers.
3 Defined as: yelling angrily at students; the use of sarcasm or public humiliation of students; and punishing a whole class when the individual miscreants could not be identified.

References and selected bibliography

Abel, T., & Kandel, E. (1998). Positive and negative regulatory mechanisms that mediate long-term memory storage. *Brain Research Reviews*, 26(2–3), 360–378.

Aberbach, D. (1995). Charisma and attachment theory: A crossdisciplinary interpretation. *International Journal of Psycho-Analysis*, 76(4), 845–855.

Ackerman, R. H., & Mackenzie, S. V. (2007). *Uncovering teacher leadership: Essays and voices from the field*. Thousand Oaks, CA: Corwin Press.

Ackerman, R. H., & Maslin-Ostrowski, P. (2002). *The wounded leader: How real leadership emerges in times of crisis*. San Francisco, CA: Jossey-Bass.

Ainsworth, M. D. S. (1962). The effects of maternal deprivation: A review of findings and controversy in the context of research strategy. *Deprivation of maternal care: A reassessment of its effects* (Vol. Public Health Papers No. 14). Geneva: World Health Organisation.

Ainsworth, M. D. S. (1967). *Infancy in Uganda: Infant care and the growth of attachment*. Baltimore, MD: Johns Hopkins University Press.

Ainsworth, M. D. S. (1969). Object relations, dependency, and attachment: A theoretical review of the infant–mother relationship. *Child Development*, 40(4), 969–1025.

Ainsworth, M. D. S. (1972). Attachment and dependency: A comparison. In J. L. Gewirtz (Ed.), *Attachment and dependency*. Oxford: V. H. Winston & Sons.

Ainsworth, M. D. S. (1979). Infant–mother attachment. *American Psychologist*, 34(10), 932–937.

Ainsworth, M. D. S. (1982). Attachment: Retrospect and prospect. In C. M. Parkes & J. Stevenson-Hinde (Eds), *The place of attachment in human behaviour* (pp. 3–30). London: Tavistock.

Ainsworth, M. D. S. (1985). Patterns of attachment. *Clinical Psychologist*, 38(2), 27–29.

Ainsworth, M. D. S. (1989). Attachments beyond infancy. *American Psychologist*, 44(4), 709–716.

Ainsworth, M. D. S. (1991). Attachments and other affectional bonds across the life cycle. In C. M. Parkes, J. Stevenson-Hinde & P. Marris (Eds), *Attachment across the life cycle* (pp. 33–51). New York: Tavistock/Routledge.

Ainsworth, M. D. S. (1992). A consideration of social referencing in the context of attachment theory and research. In S. Feinman (Ed.), *Social referencing and the social construction of reality in infancy*. New York: Plenum Press.

Ainsworth, M. D. S., & Ainsworth, L. H. (1958). *Measuring security in personal adjustment*. Oxford: Toronto Press.

Ainsworth, M. D. S., & Bell, S. M. (1970). Attachment, exploration, and separation: Illustrated by the behavior of one-year-olds in a strange situation. *Child Development*, 41(1), 49–67.

Ainsworth, M. D. S., Bell, S. M., & Stayton, D. (1974). Infant–mother attachment and social development: Socialization as a product of reciprocal responsiveness to signals. In M. P. Richards (Ed.), *The integration of a child into a social world* (pp. 9–135). New York: Cambridge University Press.

Ainsworth, M. D. S., Bell, S. M., & Stayton, D. J. (1972). Individual differences in the development of some attachment behaviors. *Merrill-Palmer Quarterly*, 18(2), 123–143.

Ainsworth, M. D. S., Bell, S. M., & Stayton, D. J. (1991). Infant–mother attachment and social development: "Socialisation" as a product of reciprocal responsiveness to signals. In M. Woodhead, R. Carr & P. Light (Eds), *Becoming a person* (Vol. 1: Child development in social context.). Florence, KY: Taylor & Francis/Routledge.

Ainsworth, M. D. S., Blehar, M. C., Waters, E., & Wall, S. (1978). *Patterns of attachment: A psychological study of the strange situation.* Oxford: Lawrence Erlbaum.

Ainsworth, M. D. S., & Bowlby, J. (1954). Research strategy in the study of mother–child separation. *Courrier*, 4, 105–131.

Ainsworth, M. D. S., & Bowlby, J. (1991). An ethological approach to personality development. *American Psychologist*, 46(4), 333–341.

Ainsworth, M. D. S., & Eichberg, C. G. (1991). Effects on infant–mother attachment of mother's unresolved loss of an attachment figure, or other traumatic experience. In C. M. Parkes, J. Stevenson-Hinde & P. Marris (Eds), *Attachment across the life cycle* (pp. 160–183). New York: Tavistock/Routledge.

Ainsworth, M. D. S., & Marvin, R. S. (1995). On the shaping of attachment theory and research: An interview with Mary D. S. Ainsworth (Fall 1994). *Monographs of the Society for Research in Child Development*, 60(2–3), 3–21.

Akyalcin, E. (2003). Contextual modular therapy for unresolved grief: A case study. *Psychotherapy in Australia*, 10(1), 42–46.

Alexander, P. A. (2008). Charting the course for the teaching profession: The energizing and sustaining role of motivational forces. *Learning and Instruction*, 18(5), 483–491.

Allen, J. G., Stein, H., Fonagy, P., Fultz, J., & Target, M. (2005). Rethinking adult attachment: A study of expert consensus. *Bulletin of the Menninger Clinic*, 69(1), 59–80.

American Psychiatric Association (2000). *Diagnostic and statistical manual of mental disorders: Text revision IV* (4th ed.). Washington, DC: American Psychiatric Association.

Amini, F., Lewis, T., Lannon, R., & Louie, A. (1996). Affect, attachment, memory: Contributions toward psychobiologic integration. *Psychiatry: Interpersonal and Biological Processes*, 59(3), 213–239.

Andersen, S. M., & Berk, M. S. (1998). The social-cognitive model of transference: Experiencing past relationships in the present. *Current Directions in Psychological Science*, 7(4), 109–115.

Anderson, A., Hamilton, R. J., & Hattie, J. (2004). Classroom climate and motivated behavior in secondary schools. *Learning Environments Research*, 7(3), 211–225.

Antonio, D. M. S., & Salzfass, E. A. (2007). How we treat one another in school. *Educational Leadership*, 64(8), 32–38.

Appleyard, K., Egeland, B., van Dulmen, M. H., & Sroufe, L. A. (2005). When more is not better: The role of cumulative risk in child behavior outcomes. *Journal of Child Psychology and Psychiatry*, 46(3), 235–245.

Ashkanasy, N., & Daus, C. S. (2002). Emotion in the workplace: The new challenge for managers. *Academy of Management Executive*, 16(1), 76–86.

Aspelmeier, J. E., & Kerns, K. A. (2003). Love and school: Attachment/exploration dynamics in college. *Journal of Social and Personal Relationships*, 20(1), 5–30.

Atkinson, L., & Zucker, K. J. (1997). *Attachment and psychopathology*. New York: Guilford Press.

Aultman, L. P., Williams-Johnson, M. R., & Schutz, P. A. (2009). Boundary dilemmas in teacher–student relationships: Struggling with "the line". *Teaching and Teacher Education*, 25(5), 636–646.

Awaya, A., McEwan, H., Heyler, D., Linsky, S., Lum, D., & Wakukawa, P. (2003). Mentoring as a journey. *Teaching and Teacher Education*, 19(1), 45–56.

Baker, D. B., & Benjamin Jr, L. T. (2000). The affirmation of the scientist-practitioner: A look back at Boulder. *American Psychologist*, 55(2), 241–247.

Bakermans-Kranenburg, M. J. (2006). Script-like attachment representations: Steps towards a secure base for further research. *Attachment & Human Development*, 8(3), 275–281.

Bakermans-Kranenburg, M. J., & IJzendoorn, M. H. V. (1993). A psychometric study of the Adult Attachment Interview: Reliability and discriminant validity. *Developmental Psychology*, 29(5), 870–879.

Baldwin, M. W. (1995). Relational schemas and cognition in close relationships. *Journal of Social and Personal Relationships*, 12(4), 547–552.

Baldwin, M. W. (2007). On priming security and insecurity. [Comment/Reply]. *Psychological Inquiry*, 18(3), 157–162.

Baldwin, M. W., Fehr, B., Keedian, E., Seidel, M., & Thomson, D. W. (1993). An exploration of the relational schemata underlying attachment styles: Self-report and lexical decision approaches. *Personality and Social Psychology Bulletin*, 19(6), 746–754.

Baldwin, M. W., Keelan, J. P. R., Fehr, B., Enns, V., & Koh-Rangarajo, E. (1996). Social-cognitive conceptualization of attachment working models: Availability and accessibility effects. *Journal of Personality and Social Psychology*, 71(1), 94–109.

Balint, M. (1968). *The basic fault*. London: Tavistock.

Bandura, A. (1973). *Aggression: A social learning analysis*. Englewood Cliffs, NJ: Prentice Hall.

Bandura, A. (2006). Toward a psychology of human agency. *Perspectives on Psychological Science*, 1(2), 164–180.

Banfield, S. R., Richmond, V. P., & McCroskey, J. C. (2006). The effect of teacher misbehaviors on teacher credibility and affect for the teacher. *Communication education*, 55(1), 63–72.

Banse, R. (1999). Automatic evaluation of self and significant others: Affective priming in close relationships. *Journal of Social and Personal Relationships*, 16(6), 803–821.

Bargh, J. A. (Ed.). (2007). *Social psychology and the unconscious: The automaticity of higher mental processes*. New York: Psychology Press.

Barth, R. S. (2004). *Learning by heart*. San Francisco, CA: Jossey Bass.

Bartholomew, K. (1990). Avoidance of intimacy: An attachment perspective. *Journal of Social and Personal Relationships*, 7(2), 147–178.

Bartholomew, K. (1994). Assessment of individual differences in adult attachment. *Psychological Inquiry*, 5(1), 23–27.

Bartholomew, K., & Horowitz, L. M. (1991). Attachment styles among young adults: A test of a four-category model. *Journal of Personality & Social Psychology*, 61(2), 226–244.

Bartholomew, K., & Shaver, P. R. (1998). Methods of assessing adult attachment: Do they converge? In J. A. Simpson & W. S. Rholes (Eds), *Attachment Theory and Close Relationships* (pp. 46–76). New York: Guilford Press.

Bartholomew, R., Moorhead, G., Ference, R., Neck, C. P., Kelman, H. C., Paul, A. M., et al. (2000). Unit 9: Group processes. In M. H. Davis (Ed.), *Annual editions: Social psychology 2000/2001* (2004th ed.) (pp. 2192–2224). Guilford, CT: Dushkin/Mcgraw-Hill.

Bartz, J. A., & Lydon, J. E. (2004). Close relationships and the working self-concept: Implicit and explicit effects of priming attachment on agency and communion. *Personality and Social Psychology Bulletin*, 30(11), 1389–1401.

Bateson, P. (1991). *The development and integration of behaviour: Essays in honour of Robert Hinde*. New York: Cambridge University Press.

Batty, G., Shipley, M., Jarrett, R., Breeze, E., Marmot, M., & Smith, G. (2005). Obesity and overweight in relation to organ-specific cancer mortality in London (UK): Findings from the original Whitehall study. *International Journal of Obesity*, 29(10), 1267–1274.

Batty, G., Shipley, M. J., Marmot, M. G., & Smith, G. D. (2003). Leisure time physical activity and disease-specific mortality among men with chronic bronchitis: Evidence from the Whitehall Study. *American Journal of Public Health*, 93(5), 817–821.

Baumeister, R. F., & Leary, M. R. (1995). The need to belong: Desire for interpersonal attachments as a fundamental human motivation. *Psychological Bulletin*, 117(3), 497–529.

Beatty, B. R., & Riley, P. (Eds). (2008). *Willing to Lead – Human leadership: Developing people*. Melbourne: Department of Education and Early Childhood Development (DEECD).

Beauchamp, C., & Thomas, L. (2009). Understanding teacher identity: An overview of issues in the literature and implications for teacher education. *Cambridge Journal of Education*, 39(2), 175–189.

Bechara, A., Damasio, A. R., & Bar-On, R. (2007). The anatomy of emotional intelligence and implications for educating people to be emotionally intelligent. In R. Bar-On, J. G. Maree & M. J. Elias (Eds), *Educating people to be emotionally intelligent* (pp. 273–290). Westport, CT: Praeger Publishers/Greenwood Publishing Group.

Beck, A., Rush, A., Shaw, B., & Emery, G. (1979). *Cognitive therapy of depression*. New York: Guilford Press.

Beijaard, D., Verloop, N., & Vermunt, J. D. (2000). Teachers' perceptions of professional identity: An exploratory study from a personal knowledge perspective. *Teaching and Teacher Education*, 16, 749–764.

Beishuizen, J., Hof, E., van Putten, C., Bouwmeester, S., & Asscher, J. (2001). Students' and teachers' cognitions about good teachers. *British Journal of Educational Psychology*, 71(2), 185–201.

Bell, D. C., & Richard, A. J. (2000). The search for a caregiving motivation. *Psychological Inquiry*, 11(2), 124–128.

Bell, S. M., & Ainsworth, M. D. (1972). Infant crying and maternal responsiveness. *Child Development*, 43(4), 1171–1190.

Beltman, S., & Volet, S. (2007). Exploring the complex and dynamic nature of sustained motivation. *European Psychologist*, 12(4).

Benbenishty, R., Zeira, A., & Astor, Ron A. (2002). Children's reports of emotional, physical and sexual maltreatment by educational staff in Israel. *Child Abuse & Neglect*, 26(8), 763–782.

Benbenishty, R., Zeira, A., Astor, A. R., et al. (2002). Maltreatment of primary school students by educational staff in Israel. *Child Abuse & Neglect*, 26(12), 1291–1309.

Bengston, J. K., & Marshik, T. T. (2007). An ecological study of intersubjectivity and the opening of closed minds. *Journal of Educational Psychology*, 99(1), 1.

Benjamin, L. T. (2000). Boulder at 50: Introduction to the section. *American Psychologist*, 55(2), 233–236.

Ben-Peretz, M., & Bromme, R. (Eds). (1990). *The nature of time in schools: Theoretical concepts, practitioner perceptions*. New York: Teachers College Press.

Bergin, C., & Bergin, D. (2009). Attachment in the classroom. *Educational Psychology Review*, 21(2), 141–170.

Berry, D., & O'Connor, E. Behavioral risk, teacher–child relationships, and social skill development across middle childhood: A child-by-environment analysis of change. *Journal of Applied Developmental Psychology*. In Press, Corrected Proof.

Bibou-Nakou, I., Stogiannidou, A., & Kiosseoglou, G. (1999). The relation between teacher burnout and teachers' attributions and practices regarding school behaviour problems. *School Psychology International*, 20(2), 209–217.

Birns, B. (1999). Attachment theory revisited: Challenging conceptual and methodological sacred cows. *Feminism & Psychology*, 9(1), 10–21.

Bishop, B. J., & Browne, A. L. (2006). There is nothing so practical as … Building myths in community psychology. *The Australian Community Psychologist*, 18(3), 68–73.

Black, A. L. (2000). *Who am I as teacher? Promoting the active positioning of self within teaching realities*. Brisbane: Queensland University of Technology.

Blackmore, J. (1996). Doing emotional labour in the educational market place: Stories from the field of women in management. *Discourse*, 17(33), 337–350.

Blehar, M. C., Lieberman, A. F., & Ainsworth, M. D. (1977). Early face-to-face interaction and its relation to later infant–mother attachment. *Child Development*, 48(1), 182–194.

Block, A. A. (2008). Why should I be a teacher? *Journal of Teacher Education*, 59(5), 416–427.

Bolger, K. E., & Patterson, C. J. (2001). Developmental pathways from child maltreatment to peer rejection. *Child Development*, 72(2), 549–568.

Borman, G. D., & Dowling, N. M. (2008). Teacher attrition and retention: A meta-analytic and narrative review of the research. *Review of Educational Research*, 78(3), 367.

Bost, K. K., Shin, N., McBride, B. A., Brown, G. L., Vaughn, B. E., Coppola, G. et al. (2006). Maternal secure base scripts, children's attachment security, and mother–child narrative styles. *Attachment & Human Development*, 8(3), 241–260.

Bouchard, M.-A., Target, M., Lecours, S., Fonagy, P., Tremblay, L.-M., Schachter, A. et al. (2008). Mentalization in adult attachment narratives: Reflective functioning, mental states, and affect elaboration compared. *Psychoanalytic Psychology*, 25(1), 47–66.

Bouquillon, E. A., Sosik, J. J., & Lee, D. (2005). "It's only a phase": Examining trust, identification and mentoring functions received across the mentoring phases. *Mentoring & Tutoring: Partnership in Learning*, 13(2), 239–258.

Bowlby, J. (1944). Forty-four juvenile thieves: Their characters and home life. *International Journal of Psychoanalysis*, 25, 1–57.

Bowlby, J. (1951). Maternal care and mental health. *World Health Organization Monograph Series*, 179, 355–533.

Bowlby, J. (1957). An ethological approach to research in child development. *British Journal of Medical Psychology*, 30, 230–240.

Bowlby, J. (1958). The nature of the child's tie to his mother. *International Journal of Psycho-Analysis*, 39 (Sep–Oct), 350–373.

Bowlby, J. (1960a). Grief and Mourning in Infancy and Early Childhood. *Psychoanalytic Study of The Child*, 15, 9–52.

Bowlby, J. (1960b). Separation anxiety. *International Journal of Psycho-Analysis*, 41, 89–113.

Bowlby, J. (1961a). Processes of mourning. *International Journal of Psychoanalysis*, 42, 317–338.

Bowlby, J. (1961b). Separation anxiety: A critical review of the literature. *Journal of Child Psychology & Psychiatry*, 1, 251–269.

Bowlby, J. (1970). Disruption of affectional bonds and its effects on behavior. *Journal of Contemporary Psychotherapy*, 75–86.

Bowlby, J. (1975). *Separation: Anxiety and anger* (Vol. 2). Harmondsworth: Penguin.

Bowlby, J. (1976). Human personality development in an ethological light. In G. Serban & A. Kling (Eds), *Animal models in human psychobiology* (pp. 27–36). New York: Plenum Press.

Bowlby, J. (1977). The making and breaking of affectional bonds: I. Aetiology and psychopathology in the light of attachment theory. *British Journal of Psychiatry*, 130 (Mar), 201–210.

Bowlby, J. (1978). Attachment theory and its therapeutic implications. *Adolescent Psychiatry*, 5, 5–33.

Bowlby, J. (1979). Psychoanalysis as art and science. *International Review of Psycho-Analysis*, 6(1), 3–14.

Bowlby, J. (1980). *Loss, sadness and depression* (Vol. 3). New York: Basic Books.

Bowlby, J. (1982). *Attachment* (2nd ed. Vol. 1). London: Harper Collins.

Bowlby, J. (1983). Attachment and loss: Retrospect and prospect. *Annual Progress in Child Psychiatry & Child Development*, 29–47.

Bowlby, J. (1984). Psychoanalysis as a natural science. *Psychoanlaytic Psychology*, 1(1), 7–21.

Bowlby, J. (1988a). *A secure base: Clinical applications of attachment theory*. London: Routledge.

Bowlby, J. (1988b). Changing theories of childhood since Freud. In E. Timms & N. Segal (Eds), *Freud in exile: Psychoanalysis and its vicissitudes* (pp. 230–240). New Haven, CT: Yale University Press.

Bowlby, J. (1988c). Defensive processes in response to stressful separation in early life. In E. J. Anthony & C. Chiland (Eds), *The child in his family, Vol. 8: Perilous development: Child raising and identity formation under stress* (pp. 23–30). Oxford: John Wiley & Sons.

Bowlby, J. (1991). Ethological light on psychoanalytical problems. In P. Bateson (Ed.), *The development and integration of behaviour: Essays in honour of Robert Hinde* (pp. 301–313). New York: Cambridge University Press.

Bowlby, J. (1994). Pathological mourning and childhood mourning. In R. V. Frankiel (Ed.), *Essential papers on object loss* (pp. 185–221). New York: New York University Press.

Bowlby, J., Robertson, J., & Rosenbluth, D. (1952). A two-year-old goes to the hospital. *The Psychoanalytic Study of the Child*, 7, 82–94.

Bowlby, R. (2004). *Fifty years of attachment theory*. London: Karnac Books.

Bradshaw, C. P., & Hazan, C. (2006). Examining views of self in relation to views of others: Implications for research on aggression and self-esteem. *Journal of Research in Personality*, 40(6), 1209–1218.

Branigan, H. P., Pickering, M. J., & McLean, J. F. (2005). Priming prepositional-phrase attachment during comprehension. *Journal of Experimental Psychology: Learning, Memory, and Cognition*, 31(3), 468–481.

Brennan, K. A., Clark, C. L., & Shaver, P. R. (1998). Self-report measures of adult attachment: An integrative overview. In J. A. Simpson & W. S. Rholes (Eds), *Attachment theory and close relationships* (pp. 46–76). New York: Guilford Press.

Bresnahan, C. G., & Mitroff, I. I. (2007). Leadership and attachment theory. *American Psychologist*, 62(6), 607–608.

Bretherton, I. (1985). Attachment theory: Retrospect and prospect. *Monographs of the Society for Research in Child Development*, 50(1–2), 3–35.

Bretherton, I. (1987). New perspectives on attachment relations: Security, communication, and internal working models. In J. D. Osofsky (Ed.), *Handbook of infant development* (2nd ed., pp. 1061–1100). Oxford: John Wiley & Sons.

Bretherton, I. (1990). Communication patterns, internal working models, and the intergenerational transmission of attachment relationships. *Infant Mental Health Journal*, 11(3), 237–252.

Bretherton, I. (1991). Pouring new wine into old bottles: The social self as internal working model. In M. R. Gunnar & L. A. Sroufe (Eds), *Self processes and development* (pp. 1–41). Hillsdale, NJ: Lawrence Erlbaum Associates.

Bretherton, I. (1992). The origins of attachment theory: John Bowlby and Mary Ainsworth. *Developmental Psychology*, 28, 759–775.

Bretherton, I. (1997). Bowlby's legacy to developmental psychology. *Child Psychiatry & Human Development*, 28(1), 33–43.

Bretherton, I. (1998). Attachment and psychoanalysis: A reunion in progress: Commentary. *Social Development*, 7(1), 132–136.

Bretherton, I. (2003). Mary Ainsworth: Insightful observer and courageous theoretician. In G. A. Kimble & M. Wertheimer (Eds), *Portraits of pioneers in psychology* (Vol. V, pp. 317–331). Washington, DC: American Psychological Association.

Bretherton, I. (2005). In pursuit of the internal working model construct and its relevance to attachment relationships. In K. E. Grossmann, K. Grossmann & E. Waters (Eds), *Attachment from infancy to adulthood: The major longitudinal studies* (pp. 13–47). New York: Guilford Press.

Bretherton, I., & Munholland, K. A. (1999). Internal working models in attachment relationships: A construct revisited. In J. Cassidy & P. R. Shaver (Eds), *Handbook of attachment: Theory, research, and clinical applications* (pp. 89–111). New York: Guilford Press.

Briesch, A. M., & Chafouleas, S. M. (2009). Review and analysis of literature on self-management interventions to promote appropriate classroom behaviors (1988–2008). *School Psychology Quarterly*, 24(2), 106–118.

Brocato, K. (2009). Studio based learning: Proposing, critiquing, iterating our way to person–centeredness for better classroom management. *Theory Into Practice*, 48(2), 138–146.

Brookfield, S. (1983). *Adult learners, adult education and the community*. Milton Keynes: Open University Press.

Brookfield, S. (1991). *The skillful teacher: On technique, trust, and responsiveness in the classroom*. San Francisco, CA: Jossey-Bass.

Brookfield, S. (1995). *Becoming a critically reflective teacher*. San Francisco, CA: Jossey-Bass.

Brookfield, S., & Preskill, S. (1999). *Discussion as a way of teaching: Tools and techniques for democratic classrooms* (1st ed.). San Francisco, CA: Jossey-Bass.

Brophy, J. E., & Good, T. L. (1974). *Teacher–student relationships: Causes and consequences*. Oxford: Holt, Rinehart & Winston.

Brotheridge, C. M., & Lee, R. T. (2003). Development and validation of the Emotional Labour Scale. *Journal of Occupational and Organizational Psychology*, 76(3), 365–379.

Brown, C. (2002). *The role of attachment in a time-limited marital therapy: Implications for practice and treatment*. Melbourne: Australian Catholic University.

Brown, C. M., Young, S. G., & McConnell, A. R. Seeing close others as we see ourselves: One's own self-complexity is reflected in perceptions of meaningful others. *Journal of Experimental Social Psychology*. In Press, Accepted Manuscript.

Brown, K. M., & Schainker, S. A. (2008). Doing all the right things: Teacher retention issues. *Journal of Cases in Educational Leadership*, 11(1), 10–17.

Brown, O., Fuller, F., & Richek, H. (1966). Differentiating prospective elementary and secondary school teachers. *Alberta Journal of Educational Research*, 12(2), 127–130.

Budd, M., & Rowe (2000). Teachers who care. *The Science Teacher*, 67(1), 30.

Burger, J. M. (2009). Replicating Milgram: Would people still obey today? *American Psychologist*, 64(1), 1–11.

Burton, N. (1998). Calculating the cost of an undergraduate Initial Teacher Education (ITE) course. *International Journal of Educational Management*, 12(6), 260–269.

Busher, H. (2002). Ethics of research in education. In M. Coleman & A. J. R. Briggs (Eds), *Research methods in educational leadership and management* (pp. 73–89). London: Paul Chapman.

Buxton, C. E. (1985). *Points of view in the modern history of psychology*. San Diego, CA: Academic Press.

Byrne, J. J. (1998). Teacher as hunger artist: Burnout: Its causes, effects, and remedies. *Contemporary Education*, 69(2), 86–92.

Cameron, M., & Rupp, A. A. (2005). A meta-analysis for exploring the diverse causes and effects of stress in teachers. *Canadian Journal of Education*, 28(3), 458–486.

Cano-Garcia, F. J., Padilla-Munoz, E. M., & Carrasco-Ortiz, M. A. (2005). Personality and contextual variables in teacher burnout. *Personality and Individual Differences*, 38(4), 929–940.

Carnelley, K. B., & Rowe, A. C. (2007). Repeated priming of attachment security influences later views of self and relationships. *Personal relationships*, 14(2), 307–320.

Carroll, D., Smith, G. D., Sheffield, D., Shipley, M. J., & Marmot, M. G. (1997). The relationship between socioeconomic status, hostility, and blood pressure reactions to mental stress in men: Data from the Whitehall II study. *Health Psychology*, 16(2), 131–136.

Carroll, D., Smith, G. D., Shipley, M. J., Steptoe, A., Brunner, E. J., Marmot, M. G. et al. (2001). Blood pressure reactions to acute psychological stress and future blood pressure status: A 10-year follow-up of men in the Whitehall II study. *Psychosomatic Medicine*, 63(5), 737–743.

Carson, R. L. (2007). *Exploring the episodic nature of teachers' emotions as it relates to teacher burnout*. West Lafayette, IN: Purdue University.

Carter, K. (1999). What is a case? What is not a case? In M. A. Lundberg, B. B. Levin & H. L. Harrington (Eds), *Who learns what from cases and how?: The research base for teaching and learning with cases*. Mahwah, NJ: Laurence Erlbaum Associates.

Cassidy, J., & Shaver, P. (1999). *Handbook of attachment: Theory, research, and clinical applications*. New York: Guilford Press.

Center for Innovative Thought (2006). *Teachers and the uncertain American future*. New York: The College Board.

Chan, D. W. (2003). Perceived emotional intelligence and self-efficacy among Chinese secondary school teachers in Hong Kong. *Personality and Individual Differences*, 36(2004), 1781–1795.

Chaplain, R. P. (2008). Stress and psychological distress among trainee secondary teachers in England. *Educational Psychology*, 28(2), 195–209.

Cheng, M. M. H., Chan, K.-W., Tang, S. Y. F., & Cheng, A. Y. N. (2009). Pre-service teacher education students' epistemological beliefs and their conceptions of teaching. *Teaching and Teacher Education*, 25(2), 319–327.

Cicchetti, D., & Sroufe, L. A. (2000). The past as prologue to the future: The times, they've been a-changin. *Development and Psychopathology*, 12(3), 255–264.

Clandinin, D. J. (2006). *Composing diverse identities: Narrative inquiries into the interwoven lives of children and teachers*. London: Routledge.

Clandinin, D. J. (2007) (Ed.). *Handbook of narrative inquiry: Mapping a methodology*. Thousand Oaks, CA: Sage Publications.

Cochran-Smith, M. (2005). The New Teacher Education: For better or for worse? *Educational Researcher*, 34(7), 3–17.

Coleman, J. (2009). Well-being in schools: Empirical measure, or politician's dream? *Oxford Review of Education*, 35(3), 281–292.

Coleman, L. J. (1994). "Being a teacher": Emotions and optimal experience while teaching gifted children. *Gifted Child Quarterly*, 38(3), 146–152.

Collins, N. L. (1996). Working models of attachment: Implications for explanation, emotion, and behavior. *Journal of Personality and Social Psychology*, 71(4), 810–832.

Collins, N. L., & Feeney, B. C. (2000). A safe heaven: An attachment theory perspective on support-seeking and caregiving in adult romantic relationships. *Journal of Personality & Social Psychology*, 78, 1053–1073.

Connelly, F. M., & Clandinin, D. J. (1999). *Shaping a professional identity: Stories of educational practice*. New York: Teachers College Press.

Contratto, S. (2002). A feminist critique of attachment theory and evolutionary psychology. In M. Ballou & L. S. Brown (Eds), *Rethinking mental health and disorder: Feminist perspectives* (pp. 29–47). New York: Guilford Press.

Corey, G. (2005). *Theory and practice of counselling and psychotherapy* (7th ed.). Florence, KY: Wadsworth/Brooks-Cole.

Cornelius-White, J. (2007). Learner-centered teacher–student relationships are effective: A meta-analysis. *Review of Educational Research*, 77(1), 113–143.

Cornille, T. A., Pestle, R. E., & Vanwy, R. W. (1999). Teachers' conflict management styles with peers and students' parents. *International Journal of Conflict Management*, 10(1), 69–79.

Craig, C. J. (2009). Flights from the field and the plight of teacher education: A personal perspective. *Journal of Curriculum Studies*, 41(5), 605–624.

Craik, K. (1943). *The nature of explanation*. Cambridge: Cambridge University Press.

Creasey, G. (2002). Associations between working models of attachment and conflict management behavior in romantic couples. *Journal of Counseling Psychology*, 49(3), 365–375.

Cristobal, R. (2003). The psychoanalytic process in the light of attachment theory. In M. Cortina & M. Marrone (Eds), *Attachment theory and the psychoanalytic process* (pp. 335–355). Philadelphia, PA: Whurr Publishers.

Crittenden, P. M., & Ainsworth, M. D. S. (1989). Child maltreatment and attachment theory. In D. Cicchetti & V. Carlson (Eds), *Child maltreatment: Theory and research on the causes and consequences of child abuse and neglect*. New York: Cambridge University Press.

Crowell, J. A., & Treboux, D. (1995). A review of adult attachment measures: Implications for theory and research. *Social Development*, 4, 294–327.

Crowell, J. A., Treboux, D., Gao, Y., Fyffe, C., Pan, H., & Waters, E. (2002). Assessing secure base behavior in adulthood: Development of a measure, links to adult attachment representations and relations to couples' communication and reports of relationships. *Developmental Psychology*, 38(5), 679–693.

Cukier, J. (1990). Patologia de la didactogenia [Pathology of diactogeny]. *Revista de Psicoanalisis*, 47(1), 140–152.

Cummings, E. M. (2003). Toward assessing attachment on an emotional security continuum: Comment on Fraley and Spieker. *Developmental Psychology*, 39(3), 405–408.

Czander, W., & Eisold, K. (2003). Psychoanalytic perspectives on organizational consulting: Transference and counter-transference. *Human relations*, 56(4), 475–490.

Dale, M., & Frye, E. M. (2009). Vulnerability and love of learning as necessities for wise teacher education. *Journal of Teacher Education*, 60(2), 123–130.

Damasio, A. R. (2004). Emotions and feelings: A neurobiological perspective. In A. S. R. Manstead, N. Frijda & A Fischer (Eds), *Feelings and emotions: The Amsterdam symposium* (pp. 49–57). New York: Cambridge University Press.

Damasio, A. R. (2007). How the brain creates the mind. In F. E. Bloom (Ed.), *Best of the brain from Scientific American* (pp. 58–67). Washington, DC: Dana Press.

Damasio, H., Tranel, D., Grabowskia, T., Adolphs, R., & Damasio, A. (2004). Neural systems behind word and concept retrieval. *Cognition*, 92(1–2), 179–229.

Darby, A. (2008). Teachers' emotions in the reconstruction of professional self-understanding. *Teaching and Teacher Education*, 24(5), 1160–1172.

Darling-Hammond, L. (2010). Teacher education and the American future. *Journal of Teacher Education*, 61(1–2), 35–47.

Davidovitz, R., Mikulincer, M., Shaver, P. R., Izsak, R., & Popper, M. (2007). Leaders as attachment figures: Leaders' attachment orientations predict leadership-related mental representations and followers' performance and mental health. *Journal of Personality and Social Psychology*, 93(4), 632–650.

Davis, H. A. (2003). Conceptualizing the role and influence of student–teacher relationships on children's social and cognitive development. *Educational Psychologist*, 38(4), 207–234.

Day, C., & Kington, A. (2008). Identity, well-being and effectiveness: The emotional contexts of teaching. *Pedagogy, Culture & Society*, 16(1), 7–23.

Day, C., & Leitch, R. (2001). Teachers' and teacher educators' lives: The role of emotion. *Teaching and Teacher Education*, 17(4), 403.

DEEWR (Department of Education, Employment and Workplace Relations). (2007). *Publications – Higher Education Statistics Collections.* Available at: www.dest.gov.au/sectors/higher_education/publications_resources/statistics/publications_higher_education_statistics_collections.htm#studpubs.

Demetriou, H., Wilson, E., & Winterbottom, M. (2009). The role of emotion in teaching: Are there differences between male and female newly qualified teachers' approaches to teaching? *Educational Studies*, 35(4), 449–473.

Dennett, D. (1995). *Darwin's dangerous idea: Evolution and the meanings of life.* London: Allen Lane/The Penguin Press.

Denzin, N. K., & Lincoln, Y. S. (2005). *The Sage Handbook of Qualitative Research* (3rd ed.). Thousand Oaks, CA: Sage Publications.

Derks, B., Inzlicht, M., & Kang, S. (2008). The neuroscience of stigma and stereotype threat. *Group Processes Intergroup Relations*, 11(2), 163–181.

Desmet, T., & Declercq, M. (2006). Cross-linguistic priming of syntactic hierarchical configuration information. *Journal of Memory and Language*, 54(4), 610–632.

Dewitte, M., DeHouwer, J., Koster, E. H. W., & Buysse, A. (2007). What's in a name? Attachment-related attentional bias. *Emotion*, 7(3), 535–545.

Diamond, M. A. (1986). Resistance to change: A psychoanalytic critique of Argyris and Schon's contributions to organization theory and intervention. *Journal of Management Studies*, 23(5), 543–562.

Diaz, E. J. (2003). *Adult attachment style and burnout in elementary school teachers.* Albuquerque, NM: University of New Mexico.

Diefendorff, J. M., Croyle, M. H., & Gosserand, R. H. (2005). The dimensionality and antecedents of emotional labor strategies. *Journal of Vocational Behavior, 66*(2), 339–359.

Diefendorff, J. M., & Gosserand, R. H. (2003). Understanding the emotional labor process: A control theory perspective. *Journal of Organizational Behavior, 24*(8), 945–959.

Dixon, N., & Henley, S. (1991). Unconscious perception: Possible implications of data from academic research for clinical practice. *Journal of nervous and mental disease, 79,* 243–251.

Docan-Morgan, T., & Manusov, V. (2009). Relational turning point events and their outcomes in college teacher–student relationships from students' perspectives. *Communication education, 58*(2), 155–188.

Dolan, A., & McCaslin, M. (2008). Student perceptions of teacher support. *Teachers College Record, 110*(11), 2423.

Donohue, K. M., Perry, K. E., & Weinstein, R. S. (2003). Teachers' classroom practices and children's rejection by their peers. *Journal of Applied Developmental Psychology, 24*(1), 91–118.

Doyle, W. (2006). Ecological approaches to classroom management. In C. M. Evertson & C. S. Weinstein (Eds), *Handbook of classroom management: Research, practice, and contemporary issues* (pp. 97–125). Mahwah, NJ: Lawrence Erlbaum Associates.

Doyle, W. (2009). Situated practice: A reflection on person-centered classroom management. *Theory Into Practice, 48*(2), 156–159.

Dunkel, C., & Kerpelman, J. (2006). *Possible selves: Theory, research, and applications.* Hauppauge, NY: Nova Science Publishers.

Edelstein, R. S. (2006). Attachment and emotional memory: Investigating the source and extent of avoidant memory impairments. *Emotion, 6*(2), 340–345.

Edelstein, R. S., & Shaver, P. R. (2004). Avoidant attachment: Exploration of an oxymoron. In D. J. Mashek & A. P. Aron (Eds), *Handbook of closeness and intimacy* (pp. 397–412). Mahwah, NJ: Lawrence Erlbaum Associates.

Education Commission of the United States (2000). *The progress of education reform 1999–2001: Teacher recruitment.* Denver, CO: Education Commission of the United States.

Egan, G. (2002). *The skilled helper: A problem-management and opportunity-development approach to helping.* Pacific Grove, CA: Brooks-Cole.

Egeland, B. R., Carlson, E., & Sroufe, L. A. (1993). Resilience as process. *Development and Psychopathology, 5*(4), 517–528.

Ehrich, L. C., Hansford, B., & Tennet, L. (2004). Formal mentoring programs in education and other professions: A review of the literature. *Educational Administration Quarterly, 40*(4), 518–540.

Eisold, K. (2000). The rediscovery of the unknown: An inquiry into psychoanalytic praxis. *Contemporary Psychoanalysis, 36*(1), 57–75.

Eisold, K. (2003a). The profession of psychoanalysis: Past failures and future possibilities. *Contemporary Psychoanalysis, 39*(4), 557–582.

Eisold, K. (2003b). "The profession of psychoanalysis: Past failures and future possibilities": Reply to discussants. *Contemporary Psychoanalysis, 39*(4), 629–636.

Ekstein, R., & Motto, R. L. (Eds). (1969). *From learning for love to love of learning: Essays on psychoanalysis and education.* New York: Brunner/Mazel.

Elbedour, S., Assor, A., Center, B. A., & Maruyama, G. M. (1997). Physical and psychological maltreatment in schools: The abusive behaviors of teachers in bedouin schools in Israel. *School Psychology International, 18*(3), 201–215.

Elliott-Kemp, J., & Rogers, C. R. (1982). *The effective teacher: A person-centred development guide*. Sheffield: PAVIC Publications.

Ellis, A. (1980). Rational-emotive therapy and cognitive behavior therapy: Similarities and differences. *Cognitive Therapy and Research*, 4(4), 325–340.

Ellis, A. (2000). *How to control your anxiety before it controls you*. New York: Citadel Press.

Etkin, A., Pittenger, C., Polan, H., & Kandel, E. R. (2005). Toward a neurobiology of psychotherapy: Basic science and clinical applications. *Journal of Neuropsychiatry & Clinical Neurosciences*, 17(2), 145–158.

Evans, R. I. (1975). *Carl Rogers: The man and his ideas* (1st ed.). New York: Dutton.

Evertson, C. M., & Weinstein, C. S. (Eds). (2006). *Handbook of classroom management: Research, practice, and contemporary issues*. Mahwah, NJ: Lawrence Erlbaum Associates.

Ewing, R. A., & Smith, D. L. (2003). Retaining quality beginning teachers in the profession. *English Teaching: Practice and Critique*, 2(1), 15–32.

Fairbairn, R. (1952). *Psychoanalytic studies of the personality*. London: Tavistock.

Fallu, J.-S., & Janosz, M. (2003). The quality of student–teacher relationships at adolescence: A protective factor against school failure. *Revue de Psychoeducation*, 32(1), 7–29.

Fearon, R., Ijzendoorn, M. H. V., Fonagy, P., Bakermans-Kranenburg, M. J., Schuengel, C., & Bokhorst, C. L. (2006). In search of shared and nonshared environmental factors in security of attachment: A behavior-genetic study of the association between sensitivity and attachment security. *Developmental Psychology*, 42(6), 1026–1040.

Feiman-Nemser, S. (2003). What new teachers need to learn. *Educational Leadership*, 60(8), 25.

Ferris, G. R., Liden, R. C., Munyon, T., Summers, J. K., Basik, K. J., & Buckley, M. R. (2009). Relationships at work: Toward a multidimensional conceptualization of dyadic work relationships. *Journal of Management*, 35(6), 1379–1403.

Filak, V. F., & Sheldon, K. M. (2008). Teacher support, student motivation, student need satisfaction, and college teacher course evaluations: Testing a sequential path model. *Educational Psychology*, 28(6), 711–724.

Fineman, S. (Ed.). (2008). *The emotional organization: Passions and power*. Malden, MA: Blackwell.

Finn, A. N., Schrodt, P., Witt, P. L., Elledge, N., Jernberg, K. A., & Larson, L. M. (2009). A meta-analytical review of teacher credibility and its associations with teacher behaviors and student outcomes. *Communication Education*, 58(4), 516–537.

Fisher, D. L., & Fraser, B. J. (1983). A comparison of actual and preferred classroom environments as perceived by science teachers and students. *Journal of Research in Science Teaching*, 20(1), 55–61.

Fisher, D., Fraser, B., & Wubbels, T. (1993). Interpersonal teacher behavior and school environment. In T. Wubbels & J. Levy (Eds), *Do you know what you look like? Interpersonal relationships in education* (pp. 103–112). Oxford: Falmer Press/Taylor & Francis.

Fisher, D. L., & Kent, H. B. (1998). Associations between teacher personality and classroom environment. *Journal of Classroom Interaction*, 33(1), 5–13.

Fisher, D., Kent, H., & Fraser, B. (1998). Relationships between teacher–student interpersonal behaviour and teacher personality. *School psychology international*, 19(2), 99–119.

Fivush, R. (2006). Scripting attachment: Generalized event representations and internal working models. *Attachment & Human Development*, 8(3), 283–289.

Fonagy, P. (1994). Mental representations from an intergenerational cognitive science perspective. *Infant Mental Health Journal*, 15(1), 57–68.

Fonagy, P. (1997). Multiple voices vs. meta-cognition: An attachment theory perspective. *Journal of Psychotherapy Integration*, 7(3), 181–194.

Fonagy, P. (1998a). An attachment theory approach to treatment of the difficult patient. *Bulletin of the Menninger Clinic*, 62(2), 147–169.

Fonagy, P. (1998b). Moments of change in psychoanalytic theory: Discussion of a new theory of psychic change. *Infant Mental Health Journal*, 19(3), 346–353.

Fonagy, P. (1999a). Male perpetrators of violence against women: An attachment theory perspective. *Journal of Applied Psychoanalytic Studies*, 1(1), 7–27.

Fonagy, P. (1999b). Points of contact and divergence between psychoanalytic and attachment theories: Is psychoanalytic theory truly different? *Psychoanalytic Inquiry*, 19(4), 448–480.

Fonagy, P. (1999c). Psychoanalytic theory from the viewpoint of attachment theory and research. In J. Cassidy & P. R. Shaver (Eds), *Handbook of attachment: Theory, research, and clinical applications* (pp. 595–624). New York: Guilford.

Fonagy, P. (2001). *Attachment theory and psychoanalysis*. New York: Other Press.

Fonagy, P. (2003a). Attachment theory and psychoanalysis. *Journal of Child Psychotherapy*, 29(1), 109–120.

Fonagy, P. (2003b). Freudian psychanalysis and the natural sciences. In J. Knox (Ed.), *Archetype, attachment analysis: Jungian psychology and the emergent mind* (pp. viii–xviii). Hove: Brunner-Routledge.

Fonagy, P., Gergely, G., Jurist, E. L., & Target, M. (2002). *Affect regulation, mentalization, and the development of the self*. New York: Other Press.

Fonagy, P., Leigh, T., Steele, M., Steele, H., Kennedy, R., Mattoon, G., et al. (1996). The relation of attachment status, psychiatric classification, and response to psychotherapy. *Journal of Consulting and Clinical Psychology*, 64(1), 22–31.

Fonagy, P., Roth, A., & Higgitt, A. (2005). Psychodynamic psychotherapies: Evidence-based practice and clinical wisdom. *Bulletin of the Menninger Clinic*, 69(1), 1–58.

Fonagy, P., Steele, M., & Steele, H. (1991). Maternal representations of attachment during pregnancy predict the organisation of infant–mother attachment at one year of age. *Child Development*, 62(5), 891–905.

Fonagy, P., Steele, M., Steele, H., Higgitt, A., & Target, M. (1994). The Emanuel Miller memorial lecture 1992: The theory and practice of resilience. *Journal of Child Psychology and Psychiatry*, 35(2), 231–257.

Fonagy, P., & Target, M. (1997). Attachment and reflective function: Their role in self-organization. *Development and Psychopathology*, 9(4), 679–700.

Fonagy, P., & Target, M. (2003). *Psychoanalytic theories: Perspectives from developmental psychopathology*. Philadelphia, PA: Whurr Publishers.

Fonagy, P., & Target, M. (2005). Commentary: Bridging the transmission gap: An end to an important mystery of attachment research? *Attachment & Human Development*, 7(3), 333–343.

Fox, S., & Spector, P. E. (2002). Emotions in the workplace: The neglected side of organizational life introduction. *Human Resource Management Review*, 12, 1–5.

Fraley, R. C., & Shaver, P. R. (1997). Adult attachment and the suppression of unwanted thoughts. *Journal of Personality and Social Psychology*, 73(5), 1080–1091.

Fraley, R. C., & Shaver, P. R. (2000). Adult romantic attachment: Theoretical developments, emerging controversies, and unanswered questions. *Review of General Psychology*, 4(2), 132–154.

Fraley, R. C., & Spieker, S. J. (2003). What are the differences between dimensional and categorical models of individual differences in attachment? Reply to Cassidy (2003),

Cummings (2003), Sroufe (2003), and Waters and Beauchaine (2003). *Developmental Psychology*, 39(3), 423–429.

Fraley, R. C., Waller, N. G., & Brennan, K. A. (2000). An item response theory analysis of self-report measures of adult attachment. *Journal of Personality and Social Psychology*, 78(2), 350–365.

Franzblau, S. H. (1999). Historicizing attachment theory: Binding the ties that bind. *Feminism & Psychology*, 9(1), 22–31.

Franzini, L. R. (2001). Humor in therapy: The case for training therapists in its uses and risks. *Journal of General Psychology*, 128(2), 170–193.

Fraser, B. J., & Fisher, D. L. (1982). Predicting students' outcomes from their perceptions of classroom psychosocial environment. *American Educational Research Journal*, 19(4), 498–518.

Fraser, B. J., & Fisher, D. L. (1983). Effects of classroom openness on science students' achievement and attitudes. *Research in Science & Technological Education*, 1(1), 41–51.

Fraser, B. J., & Fisher, D. L. (1986). Using short forms of classroom climate instruments to assess and improve classroom psychosocial environment. *Journal of Research in Science Teaching*, 23(5), 387–413.

Fraser, B. J., Nash, R., & Fisher, D. L. (1983). Anxiety in science classrooms: Its measurement and relationship to classroom environment. *Research in Science & Technological Education*, 1(2), 201–208.

Freiberg, H. J., & Lamb, S. M. (2009). Dimensions of person-centered classroom management. *Theory Into Practice*, 48(2), 99–105.

Frenzel, A. C., Goetz, T. A., Ludtke, O., Pekrun, R., & Sutton, R. E. (2009). Emotional transmission in the classroom: Exploring the relationship between teacher and student enjoyment. *Journal of Educational Psychology*, 101(3),705–716.

Freud, A. (1966). *The ego and the mechanisms of defense*. New York: International Universities Press.

Freud, S. (1928). Humour. *International Journal of Psycho-Analysis*, 9, 1–6.

Freund, L. D. (2004). A psychoanalytic reading of the reader. *Psychoanalytic Psychology*, 21(4), 601–608.

Friedel, J., Marachi, R., & Midgley, C. (2002). *"Stop embarrassing me!" Relations among student perceptions of teachers, classroom goals, and maladaptive behaviors*. Paper presented at the annual meeting of the American Educational Research Association, New Orleans, LA.

Friedman, I. A. (1994). Burnout in teachers: The concept and its unique core meaning. *Educational & Psychological Measurement*, 53(4), 1035–1044.

Friedman, I. A. (2006). Classroom management and teacher stress and burnout. In C. M. Evertson & C. S. Weinstein (Eds), *Handbook of classroom management: Research, practice, and contemporary issues* (pp. 925–944). Mahwah, NJ: Laurence Erlbaum Associates.

Fromm, E. (1978). *The crisis of psychoanalysis: Essays on Freud, Marx and social psychology*. Harmondsworth: Penguin.

Frost, D. (2008). "Teacher leadership": Values and voice. *School Leadership & Management*, 28(4), 337–352.

Fuhrman, N. L. (2000). *Correlates of student attachment and identification with school*. University Park, PA: Pennsylvania State University Press.

Fuller, F. F. (1969). Concerns of teachers: A developmental conceptualization. *American Educational Research Journal*, 6(2), 207–226.

Fuller, F., Veldman, D., & Richek, H. (1966). Tape recordings, feedback and prospective teachers' self evaluation. *Alberta Journal of Educational Research*, 12(4), 301–307.

Galand, B., & Dupont, E. (2002). Relations between perceived discrimination, school bonding, and beliefs supporting aggression. *Cahiers Internationaux de Psychologie Sociale*, 55, 64–72.

Gallant, A., & Riley, P. (2008). Consciousness structures and attachment responses to strange situations. *Asia Journal of Global Studies*, 2(1), 16–25.

Galman, S. (2009). Doth the lady protest too much? Pre-service teachers and the experience of dissonance as a catalyst for development. *Teaching and Teacher Education*, 25(3), 468–481.

Garbarino, J. J. (1998). Comparisons of the constructs and psychometric properties of selected measures of adult attachment. *Measurement and Evaluation in Counseling and Development*, 31, 28–45.

Gardner, H. (2006a). *Changing minds: The art and science of changing our own and other people's minds*. Boston, MA: Harvard Business School Press.

Gardner, H. (2006b). *The development and education of the mind: The selected works of Howard Gardner*. London: Routledge.

Gardner, H. (2009). *Five minds for the future*. Boston, MA: Harvard Business School Press.

Garet, M. S., Porter, A. C., Desimone, L., Birman, B. F., & Yoon, K. S. (2001). What makes professional development effective? Results from a national sample of teachers. *American Educational Research Journal*, 38(4), 915–945.

Gatz (2001). The reliability and validity of the "Parent Attachment Scale": A measure of adolescent perceptions of parental attachment behaviors. *Dissertation Abstracts International Section A: Humanities and Social Sciences*, 61(7–A), 2936.

Gauthier, Y. (2003). Infant mental health as we enter the third millennium: Can we prevent aggression? *Infant Mental Health Journal*, 24(3), 296–308.

Geake, J. (2008). Neuromythologies in education. *Educational Research*, 50(2), 123–133.

Geldard, D., & Geldard, K. (2005). *Basic personal counselling: A training manual for counsellors*. Frenchs Forest: Pearson

Geoffrey, D. B., & Dowling, N. M. (2008). Teacher attrition and retention: A meta-analytic and narrative review of the research. *Review of Educational Research*, 78(3), 367.

George, C., Kaplan, N., & Main, N. (1984). *Adult Attachment Interview*. Berkeley, CA: University of California.

Georgiou, S. N. (2008). Beliefs of experienced and novice teachers about achievement. *Educational Psychology*, 28(2), 119–131.

Georgiou, S. N., Demetriou, A. P., & Stavrinides, P. (2008). Attachment style and mentoring relationships in adolescence. *Educational Psychology*, 28(6), 603–614.

Gergen, K. J. (2001). Psychological science in a postmodern context. *American Psychologist*, 56(10), 803–813.

Geving, A. M. (2007). Identifying the types of student and teacher behaviours associated with teacher stress. *Teaching and Teacher Education*, 23(5), 624–640.

Gibney, P. (2003). *The pragmatics of therapeutic practice*. Melbourne: Psychoz Publications.

Gillath, O., Giesbrecht, B., & Shaver, P. R. Attachment, attention, and cognitive control: Attachment style and performance on general attention tasks. *Journal of Experimental Social Psychology*. In Press, Accepted Manuscript.

Gillath, O., Hart, J., Noftle, E. E., & Stockdale, G. D. Development and validation of a state adult attachment measure (SAAM). *Journal of Research in Personality*. In Press, Corrected Proof.

Gilligan, R. (2000). Adversity, resilience and young people: The protective value of positive school and spare time experiences. *Children & Society*, 14, 37–47.

Giluk, T. L. (2009). Mindfulness, Big Five personality, and affect: A meta-analysis. *Personality and Individual Differences*, 47(8), 805–811.

Ginott, H. G. (1972). *Teacher and child*. New York: Macmillan.

Gitlin, A., & Margonis, F. (1995). The political aspect of reform: Teacher resistance as good sense. *American Journal of Education*, 103(4), 377–405.

Glaser, B. G., & Strauss, A. L. (1967). *The discovery of grounded theory: Strategies for qualitative research*. New York: Aldine.

Globerson, S., & Malki, N. (1980). Estimating the expenses resulting from labor turnover: An Israelian study. *Management International Review (MIR)*, 20(3), 111–117.

Goddard, M. J. (2009). The impact of human intuition in psychology. *Review of General Psychology*, 13(2), 167–174.

Goetz, T., Frenzel, A. C., Pekrun, R., & Hall, N. C. (2006). The domain specificity of academic emotional experiences. *Journal of Experimental Education*, 75(1), 5–29.

Goetz, T., Frenzel, A. C., Pekrun, R., & Hall, N. C. (2007). "The domain specificity of academic emotional experiences": Erratam. *Journal of Experimental Education*, 75(2), 125.

Golby, M. (1996). Teachers' emotions: An illustrated discussion. *Cambridge Journal of Education*, 26(3), 423–434.

Goldberg, S., Muir, R., & Kerr, J. (Eds). (1995). *Attachment theory: Social, developmental, and clinical perspectives*. Hillsdale, NJ: Analytic Press.

Goleman, D. (1995). *Emotional intelligence*. New York: Bantam Books.

Goleman, D. (2006). *Social intelligence: The new science of human relationships*. New York: Bantam Books.

Goleman, D., Wilber, K., Tart, C., & Walsh, R. (1993). The riddle of consciousness. In R. Walsh & F. Vaughan (Eds), *Paths beyond ego: The transpersonal vision* (pp. 18–46). New York: Perigee Books.

Gonzales, L. (2008). *Everyday survival: Why smart people do stupid things* (1st ed.). New York: WW Norton & Co.

Gonzalez, R., & Griffin, D. (1997). On the statistics of interdependence: Treating dyadic data with respect. In S. Duck (Ed.), *Handbook of personal relationships: Theory, research and interventions* (2nd ed., pp. 271–302). Hoboken, NJ: John Wiley & Sons.

Goodman, J. F. (2009). Respect-due and respect-earned: Negotiating student–teacher relationships. *Ethics and Education*, 4(1), 3–17.

Goodnough, K., Osmond, P., Dibbon, D., Glassman, M., & Stevens, K. (2009). Exploring a triad model of student teaching: Pre-service teacher and cooperating teacher perceptions. *Teaching and Teacher Education*, 25(2), 285–296.

Gorham, J., & Chrisophel, D. M. (1992). Students' perceptions of teacher behaviours as motivating and demotivating factors in college classes. *Communication Quarterly*, 40(3), 239–252.

Gormley, B. (2008). An application of attachment theory: Mentoring relationship dynamics and ethical concerns. *Mentoring & Tutoring: Partnership in Learning*, 16(1), 45–62.

Gosserand, R. H., & Diefendorff, J. M. (2005). Emotional display rules and emotional labor: The moderating role of commitment. *Journal of Applied Psychology*, 90(6), 1256–1264.

Graham, S., & Weiner, B. (1996). Theories and principles of motivation. In D. C. Berliner & R. C. Calfee (Eds), *Handbook of educational psychology* (pp. 63–84). New York: Macmillan.

Granot, D., & Mayseless, O. (2001). Attachment security and adjustment to school in middle childhood. *International Journal of Behavioral Development*, 25(6), 530–541.

Gray, B. (2002). Emotional labour and befriending in family support and child protection in Tower Hamlets. *Child & Family Social Work*, 7(1), 13–22.

Gray, J. (2009). Staying at school: Reflective narratives of resistance and transition. *Reflective Practice: International and Multidisciplinary Perspectives*, 10(5), 645–656.

Grayson, J. L., & Alvarez, H. K. (2008). School climate factors relating to teacher burnout: A mediator model. *Teaching and Teacher Education*, 24(5), 1349–1363.

Green, J. D., & Campbell, W. (2000). Attachment and exploration in adults: Chronic and contextual accessibility. *Personality and Social Psychology Bulletin*, 26(4), 452–461.

Green, J. L., Camilli, G., & Elmore, P. B. (Eds). (2006). *Handbook of complementary methods in education research*. Mahwah, NJ: Lawrence Erlbaum Associates.

Greenberg, J., & Mitchell, S. (1983). *Object relations in psychoanalytic theory*. London: Harvard University Press.

Greenson, R. (1967). *The technique and practice of psychoanalysis*. New York: International Universities Press.

Greig, A., Minnis, H., Millward, R., Sinclair, C., Kennedy, E., Towlson, K. et al. (2008). Relationships and learning: A review and investigation of narrative coherence in looked-after children in primary school. *Educational Psychology in Practice*, 24(1), 13–27.

Griffin, D. W., & Bartholomew, K. (1994). The metaphysics of measurement: The case of adult attachment. In K. Bartholomew & D. Perlman (Eds), *Attachment processes in adulthood* (pp. 17–52). Philadelphia, PA: Jessica Kingsley Publishers.

Grossmann, K. E. (1995). The evolution and history of attachment research and theory. In S. Goldberg, R. Muir & J. Kerr (Eds), *Attachment theory: Social, developmental, and clinical perspectives* (pp. 85–121). Hillsdale, NJ: Analytic Press.

Hall, C., & Noyes, A. (2009). School self-evaluation and its impact on teachers' work in England. *Research Papers in Education*, 24(3), 311–334.

Halliday, S., & Ius, S. (2009). *Victorian Institute of Teaching Annual Report 2009*. Melbourne: Victorian Insititute of Teaching.

Harber, C. (2008). Perpetrating disaffection: Schooling as an international problem. *Educational Studies*, 34(5), 457–467.

Hargreaves, A. (1998). The emotional practice of teaching. *Teaching and Teacher Education*, 14(8), 835–854.

Hargreaves, A. (2000). Mixed emotions: Teachers' perceptions of their interactions with students. *Teaching and Teacher Education*, 16(8), 811–826.

Hargreaves, A. (2001). The emotional geographies of teachers' relations with colleagues. *International Journal of Educational Research*, 35(5), 503.

Hargreaves, A. (2002). Teaching and betrayal. *Teachers and Teaching: Theory and Practice*, 8(3), 393–407.

Hargreaves, A., & Tucker, E. (1991). Teaching and guilt: Exploring the feelings of teaching. *Teaching and Teacher Education*, 7(5–6), 491–505.

Harlow, H. (1958). The nature of love. *American Psychologist*, 13, 673–685.

Harlow, H., & Harlow, M. K. (1965). The affectional systems. In A. M. Schrier, H. F. Harlow & F. Stollnitz (Eds), *Behaviour of non-human primates* (Vol. 2, pp. 287–334). New York: Academic Press.

Harlow, H., & Zimmermann, R. R. (1959). Affectional responses in the infant monkey. *Science*, 130, 421–466.

Hart, T. (2007). Reciprocal revelation: Toward a pedagogy of interiority. *Journal of Cognitive Affective Learing*, 3(2), 1–10.

Hart, T. (2008). Interiority and education: Exploring the neurophenomenology of contemplation and its potential role in learning. *Journal of Transformative Education*, 6(4), 235–250.

Harvey, S. (2005). Emotional intelligence: The classroom story. *Teacher*, 155, 20–22, 24.

Hassin, R. R., Uleman, J. S., & Bargh, J. A. (Eds). (2005). *The new unconscious*. New York: Oxford University Press.

Hastings, W. (2008). I felt so guilty: Emotions and subjectivity in school-based teacher education. *Teachers and Teaching*, 14(5), 497–513.

Hargreaves, A., & Fink, D. (2006). *Sustainable leadership*. San Francisco, CA: Jossey-Bass.

Hazan, C., Gur-Yaish, N., & Campa, M. (2004). What does it mean to be attached? In W. S. Rholes & J. A. Simpson (Eds), *Adult attachment: Theory, research, and clinical implications* (pp. 55–85). New York: Guilford Press.

Hazan, C., & Shaver, P. R. (1987). Romantic love conceptualized as an attachment process. *Journal of Personality and Social Psychology*, 52, 511–524.

Hazan, C., & Shaver, P. R. (1990). Love and work: An attachment-theoretical perspective. *Journal of Personality and Social Psychology*, 59, 270–280.

Hazan, C., & Shaver, P. R. (1994a). Attachment as an organizational framework for research on close relationships. *Psychological Inquiry*, 5, 1–22.

Hazan, C., & Shaver, P. R. (1994b). Deeper into attachment theory: Reply to commentaries. *Psychological Inquiry*, 5, 68–79.

Hazan, C., & Zeifman, D. (1999). Pair bonds as attachments: Evaluating the evidence. In J. Cassidy & P. R. Shaver (Eds), *Handbook of attachment theory and research* (pp. 336–354). New York: Guilford Press.

Hemingway, H., Shipley, M., Macfarlane, P., & Marmot, M. (2000). Impact of socio-economic status on coronary mortality in people with symptoms, electrocardiographic abnormalities, both or neither: The original Whitehall study 25 year follow up. *Journal of Epidemiology & Community Health*, 54(7), 510–516.

Hepburn, A. (2000). Power lines: Derrida, discursive psychology and the management of accusations of teacher bullying. *British Journal of Social Psychology*, 39, 605–628.

Herr, K. (1999). Unearthing the unspeakable: When teacher research and political agendas collide. *Language Arts*, 77(1), 10–15.

Hinde, R. (1982a). Attachment: Some conceptual and biological issues. In C. M. Parkes & J. Stevensen-Hinde (Eds), *The place of attachment in human behaviour* (pp. 60–78). London: Tavistock.

Hinde, R. (1982b). *Ethology*. London: Fontana.

Hinde, R. (1987). *Individuals, relationships and culture: Links between ethology and the social sciences*. Cambridge: Cambridge University Press.

Hirschkorn, M. (2009). Student–teacher relationships and teacher induction: Ben's story. *Teacher Development: An international journal of teachers' professional development*, 13(3), 205–217.

Hochschild, A. R. (1983). *The managed heart: The commercialization of human feeling*. Berkeley, CA: University of California Press.

Hodgen, J., & Askew, M. (2007). Emotion, identity and teacher learning: Becoming a primary mathematics teacher. *Oxford Review of Education*, 33(4), 469.

Holder, A. (2005). *Anna Freud, Melanie Klein, and the psychoanalysis of children and adolescents* (P. Slotkin, Trans.). London: Karnac.

Holinger, P. C. (2008). Further issues in the psychology of affect and motivation: A developmental perspective. *Psychoanalytic Psychology*, 25(3), 425–442.

Holmes, J. (1986). Teaching the psychotherapeutic method: Some literary parallels. *British Journal of Medical Psychology*, 59(2), 113–121.

Holmes, J. (1993a). Attachment theory: A biological basis for psychotherapy? *British Journal of Psychiatry*, 163, 430–438.

Holmes, J. (1993b). *John Bowlby & attachment theory: Makers of modern psychotherapy*. London: Brunner-Routledge.

Holmes, J. (1993c). Who owns psychoanalysis? *British Journal of Psychotherapy*, 10(2), 249–252.

Holmes, J. (1994a). Attachment theory: A secure theoretical base for counselling? *Psychodynamic Counselling*, 1(1), 65–78.

Holmes, J. (1994b). The clinical implications of attachment theory. *British Journal of Psychotherapy*, 11(1), 62–76.

Holmes, J. (1996a). Attachment theory: A secure base for policy? In S. Kraemer & J. Roberts (Eds), *The politics of attachment: Towards a secure society* (pp. 27–42). London: Free Association Books.

Holmes, J. (1996b). *Attachment, intimacy, autonomy: Using attachment theory in adult psychotherapy*. Lanham, MD: Jason Aronson.

Holmes, J. (1998). The changing aims of psychoanalytic psychotherapy: An integrative perspective. *International Journal of Psycho-Analysis*, 79(2), 227–240.

Holmes, J. (1999a). Ghosts in the consulting room: An attachment perspective on intergenerational transmission. *Attachment & Human Development*, 1(1), 115–131.

Holmes, J. (1999b). Narrative, attachment and the therapeutic process. In C. Mace (Ed.), *Heart and soul: The therapeutic face of philosophy* (pp. 147–161). Florence, KY: Routledge.

Holmes, J. (1999c). The relationship in psychodynamic counselling. In C. Feltham (Ed.), *Understanding the counselling relationship* (pp. 33–54). Thousand Oaks, CA: Sage Publications.

Holmes, J. (2000). Attachment theory and psychoanalysis: A rapprochement. *British Journal of Psychotherapy*, 17(2), 157–180.

Holmes, J. (2001). *The search for the secure base: Attachment theory and psychotherapy*. New York: Brunner-Routledge.

Holmes, J. (2005). Notes on mentalizing – Old hat, or new wine? *British Journal of Psychotherapy*, 22(2), 179–197.

Holmes, J. G. (2000). Social relationships: the nature and function of relational schemas. *European Journal of Social Psychology*, 30(4), 447–495.

Holtzworth-Munroe, A., Stuart, G. L., & Hutchinson, G. (1997). Violent versus non-violent husbands: Differences in attachment patterns, dependency, and jealousy. *Journal of Family Psychology*, 11(3), 314–331.

Horney, K. (1932/1964). *New ways in psychoanalysis*. Oxford: W W Norton & Co.

Horppu, R., & Ikonen-Varila, M. (2004). Mental models of attachment as a part of kindergarten student teachers' practical knowledge about caregiving. *International Journal of Early Years Education*, 12(3), 231–243.

Hoshmand, L. T., & Polkinghorne, D. E. (1992). Redefining the science–practice relationship and professional training. *American Psychologist*, 47(1), 55–66.

Houghton, V. (2001). *Teacher/pupil emotional alienation in the classroom: Towards a theory of educational significance*. Nedlands, WA: University of Western Australia.

Hrdy, S. B. (2000). *Mother nature: Maternal instincts and how they shape the human species* (1st Ballantine Books ed.). New York: Ballantine Books.

Hrdy, S. B. (2009). *Mothers and others: The evolutionary origins of mutual understanding*. Cambridge, MA: Belknap Press.

Huberman, M. (1993). Burnout in teaching careers. *European Education*, 25(3), 47–70.

Husu, J., Toom, A., & Patrikainen, S. (2008). Guided reflection as a means to demonstrate and develop student teachers' reflective competencies. *Reflective Practice*, 9(1), 37–51.

Hyman, I. A., & Snook, P. A. (1999). *Dangerous schools: What we can do about the physical and emotional abuse of our children* (1st ed.). San Francisco, CA: Jossey-Bass.

Immordino-Yang, M., & Damasio, A. (2007). We feel therefore we learn: The relevance of affective and social neuroscience to education. *Brain, Mind and Education*, 1(1), 3–10.

Ingleby, D. (1983). Freud and Piaget: The phoney war. *New Ideas in Psychology*, 1(2), 123–144.

Ingvarson, L., Meiers, M., & Beavis, A. (2005). Factors affecting the impact of professional development programs on teachers' knowledge, practice, student outcomes & efficacy. *Education Policy Analysis Archives*, 13(10), 1–28.

Inness, S. A., & Inness, J. C. (1996). Speaking up at last: Anger in the classroom. *Transformations*, 7(1), 29.

Isenbarger, L., & Zembylas, M. (2006). The emotional labour of caring in teaching. *Teaching and Teacher Education: An International Journal of Research and Studies*, 22(1), 120–134.

Isikoglu, N., Basturk, R., & Karaca, F. (2009). Assessing in-service teachers' instructional beliefs about student-centered education: A Turkish perspective. *Teaching and Teacher Education*, 25(2), 350–356.

ISQ Briefings (2007). Managing challenging behaviour: How do we help young people with emotional, behavioural and social difficulties? *ISQ Briefings*, 11(6), 1–3.

ISQ Briefings (2008). Teachers make a difference: The central role of teachers in top-performing schools. *ISQ Briefings*, 12(1), 1–4.

Jackson, P. W. (1968). *Life in classrooms*. New York: Holt, Rinehart and Winston.

James, M. (2006). *Implementing attachment theory in Head Start to enhance social competence: A program development*. Chicago, IL: The Chicago School Of Professional Psychology.

Johnson, F. D. (2006). An inquiry of middle school teacher stress and burnout with a predictive analysis of the characteristics of teachers most likely to experience emotional exhaustion, depersonalization and low personal accomplishment with in-depth interviews. *Dissertation Abstracts International Section A: Humanities and Social Sciences*, 66(11-A), 3878.

Johnson, H. L., & Fullwood, H. L. (2006). Disturbing behaviors in the secondary classroom: How do general educators perceive problem behaviors? *Journal of Instructional Psychology*, 33(1), 20–39.

Johnson, S., Cooper, C., Cartwright, S., Donald, I., Taylor, P., & Millet, C. (2005). The experience of work-related stress across occupations. *Journal of Managerial Psychology*, 20(2), 178–187.

Johnson, S. M. (2003). Introduction to attachment: A therapist's guide to primary relationships and their renewal. In S. M. Johnson & V. E. Whiffen (Eds), *Attachment processes in couple and family therapy* (pp. 3–17). New York: Guilford Press.

Johnson, S. M., & Birkeland, S. E. (2003). The schools that teachers choose. *Educational Leadership*, 60(8), 20.

Jones, D. (2008). Constructing identities: Perceptions and experiences of male primary headteachers. *Early Child Development and Care*, 178(7), 689–702.

Jones, R. (2005). Review of psychoanalysis as education. *The Journal of Analytical Psychology*, 50(4), 552–554.

Jones, R. L., Gottfried, N. W., & Berkowitz, H. (1967). Partial construct validation of a scale developed to reflect unconscious motives fulfilled by teaching. *Educational and Psychological Measurement*, 27(1), 97–112.

Josefowitz, N., & Myran, D. (2006). Towards a person-centred cognitive behaviour therapy. *Counselling Psychology Quarterly*, 18(4), 329–336.

Kafetsios, K., & Nezlek, J. B. (2002). Attachment styles in everyday social interaction. *European Journal of Social Psychology*, 32(5), 719–735.

Kandel, E. R. (2005). *Psychiatry, psychoanalysis, and the new biology of mind*. Washington, DC: American Psychiatric Publishing.

Kearney, P., Plax, T. G., Hayes, E. R., & Ivey, M. J. (1991). College teacher misbehaviours: What students don't like about what teachers say and do. *Communication Quarterly*, 39(4), 325–340.

Kegan, R., & Lahey, L. L. (2001). *Seven languages for transformation: How the way we talk can change the way we work*. San Francisco, CA: Jossey-Bass.

Kelchtermans, G. (2005). Teachers' emotions in educational reforms: Self-understanding, vulnerable commitment and micropolitical literacy. *Teaching and Teacher Education*, 21(8), 995–1006.

Kelchtermans, G., & Strittmatter, A. (1999). Beyond individual burnout: A perspective for improved schools. Guidelines for the prevention of burnout. In R. Vandenberghe & A. M. Huberman (Eds), *Understanding and preventing teacher burnout: A sourcebook of international research and practice* (pp. 304–314). New York: Cambridge University Press.

Kelsey, D. D., Kelsey, D. M., Kearney, P., Plax, T. G., Allen, T. H., & Ritter, K. J. (2004). College students' attributions of teacher misbehaviors. *Communication education*, 53(1), 40–55.

Kennedy, J. H., & Kennedy, C. E. (2007). Applications of attachment theory in school psychology. *Journal of Early Childhood and Infant Psychology*, 3, 7–25.

Kenny, D. A., Kashy, D. A., & Cook, W. L. (2006). *Dyadic data analysis*. New York: Guilford Press.

Kesner, J. E. (2000). Teacher characteristics and the quality of child–teacher relationships. *Journal of School Psychology*, 38(2), 133–149.

Khine, M. S., & Fisher, D. L. (2004). Teacher interaction in psychosocial learning environments: cultural differences and their implications in science instruction. *Research in Science & Technological Education*, 22(1), 99–111.

Khoury-Kassabri, M., Astor, A. R., & Benbenishty, R. (2008). Student victimization by school staff in the context of an Israeli national school safety campaign. *Aggressive Behavior*, 34(1), 1–8.

Khoury-Kassabri, M., Benbenishty, R., & Astor, A. R. (2005). The effects of school climate, socioeconomics, and cultural factors on student victimization in Israel. *Social Work Research*, 29(3), 165–180.

Kieschke, U., & Schaarschmidt, U. (2008). Professional commitment and health among teachers in Germany: A typological approach. *Learning and Instruction*, 18(5), 429–437.

Kikkawa, M. (1987). Teachers' opinions and treatments for bully/victim problems among students in junior and senior high schools: Results of a fact-finding survey. *Journal of Human Development*, 23, 25–30.

Killen, D. (2006). At the heart of education. *EQ Australia*, 3, 38–39.

King, N. J., Gullone, E., & Dadds, M. R. (1990). Student perceptions of permissiveness and teacher-instigated disciplinary strategies. *British Journal of Educational Psychology*, 60(3), 322–329.

Kirkpatrick, L. A., & Hazan, C. (1994). Attachment styles and close relationships: A four-year prospective study. *Personal relationships*, 1(2), 123–142.

Kirsner, D. (2007). Fresh Freud: No longer lost in translation. *Psychoanalytic Psychology*, 24(4), 658–666.

Klein, M. (1986). *The selected Melanie Klein*. London: Penguin.

Klein, R. P., Suwalsky, J. T. D., McCarthy, M., & Gist, N. F. (1982). Convergent validity of two measures of attachment. *Educational and Psychological Measurement*, 42(1), 325–331.

Knafo, D. (2009). Freud's memory erased. *Psychoanalytic Psychology*, 26(2), 171–190.

Knapp, T. J. (1986). The emergence of cognitive psychology in the latter half of the twentieth century. In T. J. Knapp & L. C. Robertson (Eds), *Approaches to cognition: Contrasts and controversies* (pp. 13–35). Hillsdale, NJ: Lawrence Erlbaum Associates.

Knoblauch, D., & Woolfolk Hoy, A. (2008). "Maybe I can teach those kids." The influence of contextual factors on student teachers' efficacy beliefs. *Teaching and Teacher Education*, 24(1), 166–179.

Knox, J. (2003). *Archetype, attachment, analysis: Jungian psychology and the emergent mind*. New York: Brunner-Routledge.

Knox, J. (2004). From archetypes to reflective function. *Journal of Analytical Psychology*, 49(1), 1–19.

Kobak, R. R., & Hazan, C. (1991). Attachment in marriage: Effects of security and accuracy of working models. *Journal of Personality and Social Psychology*, 60(6), 861–869.

Kochenderfer-Ladd, B., & Pelletier, M. E. (2008). Teachers' views and beliefs about bullying: Influences on classroom management strategies and students' coping with peer victimization. *Journal of School Psychology*, 46(4), 431–453.

Kohl, H. (1984). *Growing minds: On becoming a teacher* (1st ed.). New York: Harper & Row.

Koomen, H. M., Verschueren, K., & Thijs, J. T. (2006). Assessing aspects of the teacher–child relationship: A critical ingredient of a practice-oriented psycho-diagnostic approach. *Educational and Child Psychology*, 23(3), 50–60.

Kovan, N. M., Chung, A. L., & Sroufe, A. L. (2009). The intergenerational continuity of observed early parenting: A prospective, longitudinal study. *Developmental Psychology*, 45(5), 1205–1213.

Kusiak, K. (2004). Negotiating the self: Identity, sexuality, and emotion in learning to teach. *Theory Into Practice*, 43(2), 162.

Kuzmic, J. (1994). A beginning teacher's search for meaning: Teacher socialization, organizational literacy, and empowerment. *Teaching and Teacher Education*, 10, 15–27.

Kyriacou, C. (2001). Teacher stress: Directions for future research. *Educational Review*, 53(1), 27–35.

Kyriacou, C. (2009). The five dimensions of social pedagogy within schools. *Pastoral Care in Education: An International Journal of Personal, Social and Emotional Development*, 27(2), 101–108.

Kyriacou, C., & Sutcliffe, J. (1978). Teacher stress: Prevalence, sources, and symptoms. *British Journal of Educational Psychology*, 48, 159–167.

Lacey, K., & Gronn, P. (2007). Letting go: Former principals reflect on their role exit. *CSE/IARTV Seminar Series*, 163 (Centre for Strategic Education Seminar Series Papers), 1–12.

Laker, A., Laker, J. C., & Lea, S. (2008). Sources of support for pre-service teachers during school experience. *Mentoring & Tutoring: Partnership in Learning*, 16(2), 125–140.

Lampela, L. (2003). Review of *Negotiating the Self: Identity, Sexuality, and Emotion in Learning to Teach*. *Teachers College Record*, 105(4), 601.

Lander, I. (2009). Repairing discordant student–teacher relationships: A case study using emotion-focused therapy. *Children & Schools*, 31(4), 229.

Laquercia, T. (2001). Is love necessary? *Modern Psychoanalysis*, 26(1), 37–53.

Larner, G. (2001). The critical-practitioner model in therapy. *Australian Psychologist*, 36(1), 36–43.

Larose, S., Bernier, A., & Soucy, N. (2005). Attachment as a moderator of the effect of security in mentoring on subsequent perceptions of mentoring and relationship quality with college teachers. *Journal of Social and Personal Relationships*, 22(3), 399–415.

Lazarus, R. S., & Folkman, S. (1984). *Stress, appraisal and coping*. New York: Springer.

Leakey, R. (2005). Our endangered siblings. *Boston Globe*, 22 September.

Learner, D. G., & Kruger, L. J. (1997). Attachment, self-concept, and academic motivation in high-school students. *American Journal of Orthopsychiatry*, 67(3), 485–492.

Leary, M. R., & Cox, C. B. (2008). Belongingness motivation: A mainspring of social action. In J. Y. Shah & W. L. Gardner (Eds), *Handbook of motivation science* (pp. 27–40). New York: Guilford Press.

LeDoux, J. E. (1996). *The emotional brain*. New York: Simon & Schuster.

Lee, Y.-S., Grossman, J., & Krishnan, A. (2008). Cultural relevance of adult attachment: Rasch modeling of the Revised Experiences in Close Relationships in a Korean sample. *Educational and Psychological Measurement*, 68(5), 824–844.

Leithwood, K. A. (2006). *Teaching for deep understanding: What every educator should know*. Thousand Oaks, CA: Corwin Press.

Leithwood, K. A., & Beatty, B. (2008). *Leading with teachers' emotions in mind*. Thousand Oaks, CA: Corwin Press.

Lemche, E., Giampietro, V. P., Surguladze, S. A., Amaro, E. J., Andrew, C. M., Williams, S. C., et al. (2006). Human attachment security is mediated by the amygdala: Evidence from combined fMRI and psychophysiological measures. *Human Brain Mapping*, 27(8), 623–635.

Levenson, E. (2001). The enigma of the unconscious. *Contemporary Psychoanalysis*, 37(2), 239–252.

Levenson, H. (2004). Time-limited dynamic psychotherapy. In J. J. Magnavita (Ed.), *Handbook of personality disorders: Theory and practice* (pp. 254–279). Hoboken, NJ: John Wiley & Sons.

Levine, S. S. (2004). To have and to hold: On the experience of having the other. *Psychoanalitic Quarterly*, 73(4), 939–969.

Levinson, H. (2006). *Harry Levinson on the psychology of leadership*. Boston, MA: Harvard Business School.

Levitt, B. E. (2008). *Reflections on human potential: Bridging the person-centered approach and positive psychology*. Ross-on-Wye: PCCS Books.

Lewis, L. (2006). Mindfulness and psychotherapy. *Bulletin of the Menninger Clinic*, 70(1), 83–84.

Lewis, R. (2001). Classroom discipline and student responsibility: The students' view. *Teaching and Teacher Education*, 17(3), 307–319.

Lewis, R. (2006). Classroom discipline in Australia. In C. M. Evertson & C. S. Weinstein (Eds), *Handbook of classroom management: Research, practice and contemporary issues* (pp. 1193–1214). Mahwah, NJ: Lawrence Erlbaum Associates.

Lewis, R. (2008). *The developmental management approach to classroom behaviour: Responding to individual neEds* Camberwell, Victoria: ACER Press.

Lewis, R., & Riley, P. (2009). Teacher misbehaviour. In L. J. Saha & A. G. Dworkin (Eds), *The international handbook of research on teachers and teaching* (pp. 417–431). Norwell, MA: Springer.

Lewis, R., Romi, S., Katz, Y. J., & Qui, X. (2008). Students' reaction to classroom discipline in Australia, Israel, and China. *Teaching and Teacher Education*, 24(3), 715–724.

Lewis, R., Romi, S., Qui, X., & Katz, Y. J. (2005). Teachers' classroom dicipline and student misbehaviour in Australia, China and Israel. *Teaching and Teacher Education*, 21, 729–741.

Lisa, R. (2003). Setting new teachers up for failure ... or success. *Educational Leadership*, 60(8), 62.

Liston, D., Whitcomb, J., & Borko, H. (2009). The end of education in teacher education: Thoughts on reclaiming the role of social foundations in teacher education. *Journal of Teacher Education*, 60(2), 107–111.

Liu, J.-j., Wei, X.-f., & Jiang, G.-r. (2009). Relationship between teacher's adult attachment and teacher interaction style. *Chinese Journal of Clinical Psychology*, 17(1), 104–106.

Logel, C., Iserman, E. C., Davies, P. G., Quinn, D. M., & Spencer, S. J. The perils of double consciousness: The role of thought suppression in stereotype threat. *Journal of Experimental Social Psychology*. In Press, Corrected Proof.

Loonstra, B., Brouwers, A., & Tomic, W. (2009). Feelings of existential fulfilment and burnout among secondary school teachers. *Teaching and Teacher Education*, 25(5), 752–757.

Lopez, F. G., Melendez, M. C., Sauer, E. M., Berger, E., & Wyssmann, J. (1998). Internal working models, self-reported problems, and help-seeking attitudes among college students. *Journal of Counseling Psychology*, 45(1), 79–83.

Lorenz, K. (1952). *King Solomon's Ring*. London: Methuen.

Lorenz, K. Z. (1935). Der kumpan in der umveld des vogels. In C. H. Schiller (Ed.), *Instinctive behaviour*. New York: International Universities Press.

Loughran, J. J. (2006). *Developing a pedagogy of teacher education: Understanding teaching and learning about teaching*. London: Routledge.

Loughran, J. J., & Northfield, J. R. (1996). *Opening the classroom door: Teacher, researcher, learner*. London: Falmer.

Lowenstein, L. F. (1991). Teacher stress leading to burnout: Its prevention and cure. *Education Today*, 14(2), 12–16.

MacDonald, F. J. (2006). *Suspended in perpetuity? Teacher professional identity in a time of educational reform*. Toronto: University of Toronto.

Macnab, F. (1991a). Psychotherapy: Focussed and integrated. *Psychoanalysis and Psychotherapy*, 9(1), 65–84.

Macnab, F. (1991b). *Psychotherapy: New directions for clinical practice*. Melbourne: Spectrum Publications.

Mader, C. E. (2009). "I will never teach the old way again": Classroom management and external incentives. *Theory Into Practice*, 48(2), 147–155.

Maguire, M. (2008). "End of term": Teacher identities in a post-work context. *Pedagogy, Culture & Society*, 16(1), 43–55.

Main, M. (1990). *A typology of human attachment organisation assessed with discourse, drawings and interviews*. New York: Cambridge University Press.

Main, M. (1999). Epilogue. Attachment: Eighteen points. In J. Cassidy & P. R. Shaver (Eds), *Handbook of attachment* (pp. 845–887). New York: Guilford Press.

Mallinckrodt, B. (2007). A call to broaden and build Mikulincer and Shaver's work on the benefits of priming attachment security. [Comment/Reply]. *Psychological Inquiry*, 18(3), 168–172.

Mallinckrodt, B., Coble, H. M., & Gantt, D. L. (1995). Toward differentiating client attachment from working alliance and transference: Reply to Robbins (1995). *Journal of counseling psychology*, 42(3), 320–322.

Malmberg, L.-E. (2008). Student teachers' achievement goal orientations during teacher studies: Antecedents, correlates and outcomes. *Learning and Instruction*, 18(5), 438–452.

Malone, M. R. (1984). Concerns Based Adoption Model (CBAM): Basis for an elementary science methods course. *Journal of Research in Science Teaching*, 21(7), 755–768.

Mamede, S., & Schmidt, H. G. (2004). The structure of reflective practice in medicine. *Medical Education*, 38(12), 1302–1308.

Mann, J. (1973). *Time-limited psychotherapy*. Cambridge, MA: Harvard University Press.

Mann, J. (1981). The core of time-limited psychotherapy: Time and the central issue. In S. Budman (Ed.), *Forms of brief therapy* (pp. 25–44). New York: Guilford Press.

Mann, J. (1991). Time-limited psychotherapy. In P. Crits-Christoph & J. Barber (Eds), *Handbook of short-term dynamic psychotherapy* (pp. 17–44). New York: Basic Books.

Marachi, R., Astor, A. R., & Benbenishty, R. (2007a). Effects of student participation and teacher support on victimization in Israeli schools: An examination of gender, culture, and school type. *Journal of Youth and Adolescence*, 36(2), 225–240.

Marachi, R., Astor, A. R., & Benbenishty, R. (2007b). Effects of teacher avoidance of school policies on student victimization. *School Psychology International*, 28(4), 501–518.

Markus, H., & Nurius, P. (1987). Possible selves: The interface between motivation and the self-concept. In K. Yardley & T. Honess (Eds), *Self and identity: Psychosocial perspectives* (pp. 157–172). Oxford: John Wiley & Sons.

Marmor, J. (1979). Short-term dynamic psychotherapy. *American Journal of Psychiatry*, 136(2), 149–155.

Marmor, J. (1982). Psychoanalysis, psychiatry and systems thinking. *Journal of the American Academy of Psychoanalysis & Dynamic Psychiatry*, 10(3), 337–350.

Marmor, J. (1983). Systems thinking in psychiatry: Some theoretical and clinical applications. *American Journal of Psychiatry*, 140(7), 833–838.

Marmot, M. G. (2006). Status syndrome: A challenge to medicine. [Editorial]. *JAMA: Journal of the American Medical Association*, 295(11), 1304–1307.

Marmot, M. G., & Smith, G. D. (1997). Socio-economic differentials in health: The contribution of the Whitehall Studies. *Journal of Health Psychology*, 2(3), 283–296.

Marris, P. (1958). *Widows and their families*. London: Routledge & Kegan Paul.

Marshak, D. (1996). The emotional experience of school change: Resistance, loss and grief. *NASSP Bulletin*, 80(577), 72–77.

Martin, A. J., & Dowson, M. (2009). Interpersonal relationships, motivation, engagement, and achievement: Yields for theory, current issues, and educational practice. *Review of Educational Research*, 79(1), 327–365.

Martin, A. J., Linfoot, K., & Stephenson, J. (1999). How teachers respond to concerns about misbehavior in their classroom. *Psychology in the Schools*, 36(4), 347–358.

Martin, W. B. W. (1987). Students' perceptions of causes and consequences of embarrassment in the school. *Canadian Journal of Education*, 12(2), 277–293.

Martinez-Inigo, D., Totterdell, P., Alcover, C. M., & Holman, D. (2007). Emotional labour and emotional exhaustion: Interpersonal and intrapersonal mechanisms. *Work & Stress*, 21(1), 30–47.

Marvin, R., Cooper, G., Hoffman, K., & Powell, B. (2002). The circle of security project: Attachment-based intervention with caregiver–pre-school child dyads. *Attachment & Human Development*, 4(1), 107–124.

Masiello, G. (2000). *Adult attachment styles as predictors of core conflictual relationships patterns*. Ann Arbor, MI: Bell & Howell Information and Learning.

Maslach, C. (1999). Progress in understanding teacher burnout. In R. Vandenberghe & A. M. Huberman (Eds), *Understanding and preventing teacher burnout: A sourcebook of international research and practice* (pp. 211–222). New York: Cambridge University Press.

Maslach, C. (2001). What have we learned about burnout and health? *Psychology & Health*, 16(5), 607–611.

Maslach, C., Jackson, S. E., & Leiter, M. P. (1996). *Maslach burnout inventory manual* (3rd ed.). Palo Alto, CA: Consulting Psychologists Press.

Maslach, C., & Leiter, M. P. (2008). Early predictors of job burnout and engagement. *Journal of Applied Psychology*, 93(3), 498–512.

Maslow, A. H. (1954). *Motivation and personality* (1st ed.). New York: Harper.

Maslow, A. H. (1968). *Toward a psychology of being* (2nd ed.). New York: Van Nostrand.

Maslowski, R. (2006). A review of inventories for diagnosing school culture. *Journal of Educational Administration; Armidale*, 44(1), 6.

Maultsby, M. C. (1984). *Rational behavior therapy*. Englewood Cliffs, NJ: Prentice Hall.

Mawhinney, T. S., & Sagan, L. L. (2007). The power of personal relationships. *Phi Delta Kappan*, 88(6), 460.

Mayer, J. D., Salovey, P., & Caruso, D. (2000). Models of emotional intelligence. In R. J. Sternberg (Ed.), *Handbook of intelligence* (pp. 396–420). New York: Cambridge University Press.

Mayer, J. D., Salovey, P., & Caruso, D. R. (2008). Emotional intelligence: New ability or eclectic traits? *American Psychologist*, 63(6), 503–517.

Mayes, C. (2008). The psychoanalytic view of teaching and learning, 1922–2002. *Journal of Curriculum Studies*, 99999(1), 1–29.

Mayseless, O., & Popper, M. (2007). Reliance on leaders and social institutions: An attachment perspective. *Attachment & Human Development*, 9(1), 73–93.

McEachern, A. G.,, Aluede, O., & Kenny, M. C. (2008). Emotional abuse in the classroom: Implications and interventions for counselors. *Journal of Counseling & Development*, 86(1), 3–10.

McGoldrick, M., Gerson, R., & Shellenberger, S. (1999). *Genograms: Assessment and intervention* (2nd ed.). New York: W.W. Norton.

McRae, D., Ainsworth, G., Groves, R., Rowland, M., & Zbar, V. (2001). *PD-2000 a national mapping of teacher professional development*. Canberra, ACT: Commonwealth Department of Education, Training and Youth Affairs.

McWilliam, E. (2008). Unlearning how to teach. *Innovations in Education and Teaching International*, 45(3), 263–269.

Meijer, P. C., Korthagen, F. A. J., & Vasalos, A. (2009). Supporting presence in teacher education: The connection between the personal and professional aspects of teaching. *Teaching and Teacher Education*, 25(2), 297–308.

Melges, F. T., & Bowlby, J. (1969). Types of hopelessness in psychopathological process. *Archives of General Psychiatry*, 20(6), 690–699.

Menter, I. (2008). Tradition, culture and identity in the reform of teachers' work in Scotland and England: Some methodological considerations. *Pedagogy, Culture & Society*, 16(1), 57–69.

Mertz, N. T. (2004). What's a mentor anyway? *Educational Administration Quarterly*, 40(4), 541–560.

Midgley, M., & Midgley, D. (2005). *The essential Mary Midgley*. London: Routledge.

Mikulincer, M., Birnbaum, G., Woddis, D., & Nachmias, O. (2000). Stress and accessibility of proximity-related thoughts: Exploring the normative and intraindividual components of attachment theory. *Journal of Personality and Social Psychology*, 78(3), 509–523.

Mikulincer, M., & Florian, V. (1995). Appraisal of and coping with a real-life stressful situation: The contribution of attachment styles. *Personality and Social Psychology Bulletin*, 21(4), 406–414.

Mikulincer, M., Gillath, O., Halevy, V., Avihou, N., Avidan, S., & Eshkoli, N. (2001). Attachment theory and reactions to others' needs: Evidence that activiation of the sense of attachment security promotes empathic responses. *Journal of Personality and Social Psychology*, 81(6), 1205–1224.

Mikulincer, M., Gillath, O., Sapir-Lavid, Y., Yaakobi, E., Arias, K., Tal-Aloni, L., et al. (2003). Attachment theory and concern for others' welfare: Evidence that activation of the sense of secure base promotes endorsement of self-transcendence values. *Basic and Applied Social Psychology*, 25(4), 299–312.

Mikulincer, M., Gillath, O., & Shaver, P. R. (2002). Activation of the attachment system in adulthood: Threat-related primes increase the accessibility of mental representations of attachment figures. *Journal of Personality and Social Psychology*, 83(4), 881–895.

Mikulincer, M., & Goodman, G. S. (2006). *Dynamics of romantic love: Attachment, caregiving, and sex*. New York: Guilford Press.

Mikulincer, M., Hirschberger, G., Nachmias, O., & Gillath, O. (2001). The affective component of the secure base schema: Affective priming with representations of attachment security. *Journal of Personality and Social Psychology*, 81(2), 305–321.

Mikulincer, M., & Shaver, P. R. (2001). Attachment theory and intergroup bias: Evidence that priming the secure base schema attenuates negative reactions to out-groups. *Journal of Personality and Social Psychology*, 81(1), 97–115.

Mikulincer, M., & Shaver, P. R. (2006). The behavioral system construct: A useful tool for building an integrative model of the social mind. In P. A. M. V. Lange (Ed.), *Bridging social psychology: Benefits of transdisciplinary approaches* (pp. 279–284). Mahwah, NJ: Lawrence Erlbaum Associates.

Mikulincer, M., & Shaver, P. R. (2007a). *Attachment in adulthood: Structure, dynamics, and change*. New York: Guilford Press.

Mikulincer, M., & Shaver, P. R. (2007b). Reflections on security dynamics: Core constructs, psychological mechanisms, relational contexts, and the need for an integrative theory. *Psychological Inquiry*, 18(3), 197–209.

Mikulincer, M., Shaver, P. R., Gillath, O., & Nitzberg, R. A. (2005). Attachment, caregiving, and altruism: Boosting attachment security increases compassion and helping. *Journal of Personality and Social Psychology*, 89(5), 817–839.

Mikulincer, M., Shaver, P. R., Sapir-Lavid, Y., & Avihou-Kanza, N. (2009). What's inside the minds of securely and insecurely attached people? The secure-base script and its associations with attachment-style dimensions. *Journal of Personality & Social Psychology*, 97(4), 615–633.

Miller, J. B., & Noirot, M. (1999). Attachment memories, models and information processing. *Journal of Social and Personal Relationships*, 16(2), 147–173.

Miller, M. L. (2008). The emotionally engaged anaylyst II: How emotions impact analytic process as illuminated by dynamic systems theory. *Psychoanalytic Psychology*, 25(2), 257–279.

Miller, R., Brickman, P., & Bolen, D. (1975). Attribution versus persuasion as a means of modifying behavior. *Journal of Personality and Social Psychology*, 31, 430–441.

Mills, J. (2008). Attachment deficits, personality structure and PTSD. *Psychoanalytic Psychology*, 25(2), 380–385.

Mills, M., Haase, M., & Charlton, E. (2008). Being the "right" kind of male teacher: The disciplining of John. *Pedagogy, Culture & Society*, 16(1), 71–84.

Milton, J. (2001). Psychoanalysis and cognitive behaviour therapy – rival paradigms or common ground? *International Journal of Psychoanalysis*, 82, 432–447.

Mitchell, J., & Riley, P. (2008, 8–11 July). *Leading professional learning in schools: Emotion in action*. Paper presented at the Teacher educators at work: What works and where is the evidence?, Sunshine Coast, Australia.

Mitchell, S. A., & Black, M. J. (1995). *Freud and beyond: A history of modern psychoanalytic thought*. New York: Basic Books.

Mockler, N. (2005). Trans/forming teachers: New professional learning and transformative teacher professionalism. *Journal of In-service Education*, 31(4), 733–746.

Molnos, A. (1995). *A question of time: Essentials of brief dynamic psychotherapy*. London: Karnac Books.

Montgomery, C., & Rupp, A. A. (2005). A meta-analysis for exploring the diverse causes and effects of stress in teachers. *Canadian Journal of Education*, 28(3), 458.

Moons, W. G., & Mackie, D. M. (2007). Thinking straight while seeing red: The influence of anger on information processing. *Personality & Social Psychology Bulletin*, 33(5), 706–720.

Moriarty, V., Edmonds, S., Blatchford, P., et al. (2001). Teaching young children: perceived satisfaction and stress. *Educational Research*, 43(1), 33–46.

Morice, L. C., & Murray, J. E. (2003). Compensation and teacher retention: A success story. *Educational Leadership*, 60(8), 40.

Morris-Rothschild, B. K., & Brassard, M. R. (2006). Teachers' conflict management styles: The role of attachment styles and classroom management efficacy. *Journal of School Psychology*, 44(2), 105–121.

Mortiboys, A. (2005). *Teaching with emotional intelligence: A step by step guide for higher and further education professionals*. London: Routledge.

Motschnig-Pitrik, R., & Lux, M. (2008). The person-centered approach meets neuroscience: Mutual support for C. R. Rogers's and A. Damasio's theories. *Journal of Humanistic Psychology*, 48(3), 287–319.

Mouton, S. G., Hawkins, J., McPherson, R. H., & Copley, J. (1996). School attachment: Perspectives of low-attached high school students. *Educational Psychology*, 16(3), 297–304.

Mulford, W., Leithwood, K. A., & Silins, H. (2004). *Educational leadership for organisational learning and improved student outcomes*. Boston, MA: Kluwer Academic Publishers.

Munn, P., Johstone, M., & Sharp, S. (2004). *Discipline in Scottish schoools: A comparative survey over time of teachers' and headteachers' perceptions*. Edinburgh: Scottish Executive Education Department.

Musselman, L. J., MacRae, H. M., Reznick, R. K., & Lingard, L. A. (2005). "You learn better under the gun": intimidation and harassment in surgical education. *Medical Education*, 39, 926–934.

Nagel, L., & Brown, S. (2003). The ABCs of managing teacher stress. *The Clearing House*, 76(5), 255.

Nakamura, J., & Csikszentmihalyi, M. (2002). The concept of flow. In C. R. Snyder & S. J. Lopez (Eds), *Handbook of positive psychology* (pp. 89–105). New York: Oxford University Press.

Naring, G., Briet, M., & Brouwers, A. (2006). Beyond demand-control: Emotional labour and symptoms of burnout in teachers. *Work & Stress*, 20(4), 303–315.

Natvig, G. K., Albrektsen, G., & Qvarnstrom, U. (2001). School-related stress experience as a risk factor for bullying behavior. *Journal of Youth and Adolescence*, 30(5), 561–575.

Neill, A. S. (1968/1985). *Summerhill: A radical approach to child-rearing*. Harmondsworth: Penguin.

Nelis, D., Quoidbach, J., Mikolajczak, M., & Hansenne, M. Increasing emotional intelligence: (How) is it possible? *Personality and Individual Differences*. In Press, Corrected Proof.

Nelson, C., Treichler, P. A., & Grossberg, L. (1992). Cultural studies: An introduction. In L. Grossberg, C. Nelson & P. A. Treichler (Eds), *Cultural studies*. New York: Routledge.

Nelson, J., Lott, L., & Glenn, H. S. (1997). *Positive discipline in the classroom* (2nd ed.). Rocklin, CA: Prima Publishing.

Neville, B. (2005). *Educating Psyche: Emotion, imagination and the unconscious in learning* (2nd ed.). Greensborough, Victoria: Flat Chat Press.

Noddings, N. (1992). *The challenge to care in schools: An alternative approach to education*. New York: Teachers College Press.

Noddings, N. (2003). *Happiness and education*. New York: Cambridge University Press.

Null, J. W. (2010). Is there a future for the teaching profession? *The Educational Forum*, 74(1), 26–36.

Nurius, P. (1991). Possible selves and social support: Social cognitive resources for coping and striving. In J. A. Howard & P. L. Callero (Eds), *The self–society dynamic: Cognition, emotion, and action* (pp. 239–258). New York: Cambridge University Press.

Nye, R. D. (1975). *Three views of man: Perspectives from Sigmund Freud, B. F. Skinner, and Carl Rogers*. Monterey, CA: Brooks-Cole.

O'Connor, K. E. (2008). "You choose to care": Teachers, emotions and professional identity. *Teaching and Teacher Education*, 24(1), 117–126.

O'Connor, P. R., & Clarke, V. A. (1990). Determinants of teacher stress. *Australian Journal of Education*, 34(2), 41–51.

O'Connor-McBrien, E. (2004). Temperament in the classroom: Understanding individual differences. *Harvard Educational Review*, 74(2), 221.

O'Loughlin, M. (2006). On knowing and desiring children: The significance of the unthought known. In G. M. Boldt & P. M. Salvio (Eds), *Love's return: Psychoanalytic essays on childhood, teaching, and learning* (pp. 185–202). New York: Routledge.

Olsen, K. (2009). *Wounded by school: Recapturing the joy in learning and standing up to old school culture*. New York: Teachers College Press.

Olweus, D. (1997). Bully/victim problems in school: Facts and intervention. *European Journal of Psychology of Education*, 12(4), 495–510.

Olweus, D. (2005). A useful evaluation design, and effects of the Olweus Bullying Prevention Program. *Psychology Crime & Law*, 11(4), 389–402.

Onwuegbuzie, A. J., Witcher, A. E., Collins, K. M. T., Filer, J. D., Wiedmaier, C. D., & Moore, C. W. (2007). Students' perceptions of characteristics of effective college teachers: A validity study of a teaching evaluation form using a mixed-methods analysis. *American Educational Research Journal*, 44(1).

Oplatka, I. (2007). Managing emotions in teaching: Toward an understanding of emotion displays and caring as nonprescribed role elements. *Teachers College Record*, 109(6), 1374.

Orr, D. (2002). The uses of mindfulness in anti-oppressive pedagogies: Philosophy and praxis. *Canadian Journal of Education*, 27(4), 477–497.

O'Sullivan, M., MacPhail, A., & Tannehill, D. (2009). A career in teaching: Decisions of the heart rather than the head. *Irish Educational Studies*, 28(2), 177–191.

Overskeid, G. (2007). Looking for Skinner and finding Freud. *American Psychologist*, 62(6), 590–595.

Pallant, J. (2007). *SPSS survival manual: A step by step guide to data analysis using SPSS* (3rd ed.). Crows Nest, Australia: Allen & Unwin.

Parker, J. D. A., & Bar-On, R. (2000). *The handbook of emotional intelligence: Theory, development, assessment, and application at home, school, and in the workplace* (1st ed.). San Francisco, CA: Jossey-Bass.

Parkes, C. M. (1986). *Bereavement: Studies of grief in adult life* (2nd ed.). Harmondsworth: Penguin.

Parkison, P. (2008). Space for performing teacher identity: Through the lens of Kafka and Hegel. *Teachers and Teaching*, 14(1), 51–60.

Parks, L., & Guay, R. P. Personality, values, and motivation. *Personality and Individual Differences*. In Press, Corrected Proof.

Pekrun, R., Goetz, T., Titz, W., & Perry, R. P. (2002). Academic emotions in students' self-regulated learning and achievement: A program of qualitative and quantitative research. *Educational Psychologist*, 37(2), 91–106.

Penlington, C. (2008). Dialogue as a catalyst for teacher change: A conceptual analysis. *Teaching and Teacher Education*, 24(5), 1304–1316.

Penuel, W., Fishman, B. J., Yamaguchi, R., & Gallagher, L. P. (2007). What makes professional development effective? Strategies that foster curriculum implementation. *American Educational Research Journal*, 44(4), 921–958.

Perel, E. (2007). *Mating in captivity: Sex, lies and domestic bliss*. London: Hodder & Stoughton.

Perlman, D. (2007). The best of times, the worst of times: The place of close relationships in psychology and our daily lives. *Canadian Psychology*, 48(1), 7–18.

Perry, L., Lennie, C., & Humphrey, N. (2008). Emotional literacy in the primary classroom: Teacher perceptions and practices. *Education 3–13*, 36(1), 27–37.

Petersen, C. A. (2007). A historical look at psychology and the scientist-practitioner model. *American Behavioral Scientist*, 50(6), 758–765.

Peterson, C., & Park, N. (2007). Attachment security and its benefits in context. [Comment/Reply]. *Psychological Inquiry*, 18(3), 172–176.

Peterson, D. R. (2000). Scientist-practitioner or scientific practitioner? *American Psychologist*, 55(2), 252–253.

Pianta, R. C., & Steinberg, M. (1992). Teacher–child relationships and the process of adjusting to school. In R. C. Pianta (Ed.), *Beyond the parent: The role of other adults in children's lives* (pp. 61–80). San Francisco, CA: Jossey-Bass.

Pianta, R. C., Steinberg, M. S., & Rollins, K. B. (1995). The first two years of school: Teacher–child relationships and deflections in children's classroom adjustment. *Development and Psychopathology*, 7(2), 295–312.

Piekarska, A. (2000). School stress, teachers' abusive behaviors, and children's coping strategies. *Child Abuse & Neglect*, 24(11), 1443–1449.

Pierce, T., & Lydon, J. (1998). Priming relational schemas: Effects of contextually activated and chronically accessible interpersonal expectations on responses to a stressful event. *Journal of Personality and Social Psychology*, 75(6), 1441–1448.

Pietromonaco, P. R., & Barrett, L. F. (2000a). Attachment theory as an organizing framework: A view from different levels of analysis. *Review of General Psychology*, 4(2), 107–110.

Pietromonaco, P. R., & Barrett, L. F. (2000b). The internal working models concept: What do we really know about the self in relation to others? *Review of General Psychology*, 4(2), 155–175.

Pillay, H., Goddard, R., & Wilss, L. (2005). Well-being, burnout and competence: Implications for teachers. *Australian Journal of Teacher Education*, 30(2), 22–33.

Pincus, D. D. M. H., Freeman, W. M. D., & Modell, A. M. D. (2007). A Neurobiological model of perception: Considerations for transference. *Psychoanalytic Psychology*, 24(4), 623–640.

Pines, A. M. (2002). Teacher burnout: A psychodynamic existential perspective. *Teachers and Teaching*, 8(2), 121–140.

Platts, H., Tyson, M., & Mason, O. (2002). Adult attachment style and core beliefs: Are they linked? *Clinical Psychology & Psychotherapy*, 9(5), 332–348.

Poehlmann, J. (2003). An attachment perspective on grandparents raising their very young grandchildren: Implications for intervention and research. *Infant Mental Health Journal*, 24(2), 149–173.

Poenaru, R., & Sava, F. A. (1998). *Teacher abuse in schools: Ethical, psychological and educational aspects*. Bucharest: Editura Danubius.

Popper, M. (2002). Narcissism and attachment patterns of personalized and socialized charismatic leaders. *Journal of Social and Personal Relationships*, 19(6), 797–809.

Popper, M. (2004). Leadership as relationship. *Journal for the Theory of Social Behaviour*, 34(2), 107–125.

Popper, M., & Amit, K. (2009). Attachment and leader's development via experiences. *The Leadership Quarterly*, 20(5), 749–763.

Popper, M., Amit, K., Gal, R., Mishkal-Sinai, M., & Lisak, A. (2004). The capacity to lead: Major psychological differences between leaders and nonleaders. *Military Psychology*, 16(4), 245–263.

Popper, M., & Lipshitz, R. (1992). Coaching on leadership. *Leadership & Organization Development Journal*, 13(7), 15–18.

Popper, M., & Lipshitz, R. (2000). Organizational learning: Mechanisms, culture, and feasibility. *Management Learning*, 31(2), 181–196.

Popper, M., & Mayseless, O. (2003). Back to basics: Applying a parenting perspective to transformational leadership. *The Leadership Quarterly*, 14(1), 41–65.

Popper, M., & Mayseless, O. (2007). The building blocks of leader development: A psychological conceptual framework. *Leadership & Organization Development Journal*, 28(7), 664–684.

Popper, M., Mayseless, O., & Castelnovo, O. (2000). Transformational leadership and attachment. *Leadership Quarterly*, 11(2), 267–289.

Pring, R. (2000). *Philosophy of educational research*. London: Continuum.

Radojevic, M. M. (1996). Adult attachment: Some considerations for family therapy. *The Australian and New Zealand journal of family therapy*, 17(1), 33–41.

Rafaeli, A., & Sutton, R. I. (1987). Expression of emotion as part of the work role. *Academy of Management Review*, 12, 23–37.

Ramachandran, V. S. (2003). *The emerging mind*. London: BBC/Profile Books.

Ramachandran, V. S. (2004). *A brief tour of human consciousness*. New York: Pi Press.

Rathunde, K., & Csikszentmihalyi, M. (2005). The social context of middle school: Teachers, friends, and activities in Montessori and traditional school environments. *The Elementary School Journal*, 106(1), 59–79.

Reese, R. J., Kieffer, K. M., & Briggs, B. K. (2002). A reliability generalization study of select measures of adult attachment style. *Educational and Psychological Measurement*, 62(4), 619–646.

Reinstein, D. K. (2006). *To hold and be held: The therapeutic school as a holding environment*. New York: Routledge.

Reis, H. T. Relationships are situations, and situations involve relationships. *Journal of Research in Personality*. In Press, Corrected Proof.

Reyna, C., & Weiner, B. (2001). Justice and utility in the classroom: An attributional analysis of the goals of teachers' punishment and intervention strategies. *Journal of Educational Psychology*, 93(2), 309–319.

Rholes, W. S., & Simpson, J. A. (2004). *Adult attachment: Theory, research, and clinical implications*. New York: Guilford Press.

Ria, L., Seve, C., Saury, J. et al. (2003). Beginning teachers' situated emotions: A study of first classroom experiences. *Journal of Education for Teaching*, 29(3), 219.

Richards, A. D., & Lynch, A. A. (2008). The identity of psychoanalysis and psychoanalysts. *Psychoanalytic Psychology*, 25(2), 203–219.

Richardson, L., & Pierre, E. A. S. (2005). Writing: A method of inquiry. In N. K. Denzin & Y. S. Lincoln (Eds), *The Sage Handbook of Qualitative Research* (3rd ed., pp. 959–978). Thousand Oaks, CA: Sage Publications.

Richardson, P. W., & Watt, H. M. G. (2006). Who chooses teaching and why? Profiling characteristics and motivations across three Australian universities. *Asia-Pacific Journal of Teacher Education*, 34(1), 27–56.

Riley, P. (2005). Changing the globe in a lighthouse school. In P. Heywood, T. McCann, B. Neville & P. Willis (Eds), *Towards re-enchantment: Education, imagination and the getting of wisdom* (pp. 105–112). Flaxton, Qld: Post Pressed.

Riley, P. (2008). Courage & opportunities, resistance & security: The human leadership domain. In B. R. Beatty & P. Riley (Eds), *Willing to lead – Human leadership: Developing people* (pp. 44–47). Melbourne: Department of Education and Early Childhood Development (DEECD).

Riley, P. (2009a). An adult attachment perspective on the student–teacher relationship & classroom management difficulties. *Teaching and Teacher Education*, 25(5), 626–635.

Riley, P. (2009b). The development and testing of a time-limited mentoring model for experienced school leaders. *Mentoring & Tutoring: Partnership in Learning*, 17(3), 233–248.

Riley, P. (2009c). *Love teaching or teaching for love? An exploration of unconscious motivation*. Paper presented at the Australian Association for Research in Education: International education research conference, Canberra, 29 Nov–3 Dec.

Riley, P. (2010). Border crossing as professional learning. In A. Berry, A. Clemens, J. J. Loughran, G. Parr, P. Riley, D. Robb & E. Tudball (Eds), *Leading Professional Learning: More cases of professional dilemmas*. Melbourne: Department of Education & Early Childhood Developement (DEECD).

Riley, P., Lewis, R. R., & Brew, C. (2010). *Teachers explain the use of legal aggresion in the classroom*. Paper presented at the 2010 AERA Annual Meeting: Understanding complex ecologies in a changing world, Denver, 30 April–4 May.

Riley, P., Lewis, R., & Brew, C.. Why did you do that? Teachers explain the use of legal aggression in the classroom. *Teaching and Teacher Education*. In press.

Riley, P., Watt, H. M. G., & Richardson, P. W. (2009). *Why are some teachers aggressive?* Paper presented at the 44th Australian Psychological Society Annual Conference, Darwin Convention Centre, 30 Sept–4 Oct.

Riley, P., Watt, H. M. G., & Richardson, P. W. (2010). *Classroom relationships strained by teachers' aggressive student management techniques*. Paper presented at the International Conference on Interpersonal Relationships in Education, Boulder, Colorado, 28–29 April.

Riviere, J. (1955). The unconscious phantasy of an inner world reflected in examples from literature. In M. P. Klien, P. Heinemann & R. Money-Kyrle (Eds), *New Directions in Psychoanalysis*. London: Hogarth.

Roberts, A. (2000). Mentoring revisited: A phenomenological reading of the literature. *Mentoring & Tutoring: Partnership in Learning*, 8(2), 145–170.

Roberts, R., Brunner, E., White, I., & Marmot, M. (1993). Gender differences in occupational mobility and structure of employment in the British civil service. *Social Science & Medicine*, 37(12), 1415–1425.

Robertson Cooper (2002). *ASSET Technical Manual*. Manchester: Robertson Cooper Ltd.

Roe, R. A. (2008). Time in applied psychology: The study of "what happens" rather than "what is". *European Psychologist*, 13(1), 37–52.

Roffey, S. (2001). The emotion in learning. *EQ Australia*, 2, 45–47.

Roffman, A. E. (2004). Is anger a thing-to-be-managed? *Psychotherapy, Theory, Research, Practice, Training*, 41(2), 161–171.

Rogers, C. R. (1951). *Client-centered therapy: Its current practice, implications and theory*. Boston, MA: Houghton Mifflin.

Rogers, C. R. (1961/1989). *On becoming a person: A therapist's view of psychotherapy*. Boston, MA: Houghton Mifflin.

Rogers, C. R. (1971). *Encounter groups*. London: Allen Lane.

Rogers, C. R. (1973). *Encounter groups*. Harmondsworth: Penguin.

Rogers, C. R. (1977). *Carl Rogers on personal power*. New York: Delacorte Press.

Rogers, C. R. (1983). *Freedom to learn for the 80s*. Columbus, OH: Charles Merrill.

Rogers, C. R. (1989). The necessary and sufficient conditions of therapeutic personality change. *Texas Association for Counselling and Development Journal*, 17(1), 53–65.

Rogers, C. R. (1990). The interpersonal relationship in the facilitation of learning. In H. Kirschenbaum & V. L. Henderson (Eds), *The Carl Rogers Reader* (pp. 304–311). London: Constable.

Rogers, C. R., Kirschenbaum, H., & Henderson, V. L. (1989a). *Carl Rogers – dialogues: conversations with Martin Buber, Paul Tillich, B.F. Skinner, Gregory Bateson, Michael Polanyi, Rollo May, and others*. Boston, MA: Houghton Mifflin.

Rogers, C. R., Kirschenbaum, H., & Henderson, V. L. (1989b). *The Carl Rogers Reader*. Boston, MA: Houghton Mifflin.

Roisman, G. I., Madsen, S. D., Hennighausen, K. H., Sroufe, L. A., & Collin, W. (2001). The coherence of dyadic behavior across parent–child and romantic relationships as mediated by the internalized representation of experience. *Attachment & Human Development*, 3(2), 156–172.

Roisman, G. I., Padron, E., Sroufe, L. A., & Egeland, B. (2002). Earned-secure attachment status in retrospect and prospect. *Child Development*, 73(4), 1204–1219.

Roisman, G. I., Tsai, J. L., & Chiang, K.-H. S. (2004). The emotional integration of childhood experience: Physiological, facial expressive, and self-reported emotional response during the adult attachment interview. *Developmental Psychology*, 40(5), 776–789.

Roland, E., & Galloway, D. (2002). Classroom influences on bullying. *Educational Research*, 44(3), 299–312.

Romano, V., Fitzpatrick, M., & Janzen, J. (2008). The secure-base hypothesis: Global attachment, attachment to counselor, and session exploration in psychotherapy. *Journal of Counseling Psychology*, 55(4), 495–504.

Romi, S., Lewis, R., & Katz, Y. J. (2009). Student responsibility and classroom discipline in Australia, China, and Israel. *Compare: A Journal of Comparative and International Education*, 39(4), 439–452.

Romi, S., Lewis, R., Roache, J., & Riley, P.. The impact of teachers' aggressive management techniques on students' attitudes to schoolwork and teachers' in Australia, China, and Israel. In press.

Rose, J. S., & Medway, F. J. (1981). Teacher locus of control, teacher behavior, and student behavior as determinants of student achievement. *Journal of Educational Research*, 74(6), 375–381.

Rosenthal, R., & Jacobson, L. (1968). *Pygmalion in the classroom: Teacher expectation and pupils' intellectual development*. New York: Holt, Rinehart & Winston.

Roudinesco, E., & Bowlby, R. (2001). *Why psychoanalysis?* New York: Columbia University Press.

Rowe, A., & Carnelley, K. B. (2003). Attachment style differences in the processing of attachment-relevant information: Primed-style effects on recall, interpersonal expectations, and affect. *Personal relationships*, 10(1), 59–75.

Royzman, E. B., & Rozin, P. (2006). Limits of symhedonia: The differential role of prior emotional attachment in sympathy and sympathetic joy. *Emotion*, 6(1), 82–93.

Rubie-Davies, C., Hattie, J., & Hamilton, R. (2006). Expecting the best for students: Teacher expectations and academic outcomes. *British Journal of Educational Psychology*, 76(3), 429–444.

Rudow, B. (1999). Stress and burnout in the teaching profession: European studies, issues, and research perspectives. In R. Vandenberghe & A. M. Huberman (Eds), *Understanding and preventing teacher burnout* (pp. 38–58). Cambridge: Cambridge University Press.

Rudrauf, D., & Damasio, A. (2006). The biological basis of subjectivity: A hypothesis. In U. Kriegel & K. Williford (Eds), *Self-representational approaches to consciousness* (pp. 423–464). Cambridge, MA: MIT Press.

Russell, T., & Loughran, J. J. (2002). *Improving teacher education practices through self-study*. London: RoutledgeFalmer.

Russell, T., & Loughran, J. J. (2007). *Enacting a pedagogy of teacher education: Values, relationships and practices*. London: Routledge.

Rutter, M. (1995). Clinical implications of attachment concepts: Retrospect and prospect. *Journal of Child Psychology and Psychiatry*, 36(4), 549–571.

Rutter, M., Colvert, E., Kreppner, J., Beckett, C., Castle, J., Groothues, C. et al. (2007). "Early adolescent outcomes for institutionally deprived and non-deprived adoptees. I: Disinhibited attachment": Erratum. *Journal of Child Psychology and Psychiatry*, 48(8), 848.

Ruys, K. I., & Stapel, D. A. (2008). The secret life of emotions. *Psychological Science*, 19(4), 385–391.

Sabini, J., Garvey, B., & Hall, A. L. (2001). Shame and embarrassment revisited. *Personality & Social Psychology Bulletin*, 27(1), 104–117.

Sadock, B. J., & Sadock, V. A. (2003). *Kaplan & Sadock's synopsis of psychiatry: Behavioural sciences/clinical psychiatry*. Philadelphia, PA: Lippincott Williams & Wilkins.

Salzberger-Wittenberg, I., Henry, G., & Osborne, E. (1992). *The emotional experience of learning and teaching*. Cornwall: T.J. Press.

Santavirta, N., Solovieva, S., & Theorell, T. (2007). The association between job strain and emotional exhaustion in a cohort of 1,028 Finnish teachers. *British Journal of Educational Psychology*, 77(1), 213.

Saribay, S., & Andersen, S. M. (2007). Are past relationships at the heart of attachment dynamics? What love has to do with it. *Psychological Inquiry*, 18(3), 183–191.

Sava, F. A. (2002). Causes and effects of teacher conflict-inducing attitudes towards pupils: A path analysis model. *Teaching and Teacher Education*, 18(2002), 1007–1021.

Scarvalone, P., Fox, M., & Safran, J. D. (2005). Interpersonal schemas: Clinical theory, research, and implications. In M. W. Baldwin (Ed.), *Interpersonal cognition* (pp. 359–387). New York: Guilford Press.

Scaturo, D. J. (2002). Technical skill and the therapeutic relationship: A fundamental dilemma in cognitive-behavioral and insight-oriented therapy. *Family therapy*, 29(1), 1–22.

Scharfe, E., & Bartholomew, K. (1994). Reliability and stability of adult attachment patterns. *Personal Relationships*, 1, 23–43.

Scheinkman, M., & Fishbane, M. D. (2004). The vulnerabiltiy cycle: Working with imasses in couples therapy. *Family Process*, 43(3), 279–299.

Schepens, A., Aelterman, A., & Vlerick, P. (2009a). Student teachers' professional identity formation: between being born as a teacher and becoming one. *Educational Studies*, 35(4), 361–378.

Scherer, L. D., & Lambert, A. J. (2009). Contrast effects in priming paradigms: Implications for theory and research on implicit attitudes. *Journal of Personality & Social Psychology*, 97(3), 383–403.

Scherff, L. (2008). Disavowed: The stories of two novice teachers. *Teaching and Teacher Education*, 24(5), 1317–1332.

Schmidt, M., & Datnow, A. (2005). Teachers' sense-making about comprehensive school reform: The influence of emotions. *Teaching and Teacher Education*, 21(8), 949–965.

Schön, D. A. (1987). *Educating the reflective practitioner*. San Francisco, CA: Jossey-Bass.

Schön, D. A. (1995). *Reflective practitioner: How professionals think in action*. Aldershot: Arena.

Schore, A. N. (1994). *Affect regulation and the origin of the self: The neurobiology of emotional development*. Hillsdale, NJ: Lawrence Erlbaum Associates.

Schore, A. N. (1997). A century after Freud's project: Is a rapprochement between psychoanalysis and neurobiology at hand? *Journal of the American Psychoanalytic Association*, 45(3), 807–840.

Schore, A. N. (1998). The experience-dependent maturation of an evaluative system in the cortex. In K. H. Pribram (Ed.), *Brain and values: Is a biological science of values possible?* (pp. 337–358). Mahwah, NJ: Lawrence Erlbaum Associates.

Schore, A. N. (2000a). Attachment and the regulation of the right brain. *Attachment & Human Development*, 2(1), 23–47.

Schore, A. N. (2000b). The self-organization of the right brain and the neurobiology of emotional development. In M. D. Lewis & I. Granic (Eds), *Emotion, development, and self-organization: Dynamic systems approaches to emotional development* (pp. 155–185). New York: Cambridge University Press.

Schore, A. N. (2001a). Effects of a secure attachment relationship on right brain development, affect regulation, and infant mental health. *Infant Mental Health Journal*, 22(1–2), 7–66.

Schore, A. N. (2001b). The effects of early relational trauma on right brain development, affect regulation, and infant mental health. *Infant Mental Health Journal*, 22(1–2), 201–269.

Schore, A. N. (2001c). The right brain as the neurobiological substratum of Freud's dynamic unconscious. In D. E. Scharff (Ed.), *The psychoanalytic century: Freud's legacy for the future* (pp. 61–88). New York: Other Press.

Schore, A. N. (2002a). Advances in neuropsychoanalysis, attachment theory, and trauma research: Implications for self psychology. *Psychoanalytic Inquiry*, 22(3), 433–484.

Schore, A. N. (2002b). Clinical implications of a psychoneurobiological model of projective identification. In S. Alhanati (Ed.), *Primitive mental states: Psychobiological and psychoanalytic perspectives on early trauma and personality development* (Vol. 2, pp. 1–65). London: Karnac Books.

Schore, A. N. (2002c). The neurobiology of attachment and early personality organization. *Journal of Prenatal & Perinatal Psychology & Health*, 16(3), 249–263.

Schore, A. N. (2003a). *Affect dysregulation and disorders of the self*. New York: W W Norton & Co.

Schore, A. N. (2003b). *Affect regulation and the repair of the self*. New York: W W Norton & Co.

Schore, A. N. (2005). A neuropsychoanalytic viewpoint: Commentary on paper by Steven H. Knoblauch. *Psychoanalytic Dialogues*, 15(6), 829–854.

Schussler, D. L. (2009). Beyond content: How teachers manage classrooms to facilitate intellectual engagement for disengaged students. *Theory Into Practice*, 48(2), 114–121.

Schutz, P. A., Pekrun, R., & Phye, G. (Eds). (2007). *Emotion in education*. Amsterdam: Academic Press.

Schwartz, E., & Davis, A. S. (2006). Reactive attachment disorder: Implications for school readiness and school functioning. *Psychology in the Schools*, 43(4), 471–479.

Schwartz, J. M., & Begley, S. (2002). *The mind and the brain: Neuroplasticity and the power of mental force*. New York: Harper Collins.

Seers, A., & Graen, G. B. (1984). The dual attachment concept: A longitudinal investigation of the combination of task characteristics and leader-member exchange. *Organizational Behavior & Human Performance*, 33(3), 283–306.

Senge, P. M. (1992). *The fifth discipline: The art and practice of the learning organization*. Milsons Point, NSW: Random House Australia.

Senge, P. M. (2006). *The fifth discipline: The art and practice of the learning organization* (2nd ed.). London: Random House.

Sergiovanni, T. J. (2001). *Leadership: What's in it for schools?* London: Routledge/Falmer.

Sergiovanni, T. J. (2005a). *Strengthening the heartbeat: Leading and learning together in schools*. San Francisco, CA: Jossey-Bass.

Sergiovanni, T. J. (2005b). The virtues of leadership. *The Educational Forum*, 69, 112–123.

Sewell, K., Cain, T., Woodgate-Jones, A., & Srokosz, A. (2009). Bullying and the post-graduate trainee teacher: a comparative study. *Journal of Education for Teaching: International research and pedagogy*, 35(1), 3–18.

Seymour, M. (2004). *Educating for humanity: Rethinking the purposes of education*. Boulder, CO: Paradigm Publishers

Shalom, Y. B., & Schechet, N. (2008). Reflective practice: A student-oriented pedagogy for veteran teachers. *Teaching Education*, 19(3), 211–221.

Shaughnessy, J. J., & Zechmeister, E. B. (1994). *Reseach methods in psychology*. New York: McGraw Hill.

Shaver, P. R., & Brennan, K. A. (1992). Attachment styles and the "Big Five" personality traits: Their connections with each other and with romantic relationship outcomes. *Personality and Social Psychology Bulletin*, 18(5), 536–545.

Shaver, P., & Hazan, C. (1987). Being lonely, falling in love: Perspectives from attachment theory. *Journal of Social Behavior & Personality*, 2(2, Pt 2), 105–124.

Shaver, P., & Hazan, C. (1988). A biased overview of the study of love. *Journal of Social and Personal Relationships*, 5(4), 473–501.

Shaver, P. R., & Mikulincer, M. (2002). Attachment-related psychodynamics. *Attachment & Human Development*, 4(2), 133–161.

Shaver, P. R., & Mikulincer, M. (2004). What do self-report attachment measures assess? In W. S. Rholes & J. A. Simpson (Eds), *Adult attachment: Theory, research, and clinical implications* (pp. 17–54). New York: Guilford Press.

Sherwood, F. (2001). Influence of perceptions: Listening to early childhood preservice teachers. *Journal of Early Childhood Teacher Education*, 22(3), 215–220.

Shulman, S., Becker, A., & Sroufe, L. A. (1999). Adult–child interactions as related to adult's family history and child's attachment. *International Journal of Behavioral Development*, 23(4), 959–976.

Shumba, A. (2002). The nature, extent and effects of emotional abuse on primary school pupils by teachers in Zimbabwe. *Child Abuse & Neglect*, 26(8), 783–791.

Sibley, C. G., Fischer, R., & Liu, J. H. (2005). Reliability and validity of the revised experiences in close relationships (ECR-R) self-report measure of adult romantic attachment. *Personality and Social Psychology Bulletin*, 31(11), 1524–1536.

Sibley, C. G., & Liu, J. H. (2004). Short-term temporal stability and factor structure of the revised experiences in close relationships (ECR-R) measure of adult attachment. *Personality and Individual Differences*, 36(4), 969–975.

Simpson, J. A., Campbell, L., & Weisberg, Y. J. (2006). Daily perceptions of conflict and support in romantic relationships: The ups and downs of anxiously attached individuals. In M. Mikulincer & G. S. Goodman (Eds), *Dynamics of romantic love: Attachment, caregiving, and sex* (pp. 216–239). New York: Guilford Press.

Simpson, J. A., & Rholes, W. S. (1998). *Attachment theory and close relationships*. New York: Guilford Press.

Simpson, J. A., Rholes, W. S. & Steven, W. (1998). *Attachment theory and close relationships*. New York: Guilford Press.

Singer, J. A., & Singer, J. L. (1994). Social-cognitive and narrative perspectives on transference. In J. M. Masling & R. F. Bornstein (Eds), *Empirical perspectives on object relations theory* (pp. 157–193). Washington, DC: American Psychological Association.

Skaalvik, E. M., & Skaalvik, S. (2009). Does school context matter? Relations with teacher burnout and job satisfaction. *Teaching and Teacher Education*, 25(3), 518–524.

Skinner, B. F. (1974). *About behaviorism*. New York: Knopf.

Skynner, R., & Cleese, J. (1993). *Life and how to survive it*. London: Methuen.

Sloan, D., & Kettering, C. F. (1984). *Toward the recovery of wholeness: Knowledge, education, and human values*. New York: Teachers College, Columbia University.

Slotter, E. B., & Gardner, W. L. (2009). Where do you end and I begin?: Evidence for anticipatory, motivated self–other integration between relationship partners. *Journal of Personality & Social Psychology*, 96(6), 1137–1151.

Smeesters, D., Wheeler, C. S., & Kay, A. C. (2009). The role of interpersonal perceptions in the prime-to-behavior pathway. *Journal of Personality & Social Psychology*, 96(2), 395–414.

Smith, A. A. (2007). Mentoring for experienced school principals: Professional learning in a safe place. *Mentoring & Tutoring: Partnership in Learning*, 15(3), 277–291.

Smith, E. R., Murphy, J., & Coats, S. (1999). Attachment to groups: Theory and management. *Journal of Personality and Social Psychology*, 77(1), 94–110.

Smith, L. (2008). *Schools that change: Evidence-based improvement and effective change leadership*. Thousand Oaks, CA: Corwin Press

Smith, M., & Bourke, S. (1992). Teacher stress: Examining a model based on context, workload, and satisfaction. *Teaching and Teacher Education*, 8(1), 31–46.

Solberg, M. E., & Olweus, D. (2003). Prevalence estimation of school bullying with the Olweus Bully Victim Questionnaire. *Aggressive Behavior*, 29(3), 239–268.

Solbereg, M. E., Olweus, D., & Endresen, I. M. (2007). Bullies and victims at school: Are they the same pupils? *British Journal of Educational Psychology*, 77, 441–464.

Sollars, F. R. (2004). Mourning, trauma, and working through. *Psychoanalytic Review*, 91(2), 201–219.

Sorenson, R. D. (2007). Stress management in education: Warning signs and coping mechanisms. *Management in Education* 21, 10, 21(3), 10–13.

Sparrow, J. (2009). Impact of emotions associated with reflecting upon the past. *Reflective Practice: International and Multidisciplinary Perspectives*, 10(5), 567–576.

Sperling, M. B., Berman, W. H., West, M. L., Sheldon-Keller, A. E., & Kirkpatrick, L. A. (1996). New developments in adult attachment: A call for re-Bowlbyization. *PsycCRITIQUES August*, 41(8), 811–813.

Sperling, M. B., Foelsch, P., & Grace, C. (1996). Measuring adult attachment: Are self-report instruments congruent? *Journal of Personality Assessment*, 67(1), 37–51.

Spiegel, R. (1981). Review of *Loss: Sadness and depression* by John Bowlby. *American Journal of Psychotherapy*, 35, 598–600.

Sroufe, L. A. (1986). Appraisal: Bowlby's contribution to psychoanalytic theory and developmental psychology – attachment, separation, loss. *Journal of Child Psychology and Psychiatry*, 27(6), 841–849.

Sroufe, L. A. (1996). *Emotional development: The organization of emotional life in the early years*. New York: Cambridge University Press.

Sroufe, L. A. (2003). Attachment categories as reflections of multiple dimensions: Comment on Fraley and Spieker (2003). *Developmental Psychology*, 39(3), 413–416.

Sroufe, L. A. (2005). Attachment and development: A prospective, longitudinal study from birth to adulthood. *Attachment & Human Development*, 7(4), 349–367.

Sroufe, L. A., & Sampson, M. C. (2000). Attachment theory and systems concepts. *Human Development*, 43(6), 321–326.

St. Clair, M. (1986) Object relations theories and self psychology. In M. St.Clair (Ed.), *Object relations and self psychology* (pp. 1–20). Florence, KY: Wadsworth/Brooks-Cole.

Stammers, P. (1992). The Greeks had a word for it (five millennia of mentoring). *The British Journal of In-Service Education*, 18(2), 76–80.

Stayton, D. J., & Ainsworth, M. D. (1973). Individual differences in infant responses to brief, everyday separations as related to other infant and maternal behaviors. *Developmental Psychology*, 9(2), 226–235.

Stayton, D. J., Ainsworth, M. D., & Main, M. B. (1973). Development of separation behavior in the first year of life: Protest, following, and greeting. *Developmental Psychology*, 9(2), 213–225.

Stayton, D. J., Hogan, R., & Ainsworth, M. D. (1971). Infant obedience and maternal behavior: The origins of socialization reconsidered. *Child Development*, 42(4), 1057–1069.

Stein, H., Fonagy, P., Ferguson, K. S., & Wisman, M. (2000). Lives through time: An ideographic approach to the study of resilience. *Bulletin of the Menninger Clinic*, 64(2), 281–305.

Stein, H., Jacobs, N. J., Ferguson, K. S., Allen, J. G., & Fonagy, P. (1998). What do adult attachment scales measure? *Bulletin of the Menninger Clinic*, 62(1), 33–82.

Stein, H., Koontz, A. D., Fonagy, P., Allen, J. G., Fultz, J., Brethour, J. R., et al. (2002). Adult attachment: What are the underlying dimensions? *Psychology and Psychotherapy: Theory, Research and Practice*, 75, 77–91.

Stern, G. G., Masling, J., Denton, B., Henderson, J., & Levin, R. (1960). Two scales for the assessment of unconscious motivations for teaching. *Educational and Psychological Measurement*, 20, 9–29.

Stern, G. G., & Masling, J. M. (1958). *Unconscious factors in career motivation for teaching*. New York: Syracuse University Research Institute.

Sternberg, R. (2008). Applying psychological theories to educational practice. *American Educational Research Journal*, 45(1), 150–165.

Stevens, B. (2005). What ghosts do in the parlour: Elements of a corrective relational experience. *Australian Journal of Psychotherapy*, 24(2), 8–34.

Stewart, D. J., & Knott, A. E. (2002). *Schools, courts and the law: Managing student welfare*. Frenchs Forest, NSW: Pearson Education.

Suhd, M. (1995). *Positive regard: Carl Rogers and other notables he influenced*. Palo Alto, CA: Science and Behavior Books.

Sullivan, H. S. (1948). The meaning of anxiety in psychiatry and in life. *Psychiatry: Journal for the Study of Interpersonal Processes*, 11, 1–13.

Sullivan, H. S. (1949). The theory of anxiety and the nature of psychotherapy. *Psychiatry: Journal for the Study of Interpersonal Processes*, 12, 3–12.

Sullivan, H. S. (1950). The illusion of personal individuality. *Psychiatry: Journal for the Study of Interpersonal Processes*, 13, 317–332.

Sullivan, H. S. (1953a). *Conceptions of modern psychiatry*. New York: W W Norton & Co.

Sullivan, H. S. (1953b). *The interpersonal theory of psychiatry*. New York: W W Norton & Co.

Sullivan, H. S. (1954a). Basic concepts in the psychiatric interview. *Pastoral Psychology*, 5(48), 39–46.

Sullivan, H. S. (1954b). *The psychiatric interview*. Oxford: W W Norton & Co.

Sullivan, H. S. (1956/1973). *Clinical studies in psychiatry*. Oxford: W W Norton & Co.

Sullivan, H. S. (1995). The data of psychiatry. In D. B. Stern, C. H. Mann & S. Kantor (Eds), *Pioneers of interpersonal psychoanalysis* (pp. 1–26). Hillsdale, NJ: Analytic Press.

Sullivan, H. S. (2000). Psychiatry: Introduction to the study of interpersonal relations. *Psychiatry: Interpersonal and Biological Processes*, 63(2), 113–126.

Sultanoff, S. M. (2003). Integrating humor into psychotherapy. In C. E. Schaefer (Ed.), *Play therapy with adults* (pp. 107–143). Hoboken, NJ: John Wiley & Sons.

Sutton, R. E. (2000). *The emotional experience of teachers*. Paper presented at the Annual meeting of the American Educational Research Association.

Sutton, R. E. (2005). Teachers' emotions and classroom effectiveness: Implications from recent research. *The Clearing House*, 78(5), 229.

Sutton, R. E., Mudrey-Camino, R., & Knight, C. C. (2009). Teachers' emotion regulation and classroom management. *Theory Into Practice*, 48(2), 130–137.

Sutton, R. E., & Wheatley, K. F. (2003). Teachers' emotions and teaching: A review of the literature and directions for future research. *Educational Psychology Review*, 15(4), 327–358.

Swars, S. L., Meyers, B., Mays, L. C., & Lack, B. (2009). A two-dimensional model of teacher retention and mobility: Classroom teachers and their university partners take a closer look at a vexing problem. *Journal of Teacher Education*, 60(2), 168–183.

Tatar, M., & Yahav, V. (1999). Secondary school pupils' perceptions of burnout among teachers. *British Journal of Educational Psychology*, 69, 457–468.

Tauber, R. T. (2007). *Classroom management: Sound theory and effective practice* (4th ed.). Westport, CT: Praeger Publishers.

Taylor, S. (1998). Emotional labour and the new workplace. In P. Thompson & C. Warhurst (Eds), *Workplaces of the future* (pp. 84–103). London: Macmillan.

Taylor, S. E., Klein, L. C., Lewis, B. P., Gruenewald, T. L., Gurung, R. A. R., & Updegraff, J. A. (2000). Biobehavioral responses to stress in females: Tend-and-befriend, not fight-or-flight. *Psychological Review*, 107(3), 411–429.

Taylor, V. S., Erwin, K. W., Ghose, M. et al. (2001). Models to increase enrollment of minority females in science-based careers. *Journal of the National Medical Association*, 93(2), 74–77.

Teven, J. J., & McCroskey, J. C. (1997). The relationship of perceived teacher caring with student learning and teacher evaluation. *Communication education*, 46(1), 1.

Teyber, E. (2006). *Interpersonal process in therapy: An integrative model* (5th ed.). Belmont: Thompson.

Thorne, B. (2003). *Carl Rogers* (2nd ed.). Thousand Oaks, CA: Sage Publications.

Thornton, M., & Bricheno, P. (2008). Entrances and exits: Changing perceptions of primary teaching as a career for men. *Early Child Development and Care*, 178(7), 717–731.

Thweatt, K. S., & McCroskey, J. C. (1998). The impact of teacher immediacy and misbehaviors on teacher credibility. *Communication education*, 47(4), 348–358.

Tigchelaar, A., & Korthagen, F. (2004). Deepening the exchange of student teaching experiences: Implications for the pedagogy of teacher education of recent insights into teacher behaviour. *Teaching and Teacher Education*, 20, 665–679.

Tomlin, R. B. (2008). *U.S. graduate teacher education and early career persistence of women K-12 teachers*. Denver, CO: University of Denver.

Tracy, R. L., & Ainsworth, M. S. (1981). Maternal affectionate behavior and infant–mother attachment patterns. *Child Development*, 52(4), 1341–1343.

Tracy, R. L., Lamb, M. E., & Ainsworth, M. D. (1976). Infant approach behavior as related to attachment. *Child Development*, 47(3), 571–578.

Tran, S., & Simpson, J. A. (2009). Prorelationship maintenance behaviors: The joint roles of attachment and commitment. *Journal of Personality & Social Psychology*, 97(4), 685–698.

Treml, J. N. (2001). Bullying as a social malady in contemporary Japan. *International Social Work*, 44, 107–117.

Troman, G. (2000). Teacher stress in the low-trust society. *British Journal of Sociology of Education*, 21(3), 331.

Troman, G., & Raggl, A. (2008). Primary teacher commitment and the attractions of teaching. *Pedagogy, Culture & Society*, 16(1), 85–99.

Tuell, J. M. (2006). *Principal and teacher relationships and teacher job satisfaction*. Orono: University of Maine.

Tulley, M., & Chiu, L. H. (1995). Student teachers and classroom discipline. *Journal of Educational Research*, 88(3), 164–171.

Tulley, M., & Chiu, L. H. (1998). Children's perceptions of the effectiveness of classroom discipline techniques. *Journal of instructional psychology*, 25(3), 189–197.

Twemlow, S. W., Fonagy, P., & Sacco, F. C. (2001). An innovative psychodynamically influenced approach to reduce school violence. *Journal of the American Academy of Child & Adolescent Psychiatry*, 40(3), 377–379.

Twemlow, S. W., Fonagy, P., & Sacco, F. C. (2002). Feeling safe in school. *Smith College Studies in Social Work*, 72(2), 303–326.

Twemlow, S. W., Fonagy, P., & Sacco, F. C. (2005a). A developmental approach to mentalizing communities: I. A model for social change. *Bulletin of the Menninger Clinic,* 69(4), 265–281.

Twemlow, S. W., Fonagy, P., & Sacco, F. C. (2005b). A developmental approach to mentalizing communities: II. The Peaceful Schools experiment. *Bulletin of the Menninger Clinic,* 69(4), 282–304.

Uitto, M., & Syrjälä, L. (2008). Body, caring and power in teacher–pupil relationships: Encounters in former pupils' memories. *Scandinavian Journal of Educational Research,* 52(4), 355–371.

Vanboven, A. M. (2005). *Students' adjustment over the transition to middle school: The role of caregiver and teacher attachments.* Urbana–Champaign, IL: University of Illinois Press.

Vandenberghe, R., & Huberman, A. M. (Eds). (1999). *Understanding and preventing teacher burnout: A sourcebook of international research and practice.* New York: Cambridge University Press.

van der Horst, F. C. P., van der Veer, R., & van Ijzendoorn, M. H. (2007). John Bowlby and ethology: An annotated interview with Robert Hinde. *Attachment and Human Development,* 9(1), 1–15.

Van Dijk, P. A., & Brown, A. K. (2006). Emotional labour and negative job outcomes: An evaluation of the mediating role of emotional dissonance. *Journal of Management & Organization,* 12(2), 101–115.

Vangelisti, A. L., & Perlman, D. (2006). *The Cambridge handbook of personal relationships.* Cambridge: Cambridge University Press.

Vanheule, S., Lievrouw, A., & Verhaeghe, P. (2003). Burnout and intersubjectivity: A psychoanalytical study from a Lacanian perspective. *Human Relations,* 56(3), 321–338.

Van Marle, S., & Holmes, J. (2002). Supportive psychotherapy as an integrative psycho-therapy. In J. Holmes & A. Bateman (Eds), *Integration in psychotherapy: Models and methods* (pp. 175–193). New York: Oxford University Press.

Van Morrow, L. (1991). Teachers' descriptions of experiences with their own teachers that made a significant impact on their lives. *Education,* 112(1), 96–103.

Vanoverbeke, C., & Cavanaugh, J. (2001). How do teachers avoid emotional involvement with students? *English Journal,* 91(2), 31.

van Tartwijk, J., Brekelmans, M., Wubbels, T., Fisher, D. L., & Fraser, B. J. (1998). Students' perceptions of teacher interpersonal style: The front of the classroom as the teacher's stage. *Teaching and Teacher Education,* 14(6), 607–617.

Vaughn, B. E., Waters, H. S., Coppola, G., Cassidy, J., Bost, K. K., & Verissimo, M. (2006). Script-like attachment representations and behavior in families and across cultures: Studies of parental secure base narratives. *Attachment & Human Development,* 8(3), 179–184.

Vinokur, A., & Ajzen, I. (1982). Relative importance of prior and immediate events: A causal primacy effect. *Journal of Personality and Social Psychology,* 42(5), 820–829.

Vygotsky, L. S., Knox, J. E., Stevens, C. B., Rieber, R. W., & Carton, A. S. (1993). *The collected works of L. S. Vygotsky, Vol. 2: The fundamentals of defectology (abnormal psychology and learning disabilities).* New York: Plenum Press.

Vygotsky, L. S., Rieber, R. W., & Carton, A. S. (1987). *The collected works of L. S. Vygotsky, Vol. 1: Problems of general psychology.* New York: Plenum Press.

Vygotsky, L. S., Rieber, R. W., & Hall, M. J. (1997). *The collected works of L. S. Vygotsky, Vol. 4: The history of the development of higher mental functions.* New York: Plenum Press.

Vygotsky, L. S., Rieber, R. W., & Hall, M. J. (1998). *The collected works of L. S. Vygotsky, Vol. 5: Child psychology.* New York: Plenum Press.

Vygotsky, L. S., Rieber, R. W., & Hall, M. J. (1999). *The collected works of L. S. Vygotsky, Vol. 6: Scientific legacy*. Dordrecht, Netherlands: Kluwer Academic Publishers.

Vygotsky, L. S., Rieber, R. W., Wollock, J., & van der Veer, R. (1997). *The collected works of L. S. Vygotsky, Vol. 3: Problems of the theory and history of psychology*. New York: Plenum Press.

Wachtel, P. L. (2009). Knowing oneself from the inside out, knowing oneself from the outside in: The "inner" and "outer" worlds and their link through action. *Psychoanalytic Psychology*, 26(2), 158–170.

Waddington, C. (1977). *Tools for thought*. London: Cape.

Walker, J. M. T. (2009). This issue: A person-centered approach to classroom management. *Theory Into Practice*, 48(2), 95–98.

Wampler, K. S., Riggs, B., & Kimball, T. G. (2004). Observing attachment behaviour in couples: The adult attachment behavior Q-set (AABQ). *Family Process*, 43(3), 315–335.

Wanzer, M. B., & McCroskey, J. C. (1998). Teacher socio-communicative style as a correlate of student affect toward teacher and course material. *Communication education*, 47(1), 43–52.

Warme, G. E., Bowlby, J., Crowcroft, A., & Rae-Grant, Q. A. (1980). Current issues in child psychiatry: A dialogue with John Bowlby. *Canadian Journal of Psychiatry*, 25(5), 367–376.

Waters, E., & Beauchaine, T. P. (2003). Are there really patterns of attachment? Comment on Fraley and Spieker. *Developmental Psychology*, 39(3), 417–422.

Waters, H. S., & Waters, E. (2006). The attachment working models concept: Among other things, we build script-like representations of secure base experiences. *Attachment & Human Development*, 8(3), 185–197.

Watson, D. (2005). Don Watson's trip down memory lane. *Iteach: The Victorian Institute of Teaching's Newsletter*, 2, 7.

Watson, D. I. (1999). "Loss of Face" in Australian Classrooms. *Teaching in Higher Education*, 4(3), 355–362.

Watt, H. M. G., & Richardson, P. W. (2008a). *A new multidimensional measure of teaching self-efficacy: The SET Scale*. Paper presented at the AARE Annual Conference, Brisbane, 30 Nov–4 Dec.

Watt, H. M. G., & Richardson, P. W. (2008b). Motivation for teaching. *Learning and Instruction*, 18(5), 405–407.

Watt, H. M. G., & Richardson, P. W. (2008c). Motivations, perceptions, and aspirations concerning teaching as a career for different types of beginning teachers. *Learning and Instruction*, 18(5), 408–428.

Watt, H. M. G., Richardson, P. W., & Tysvaer, N. M. (2007). Profiles of beginning teachers' engagement and career development aspirations. Under review.

Wei-li, W., & Li, F. (2004). The assessment of adult attachment. *Zhong guo lin chuang xin li xue za zhi*, 12(2), 217–220.

Weiner, B. (2000). Intrapersonal and interpersonal theories of motivation from an attributional perspective. *Educational Psychology Review*, 12(1), 1–14.

Weiner, B. (2003). The classroom as a courtroom. *Social Psychology of Education*, 6(1), 3–15.

Weinstein, C. S. (1989). Teacher education students' preconceptions of teaching. *Journal of Teacher Education*, 40(2), 53–60.

Weinstein, C. S., & Woolfolk, A. E. (1981). The classroom setting as a source of expectations about teachers and pupils. *Journal of Environmental Psychology*, 1(2), 117–129.

Weiss, E. M. (1999). Perceived workplace conditions and first-year teachers' morale, career choice commitment, and planned retention: A secondary analysis. *Teaching and Teacher Education*, 15(8), 861–879.

Wentzel, K. R. (2002). Are effective teachers like good parents? Teaching styles and student adjustment in early adolescence. *Child Development*, 73(1), 287–301.

West, R. (1994). Teacher–student communication: A descriptive typology of students' interpersonal experiences with teachers. *Communication Reports*, 7(2), 109–119.

Whitcomb, J. A., Borko, H., & Liston, D. (2008). Why teach? *Journal of Teacher Education*, 59(1), 3–9.

Whitehead, A. N. (1929). *The aims of education and other essays*. New York: Macmillan.

Wideen, M., Mayer-Smith, J., & Moon, B. (1998). A critical analysis of the research on learning to teach: Making the case for an ecological perspective on inquiry. *Review of Educational Research*, 68(2), 130–178.

Wilhelm, K., Dewhurst-Savellis, J., & Parker, G. (2000). Teacher stress? An analysis of why teachers leave and why they stay. *Teachers and Teaching: Theory and Practice*, 6(3), 291–304.

Wilkinson, J., Meiers, M., & Knight, P. (2008). *Research digest: Managing classroom behaviour*. Melbourne: Victorian Institute of Teaching.

Wilkinson, R. (2008). Development and properties of the adolescent friendship attachment scale. *Journal Youth Adolescence*, 37, 1270–1279.

Wilkinson, R. B. Best friend attachment versus peer attachment in the prediction of adolescent psychological adjustment. *Journal of Adolescence*. In Press, Corrected Proof.

Wilkinson, S. R. (2003). *Coping and complaining: Attachment and the language of dis-ease*. New York: Brunner-Routledge.

Williams, J. S. (2003). Why great teachers stay. *Educational Leadership*, 60(8), 71.

Wilson, T. D. (2002). *Strangers to ourselves: Discovering the adaptive unconscious*. London: Belknap.

Winnicott, D. W. (1965). *The maturational process and the facilitating environment*. London: Hogarth.

Winnicott, D. W. (1992a). Anxiety associated with insecurity. In D. W. Winnicott (Ed.), *Through paediatrics to psycho-analysis: Collected papers* (pp. 97–100). London: Brunner-Routledge.

Winnicott, D. W. (1992b). Hate in the counter-transference. In J. R. Brandell (Ed.), *Countertransference in psychotherapy with children and adolescents* (pp. 47–57). Lanham, MD: Jason Aronson.

Winnicott, D. W. (1993a). The value of the therapeutic consultation. In D. Goldman (Ed.), *In one's bones: The clinical genius of Winnicott* (pp. 95–100). Lanham, MD: Jason Aronson.

Winnicott, D. W. (1993b). Transitional objects and transitional phenomena: A study of the first not-me possession. In G. H. Pollock (Ed.), *Pivotal papers on identification* (pp. 139–157). Madison, CT: International Universities Press.

Winnicott, D. W. (1994). Letter to Melanie Klein (17 November 1952). *Percurso Revista de Psicanalise*, 7(12), 80–82.

Winnicott, D. W. (2002). *Winnicott on the child*. Cambridge, MA: Perseus Publishing.

Winnicott, D. W., Winnicott, C., Shepherd, R., & Davis, M. (1986). *Home is where we start from: Essays by a psychoanalyst*. Harmondsworth: Penguin.

Winograd, K. (2003). The functions of teacher emotions: The good, the bad, and the ugly. *Teachers College Record*, 105(9), 1641–1673.

Witmer, M. M. (2005). The Fourth R in Education – Relationships. *The Clearing House*, 78(5), 224.

Wong, E. H., Wiest, D. J., & Cusick, L. B. (2002). Perceptions of autonomy support, parent attachment, competence and self-worth as predictors of motivational orientation and academic achievement: An examination of sixth-and-ninth-grade regular education students. *Adolescence*, 37(146), 255–266.

Woolfolk Hoy, A. (1999). Psychology applied to education. In A. Stec & D. A. Bernstein (Eds), *Psychology: Fields of application* (pp. 61–81). Boston, MA: Houghton, Mifflin.

Woolfolk Hoy, A. (2008). What motivates teachers? Important work on a complex question. *Learning and Instruction*, 18(5), 492–498.

Wright, B. (1977). Our reason for teaching. *Theory Into Practice*, 16(4), 225–230.

Wright, B., & Sherman, B. (1963). Who is the teacher? *Theory Into Practice*, 2(2), 67–72.

Wright, B., & Sherman, B. (1965). Love and mastery in the child's image of the teacher. *The School Review*, 73(2), 89–101.

Yamamoto, K., & Suzuki, N. (2005). The effects of personal relationships on facial displays. *Japanese Journal of Psychology*, 76(4), 375–381.

Yamamoto, K., & Suzuki, N. (2008). Facial expressions in the course of relationship formation. *Japanese Journal of Psychology*, 78(6), 567–574.

Yariv, E., & Coleman, M. (2005). Managing "challenging" teachers. *International Journal of Educational Management*, 19(4), 330–346.

Yates, T. M., Egeland, B., & Sroufe, L. A. (2003). Rethinking resilience: A developmental process perspective. In S. S. Luthar (Ed.), *Resilience and vulnerability: Adaptation in the context of childhood adversities* (pp. 243–266). New York: Cambridge University Press.

Zajac, K., & Kobak, R. (2006). Attachment. In G. G. Bear & K. M. Minke (Eds), *Children's needs III: Development, prevention, and intervention* (pp. 379–389). Washington, DC: National Association of School Psychologists.

Zapf, D., Vogt, C., Seifert, C., Mertini, H., & Isic, A. (1999). Emotion work as a source of stress: The concept and development of an instrument. *European Journal of Work & Organizational Psychology*, 8(3), 371–400.

Zeidner, M., Roberts, R. D., & Matthews, G. (2008). The science of emotional intelligence: Current consensus and controversies. *European Psychologist*, 13(1), 64–78.

Zeifman, D. M. (2001). An ethological analysis of human infant crying: Answering Tinbergen's four questions. *Developmental Psychobiology*, 39(4), 265–285.

Zembylas, M. (2006). Witnessing in the classroom: The ethics and politics of affect. *Educational Theory*, 56(3), 305–324.

Zembylas, M. (2007a). Emotional ecology: The intersection of emotional knowledge and pedagogical content knowledge in teaching. *Teaching and Teacher Education: An International Journal of Research and Studies*, 23(4), 355–367.

Zembylas, M. (2007b). Risks and pleasures: A Deleuzo-Guattarian pedagogy of desire in education. *British Educational Research Journal*, 33(3), 331–347.

Zembylas, M., & Barker, H. B. (2002). Preservice teacher attitudes and emotions: Individual spaces, community conversations and transformations. *Research in Science Education*, 32(3), 329–351.

Zetzel, E. (1956). Current concepts of transference. *International Journal of Psychoanalysis*, 37, 369–376.

Zhang, F. The relationship between state attachment security and daily interpersonal experience. *Journal of Research in Personality*. In Press, Corrected Proof.

Zhang, F., & Hazan, C. (2002). Working models of attachment and person perception processes. *Personal relationships*, 9(2), 225–235.

Zhang, Q., & Zhu, W. (2008). Exploring emotion in teaching: Emotional labor, burnout, and satisfaction in Chinese higher education. *Communication education*, 57(1), 105–122.

Zimmerman, B. J. (2008). Investigating self-regulation and motivation: Historical background, methodological developments, and future prospects. *American Educational Research Journal*, 45(1), 166–183.

Zionts, L. T. (2005). Examining relationships between students and teachers: A potential extension of attachment theory? In K. A. Kerns & R. A. Richardson (Eds), *Attachment in middle childhood* (pp. 231–254). New York: Guilford Press.

Index

Printed in Great Britain
by Amazon

35508119R00115